RESOLVED.
Following Jesus in an Age of Quitters

The *Resolutions* of Jonathan Edwards for Today

***

Myrrh
Books
Overland Park, Kansas

RESOLVED. Following Jesus in an Age of Quitters
The *Resolutions* of Jonathan Edwards for Today

ISBN: 9798502735858

LCCN: 2021910300

Special thanks to Mark Whiting for his red pen.

Special thanks to Lauren Wilson for formatting help.

Special thanks to Dee Molton for editing, and for content and manuscript advice.

Foreword

by Trace Thurlby, President, The Global Orphan Project. [1]

Quitting is easy. No one needs to write a book teaching us how to quit. Still, the topic has captured our attention in numerous ways over the years. In 1975, Paul Simon wrote a hit song about how easy it is to quit on relationships:

Just slip out the back, Jack.
Make a new plan, Stan.
Hop on the bus, Gus.
Don't need to discuss much…
Just drop off the key, Lee, and get yourself free.[2]

From emphatically ejecting to subtly disengaging, quitting takes many forms and has many faces. Look around. People quit all the time, and it goes beyond superficial quitting on diets or gym memberships. Leaders are quitting on sacred promises and commitments like marriage, family, and ministry. From Judas' betrayal to this year's headlines, history is filled with the stories of men who walked closely with Jesus for a time but did not finish well.

Somewhere along the way, it seems they quit relying on His promises and power. They stopped following. The results are tragic, easy to criticize, and even mock. Other times, quitting hits too close to home. Our relationships fail. Our families fracture. Our heroes fall. In moments of doubt and pain, we're left questioning whether we, too, are destined to quit.

---

[1] https://goproject.org/

[2] Simon, P. (1975) https://www.paulsimon.com/track/50-ways-to-leave-your-lover-6/

RESOLVED.

As a young man, surrounded by this sobering reality, I asked myself if it was even possible to follow Jesus to the end.

The answer is a resounding 'Yes!'

Exhortation and encouragement are part of the solution. Words matter. In response to our desperate need for the Truth of Jesus Christ distilled in words, Pastor John tees up Kingdom treasure, tying together Jonathan Edwards' Resolutions with practical application for lives of personal holiness. As thankful as I am for this book, I am even more grateful for John's example. The world needs men who follow Jesus faithfully. By God's grace, Pastor John Gillespie is such a man. He does not quit, though he has had many opportunities to do so.

In 1994, pastoring in the United Kingdom, John could have quit when his church denomination ousted him for holding the line on an authoritative view of Scripture. The British press picked up the story. It went national. John got his 15 minutes of fame and could have walked off the playing field with his head held high. Instead, he stayed local, went across town, started over, and kept teaching the Word.

Later, John taught God's Word to pastors in some of the most underserved and under-resourced countries on earth. Year after year, he endured tens of thousands of miles of travel, spartan accommodations, foreign food, time away from family, and varying attendance with no fanfare. One hot, Haitian afternoon, I sat in an unconditioned, cinder block room as John led dozens of pastors, most of whom never had the opportunity to go to seminary, through the challenging book of *Romans*.

In that setting, with his brothers in Christ, John was fully alive! He loved it but was again faced with a significant challenge when his heart failed a few years ago. God brought healing, extending his life, while at the same time removing John's capacity to go to the ends of the earth.

RESOLVED.

Once more, he could have hung it up, retired, and finally gotten serious about his golf game. Instead, he embraced a call to return to the pulpit, teach the Word, and shepherd Westbrooke, a faithful church in Overland Park, Kansas.

For 39 years, John has faithfully loved his wife, Tessa, and his ever-growing family of seven children, their spouses and 22 grandchildren. Watching his family walk with the Lord brings him great joy. He has written eight books, preached more than 6,000 sermons, baptizing and discipling many along the way. I know because I am one of them.

Obviously, I love and respect John greatly. One of the most encouraging things about him is that, in so many respects, he is a normal guy. In addition to having a sweet golf swing, he likes to bike, lift weights, and have a good laugh. He would love it if you asked him about his favourite guitar. He has no desire to impress others to elevate himself. Like me, he has little regard for fashion, but do not mistake that for lacking style. If you ask John about one of his passions, you will likely find yourself hanging on his words and time passing quickly.

He can also be a little grumpy and sarcastic at times. On those off days, he is quick to repent. In an era of posers, John is a classic.

Most importantly, John is fully convinced that he has no hope of following Jesus faithfully without the supernatural, abundant grace of God. His awareness of this personal need comes across clearly in his exploration of these *Resolutions*. The overriding desire of John's heart is a deeper relationship with Jesus, for himself and for others. The process of writing imprints truth in the author's heart and mind as much (or more) as reading does in ours, and that's part of why he writes.

John also writes because God wills it. We need it, and God knows it.

RESOLVED.

Paul Simon was right in one respect. There are at least 50 ways to quit. But he was quite wrong in another. Quitting is not the way to 'get yourself free'. True freedom is found in following Jesus: in leaning in – not walking away.

In a world where it often feels like *we can't* - where excuses are the norm - the truth is, *we can!* In the power of the Holy Spirit, we can resolve to follow Jesus, like Jonathan Edwards did and like John Gillespie does. I am so grateful for him showing us how – in word and deed.

Lean in!

Trace

I have been crucified with Christ and I no longer live, but Christ lives in me. The life I now live in the body, I live by faith in the Son of God, who loved me and gave himself for me.

Galatians 2:20

RESOLVED.

Welcome

Dear Friends,

I have known failure. I have at times been a quitter. Jesus has been so, *so* gracious to me.

He has not defined me by my failure but by His faithfulness.

And He has given me grace to want to rise above the spirit of my age … a spirit that gives up quickly. He has put many men and women into my life who have inspired me to get back up and keep running the race.

One is a young man who lived three hundred years ago.

For years now I have been wrestling with him. I have tried to escape, but this youngster keeps taking me down to the mat and I think he has all but pinned me.

So….

Come back with me to the year 1722. Brace yourself. We are going to meet an eighteen-year-old man. (Notice I do not say boy. These days we would rarely refer to an eighteen-year-old as a man, but not in those days.) He was a new follower of Jesus. He had exchanged death for life, darkness for light, lies for truth. God had begun a work of transforming grace in his young life.

Born in 1703, Jonathan Edwards was to become perhaps the greatest thinker and theologian in American history. His life was not only useful in his own day; his influence has grown over the centuries.

But his development was no accident.

RESOLVED.

The young man applied himself to Christ.

Jonathan Edwards lived an extraordinary life because he was a normal Christian (never confuse *average* or *common* for *normal*).

In his nineteenth year Edwards began to set down seventy *Resolutions* to which, by the grace of God, he held himself accountable for the rest of his life. The first thirty-four *Resolutions* were conceived and written in just two sittings. The rest came into being over the following year and a half.

The fact that he wrote these over the course of eighteen months indicates that they were not just reflecting a fleeting mood but arose from a deeply convinced disposition.

Thus, by 1723, Edwards had committed himself to these seventy *Resolutions*: to read them prayerfully once a week, for the sake of his soul, for the sake of his usefulness, for the sake of his walk with Jesus. This he did for the next 35 years (that is, over eighteen-hundred times!) until his death in 1758.

So, what I want to *attempt* (pray that I can do this!) is to open up each *Resolution* to us, so that we can explore it in the light of Scripture, and have our lives impacted by it, by Jonathan, and ultimately by God.

I think this will be the toughest writing project I have ever attempted (including my 10th Grade book report on *The Red Badge of Courage,* which I think I got a 'D' on). So please join me and pray for my efforts to open up these *Resolutions*. They could bear much fruit in our lives today!

But beware! A warning should be attached:

RESOLVED.

These *Resolutions* will be hazardous to our love of ease, comfort, and self.

We are about to explore the heart of a man who did well. The jury is *in* on him, but still *out* on us. The ancient warning from Israel's King to the overconfident Ben-Hadad is timely for us as we embark:

One who puts on his armour should not boast like one who takes it off.
(1 Kings 20:11)

So, we will approach with reverence, humility, readiness and confidence in the Lord as we together see the resolve of one uncommon but not abnormal brother in Christ. These will not be for the casual, the shallow, the indifferent. They are for those who, knowing they have been apprehended by grace, set out to run well the race marked out before them.

I offer these simple expositions upon Edwards' *Resolutions* in the hope that something of the robust Jesus-following of his life may be birthed in us. May they serve to provoke us to valiant, dangerous, radical, world-defying - in short, normal - Christianity.

As to my method, Jonathan's *Resolutions* came from his heart in no special order. They did not arrive in neat categories, Themes are repeated. Nothing is systematized. I thought about trying to collate them to eliminate the repeats but, after several failed attempts (over years), I finally thought it best to take them all as they come ... from Jonathan's heart to ours. If he thought it necessary to repeat a theme, then perhaps we need to see something again in a slightly different light, take another dose of the medicine, or enjoy another slice of the pie. So, I make no apologies for any repeats. Take them not as redundant but as needed.

RESOLVED.

These first appeared as weekly *Pastoral Letters* to my dear congregation at Westbrooke Church, Overland Park, Kansas, and to our many mission partners in the UK and around the world.

Will you join me on this journey? If you are ready and willing you might want to begin by praying the simple and profound prayer of Augustine:

'O God, command what you will, and give what you command'.

Excited!
John G

***

A few warnings before you proceed:

1) Beware of the modern cry of 'legalism' to anything that approaches diligence. The two are not the same. They are not even remotely related. Diligence is a worthy response to the empowering grace of God. Legalism is labour in ignorance of the grace of God. These *Resolutions* are not the efforts of a religious man trying to find favour with a distant God. They are the proper responses of a man who has received God's favour.

2) Beware of thinking of any of these as 'quaint' and therefore not really weighty or relevant for you today. Such a move would betray modern arrogance when what is needed is a humble readiness to learn from one who has already run well and finished his course.

3) Beware of the emergent attitude which dares to suggest that we have arrived at some new understanding of discipleship while chuckling at the past. Humility is called for here. A teachable attitude which values history and honours those who have gone before will accomplish far more than a closed mind which disdains anything more than five years old.

4) Beware of confusing grace with licence. Grace empowers to change. Licence excuses the refusal to change. The prevailing attitude today is that 'grace' means 'sin really does not matter', and that the Gospel is God saying, 'Aw shucks, don't worry about it'. Nothing could be further from the truth. Old-timers understood that sin is truly wicked, God is truly holy, Hell is truly deserved, that the Gospel is truly amazing, and that one's salvation, while never earned is always proven by the pursuit of holiness empowered by grace.

5) Beware of trying to live these out 'solo'. The Christian life is meant to be lived and experienced within Christian community. If 'it takes a village to raise a child', it takes a church to raise a Jesus-follower. You will fail on your own. You need the discipline, direction, and love of a faithful family of believers around you.

6) Never forget that, in the end, you will be as holy and as happy as you want to be. God is not short on the supply of grace. His promises are sure and His willingness to work in you to your good and His Glory is not in question. Laziness will be rewarded with little joy and little transformation. Diligence will be rewarded with much joy and much transformation.

"If the LORD, whom I serve, has been pleased to favour me with that mediocrity of talent, which may qualify me for usefulness to the weak and poor of his flock, without quite disgusting persons of superior discernment, I have reason to be satisfied"

John Newton, Preface to *Olney Hymns,* 1779

Being sensible that I am unable to do anything without God's help, I do humbly entreat Him by his grace to enable me to keep these *Resolutions*, so far as they are agreeable to His will, for Christ's sake.

Jonathan Edwards

RESOLVED.

In all your course, walk with God and follow Christ as a little, poor, helpless child, taking hold of Christ's hand, keeping your eye on the mark of the wounds on his hand and side.

Jonathan Edwards in a pastoral letter to Deborah Hatheway

To Bruce Montgomery,
who first showed me how to
follow Jesus.

RESOLVED.

Resolved 1

Resolved, before all else, to do whatever will promote God's Glory, and my own good, profit and joy. And, as my happy duty, resolved to promote the good, profit and joy of others. I resolve to do this for the whole of my life, no matter how long it takes and no matter what challenges come my way, from now and into eternity.[1]

Whoever finds their life will lose it, and whoever loses their life,
for my sake, will find it.
(Matthew 10:39)

Delight yourself also in the Lord: and he shall give you
the desires of your heart.
(Psalm 37:4, NKJV)

Friends,

These *Resolutions* tumble from Jonathan's heart like precious gems spilled from a purse. We will take them as they come, warts and all (they are not Scripture!), knowing that they helped shape the soul of a good and useful servant of Jesus. May they do the same for us!

Our young Jonathan gets it right from the start: The goal and purpose of life is to live to and promote the Glory of God. To live for anything less (worldly comfort, acclaim, pleasure) is to live beneath our purpose. It is idolatry to seek to exalt anything above God and His Glory in our lives. And, since idols are impossible to please, idolatry always leads to brokenness. We are created and redeemed from sin so

---

[1] Throughout I have modernized Jonathan's wording. The originals are in the Appendix.

1

that we can promote, declare, and *enjoy* the wonder and goodness of God.

Look what Jonathan puts together, right in the same sentence: the Glory of God *and* his own good, profit, and joy. How can that be? How can we live for the Glory of God *and* at the same time, live for our own pleasure? Are we not called to deny ourselves, take up our cross, and follow Jesus?

Yes! Absolutely! But here is the wonder of this Christian Life: As we battle to dethrone *all* lesser 'gods' and enthrone Jesus solely and supremely in our lives, repenting with tears, refusing all pretenders and false lords to the thrones of our hearts, we discover *Jesus is the source and supply of all true joy, good, profit, and pleasure.*

There is no conflict between *true* pleasure and pleasure in God. There is great conflict between all lesser contenders for our hearts' affections and happiness in God.

We were *made* for joy as certainly as we were made for Jesus. We were *made* for pleasure as surely as we were made for God Himself. It is when we seek joy and pleasure apart from having God enthroned and glorified in our hearts and lives that the pursuit of our pleasure, profit, and good becomes idolatrous and destructive.

If we 'delight [ourselves] in the Lord', He will give us the 'desires of [our] heart[s]' (Psalm 37:4). *And* if we are delighted in Him, *He* will be the desire of our hearts that we receive!

The *Westminster Catechism* in 1648 said it perfectly:

Question: What is the chief end [grand purpose] of Man?
Answer: Man's chief end is to glorify God *and enjoy Him forever.*

2

RESOLVED.

C.S. Lewis famously put it as only he can:

> It would seem that Our Lord finds our desires not too strong, but too weak. We are half-hearted creatures, fooling about with drink and sex and ambition when infinite joy is offered us, like an ignorant child who wants to go on making mud pies in a slum because he cannot imagine what is meant by the offer of a holiday at the sea. We are far too easily pleased.[2]

George Muller put it this way:

> The first great and primary business to which I ought to attend every day is to have my soul happy in the Lord.[3]

Friend, go after the Glory of God! Go after the unrivalled pre-eminence of Jesus Christ – in every area of your life! Seek to promote the same in the lives and culture around you! Refuse all lesser rivals and pretenders! Battle for this daily, no matter how long it takes, how much repenting, refusing, and re-focusing it requires! Your true joy, good, and profit will be the inevitable and fitting result of your pursuit of God being rightly honoured in every facet of your life.

Let nothing deter, discourage, or distract you from seeking all your joy and profit in the promotion of the Lordship of Jesus in every corner of your life, and every corner of this world.

That marvellous Christian! He loses everything to gain all things. He goes down to go up. He is slave to all and slave to none. He is bound to Christ and yet the freest of all. He dies that he might live. He denies

---

[2] Lewis, C. S. (2001). *The Weight of Glory*, p.1. Grand Rapids, Michigan: Zondervan.

[3] Müller, G. (1855). *A Narrative of Some of the Lord's Dealings with George Müller: Written by Himself. II.* p. 417.

RESOLVED.

himself yet discovers himself. He despises his own glory as he pursues God's, and yet discovers total joy in the journey.
That marvellous Christian!

You make known to me the path of life; you will fill me with joy in your presence, with eternal pleasures at your right hand.
(Psalm 16:11)

'O Shepherd. You said you would make my feet like hinds' feet and set me upon High Places.

"Well", he answered, "the only way to develop hinds' feet is to go by the paths which the hinds use."'
(Hannah Hurnard) [4]

---

[4] Hurnard, H. (1979). *Hinds' Feet on High Places.* p.78, Tyndale House Publishers, Inc.

Resolved 2

Resolved to be always discovering new ways to Glorify God in my life and increase both my joy in Jesus and that of others.

The kingdom of heaven is like treasure hidden in a field. When a man found it, he hid it again, and then in his joy went and sold all he had and bought that field.
(Matthew 13:44)

Whoever wants to be my disciple must deny themselves and take up their cross daily and follow me.
(Luke 9:230

Dear Glory Seekers,

I want to begin with a caution.

I can almost hear someone charging young Jonathan with over-active zeal, perhaps chuckling a bit at the youthful idealism he expresses. For this I have two thoughts:

First, perhaps Jonathan, at times, needs some balance. Who doesn't? Maybe our adventure will offer some. But I caution against any of *us* (modern, Western Christians) being too quick to judge Christians of previous generations or contemporary Christians in far-off lands. *We* are not the 'Gold Standard' by which true discipleship is measured. Sorry if that hurts, but it is true. Jonathan (and perhaps your grandmother) was probably closer to a *normal* Christian than we are. What we write off as idealism may be just what Jesus meant when he likened the Kingdom-life to a merchant who *joyfully* sold all he had to buy a treasure-laden field. And Jonathan's 'over-active zeal' might match Jesus' when He declared that all comers must be self-denying cross bearers.

But secondly, when I read and think on Jonny's youthful resolve, I remember a time when I too, as a young Jesus-follower, was like him - before I became 'mature' and 'balanced' (horrible, self-conscious words!). During my middle years I would have read these *Resolutions* and thought, 'A bit much, these. Calm yourself, Jonathan!' But now that my earthly life is – statistically – 6/7ths *over*, I find myself thinking like Jonathan once again: Life is brief, Heaven is near, the Kingdom of God is what counts, Jesus is worth my very best all the time and in every way. Nowadays I read Jonny's *Resolutions* and say a hearty, 'Yes! Way to go Jonny! Keep bringing it!'

I need a good dose of his zeal and idealism!

We love, we admire, we applaud a 'go get 'em' attitude in a businessman, a mind for discovery in a scientist, creativity in an artist, or an urge to climb higher in an adventurer. Well, here is a young man who is applying just such an attitude toward the most wonderful thing in all the universe: God.

Do you see the sense of *adventure* in this *Resolution*?

> He is not lamenting,

> 'Why do I *have* to pursue God and His Glory?'

> He is not complaining,

> 'Why do I *have* to seek my good, joy, and profit in *Jesus*?'

> He is not moaning,

RESOLVED.

'Why *must* I seek that others discover their fullness in Christ?'

Just the opposite! He is saying, 'I want to forever be finding new ways to apprehend, and be apprehended by, the wonders of God! I want my Bible open and my mind engaged. I am ready to repent when I find sin within, and on the lookout for joy-robbing, God-dishonouring idols. I do not want *anything* to keep me from loving God, my own soul, and others, and I want to always be discovering how I can better promote the Glory of God in myself and in my world'.

He has *seen something*. He is *in the grip of something*. He is on a journey of discovery and the object is not a woman, a hobby, a passing treasure. It is nothing other than the Eternal God. Now get this: As *uncommon* as this may be to our time-bound values, it is *normal* for the child of grace. It is what we have been created and redeemed for. A hunger for God, for Him to capture our hearts and those of our fellows, should be the *normal* desire of the child of grace.

But you don't have to take it from me!

Take it from King David:

> *One thing I ask from the Lord,*
> *this only do I seek:*
> *that I may dwell in the house of the Lord*
> *all the days of my life,*
> *to gaze on the beauty of the Lord*
> *and to seek him in his temple.*
> (Psalm 27:4)

Take it from Paul:

RESOLVED.

My goal is that they may be encouraged in heart and united in love, so that they may have the full riches of complete understanding, in order that they may know the mystery of God, namely, Christ, in whom are hidden all the treasures of wisdom and knowledge.
(Colossians 2:2,3)

Take it from Jesus!

The kingdom of heaven is like treasure hidden in a field. When a man found it, he hid it again, and then in his joy went and sold all he had and bought that field.
(Matthew 13:44)

Friends, let's get back a sense of *adventure* in our pursuit of the Glory of God and our joy in Him! We dare not drag our feet as though we were being reluctantly hauled into the doctor's office! We are being invited into an eternity-long journey of discovery. Any reluctance betrays a poor view of God and an over-love of lesser things. I promise you, the most learned theologian, the most advanced follower of Jesus, has barely begun this glorious journey of discovery. May we join with Jonathan and stir our hearts heaven-ward. May we always be discovering new ways to glorify God in our lives and increase both our joy in Jesus and that of others.

The Lord be exalted, who delights in the well-being of his servant.
(Psalm 35:27)

'Now the Lord give you that grace to be humble; and then, according to his promise, he will make you rich in every other grace.'[1]
(Philip Henry to his son Matthew)

---

[1] Henry, M. (1839). *The Life of the Rev. Philip Henry, AM.* W. Ball.

8

RESOLVED.

Resolved 3

Resolved that, if and when I become lazy or dull and begin to neglect my spiritual well-being and these *Resolutions*, I will earnestly and quickly repent.

Godly sorrow brings repentance that leads to salvation and leaves no regret, but worldly sorrow brings death.
(2 Corinthians 7:10)

He restores my soul…
(Psalm 23:1)

Friend,

I have some very good news for you: God's Grace is not in short supply. We have a willing God and an open Heaven. God's supply is not a puddle, not even a lake, but an unending river of grace. And grace gives power: power to live life to the Glory of God.

Diligence with your heart will be repaid a thousand times over. No man or woman, has got, or ever will get to the end of their earthly journey and say, 'Dang! I was too diligent with my soul. I should have been less careful!'

But there is a need for watchfulness, carefulness over our hearts. It is dangerously easy to become lazy, dull, negligent, distracted. Hopefully, none of us will ever flat-out deny Jesus, but all of us face the very real danger of neglect, laziness, taking our eye off the ball. Nothing prospers without input. No garden thrives without attention. No one's body is healthy without deliberate intent.

RESOLVED.

Laziness might not keep you from Heaven, but it will keep you from *fullness*. Carelessness is costly. Jonathan knows himself. He is not so brash, so brave, as to believe that he cannot grow dull in his pursuit of God's Glory and his joy in Jesus. He knows that he can grow cold. Distractions abound. Sickness of soul often begins with neglect. It does not take outright rebellion to take one off course.

So, he factors *repentance* into his *Resolutions* right from the start.

I once asked a pilot, 'If you left London bound for New York, and began *one degree* off course, left uncorrected, how far would you be amiss of JFK airport at the end of the flight?'

'Three hundred miles.'

Would you be happy to be a passenger on *that* plane?

Let's remember, diligence is not legalism. It is a fitting response to the wonderful saving work of God. So, Jonathan resolves to repent when he finds himself growing lazy and dull. He has not committed adultery! He has not robbed a bank …yet! But he realizes that 'gross sin' begins with little acts of neglect. So, rather than let things get out of hand, he wisely resolves to be diligent with the little habits of life.

So, let's ask ourselves a few questions. These do not represent rules. They represent *responses* to Jesus.

> - How is my daily prayer time? Am I opening my heart to Heaven every day, even as I open my mouth to food?
> - How is my time in God's Word? Am I renewing my mind with Truth or am I neglecting to do so, allowing the world to shape my thinking?

10

RESOLVED.

- With whom am I keeping company? Am I running with the wise or stumbling with the foolish?
- How is my private world? Am I doing anything in secret that I would be ashamed to have known in public?
- How is my conversation? Is it sweet and edifying, or bitter and discouraging? Am I remembering that I will give an account for every careless word spoken?
- How is my thought life? Am I seeking to honour Jesus with the meditations of my heart? If my thought life were a movie, what would it be rated?

If I find myself slacking in these right and good responses to the love of God, I need to quickly correct my course. Listen! Real Christians can make a real mess of things! Spiritual health and spiritual disease begin in these tell-tale areas. No real Christian ever wakes up and out of the blue decides to deny Christ and do some horrible thing. It begins with neglect, laziness, distraction. To know yourself, to examine your life, is not over-doing it: It is *basic discipleship,* and it bears sweet fruit.

The renowned violinist, Jascha Heifetz, said, 'If I don't practice one day, I know it; two days, the critics know it; three days, the public knows it'.

King David … who certainly knew what it was like to get careless with his heart and make a huge mess of things, put it this way:

Search me, God, and know my heart, test me and know
my anxious thoughts.
See if there is any offensive way in me, and lead me
in the way everlasting....
... May the words of my mouth and the meditation of my heart
be pleasing in your sight, O Lord, my Rock and my Redeemer.
(Psalm 139:23,24; Psalm 19:14)

RESOLVED.

Oh Friend, let us learn the wonderful help of repenting quickly! Let us never be too afraid, ashamed, proud, or slow to run to Jesus with our sin! Let us learn and understand our hearts and become accustomed to the sound of sin's stealthy approaches. Let us believe that big failings begin in the small places - little words, secret thoughts, prayerless days.

God has such joy for us, such purpose, abundant goodness! He *wants* us to be captivated by Him and pursue Him. I cannot tell you, with any degree of confidence or accuracy, what God has in store for this nation. I do not know if He will send a yearned-for revival or a deserved judgment. But I can say with *certainty* what God will do for you, and for me: If we will be desirous of Him above all else and live a life where repentance from the little sins that lead to the big sins marks our way, then I am sure that He will show Himself to us and lead us into usefulness and fullness that will bring Him much Glory and much good to us and those around us.

> *But one thing I do: forgetting what is behind and straining*
> *towards what is ahead, I press on towards the goal to win the*
> *prize for which God has called me heavenwards in Christ Jesus.*
> (Philippians 3:13,14)

'Many sensational gifts and talents don't mean much over the
long haul. The longer I live, the more I treasure people who just
keep walking with God.'[1]
(Jim Cymbala)

---

[1] Cymbala, J. (2003). *Fresh faith: What Happens When Real Faith Ignites God's People*. Grand Rapids, Michigan: Zondervan.

Resolved 4

Resolved to do all things with my whole being, body and soul, big or small, to the Glory of God, and, so far as possible, to avoid anything which offends God and His Glory.

And whatever you do, whether in word or deed, do it all in the
name of the Lord Jesus, giving thanks to
God the Father through him.
(Colossians 3:17)

This is the word of the Lord to Zerubbabel: 'Not by
might nor by power, but by my Spirit,'
says the Lord Almighty.
(Zechariah 4:6)

Question:

How does a young man on the frontier of civilization, far from the power centres of his world, with little money and few worldly helps, rise to become a shaper not only of his generation, but of generations and even nations to come? What was it about this man that made him so useful to God? How was it that the Gospel advanced so much in his hands? How did Jonathan Edwards become Jonathan Edwards?

I am not sure if the Gospel has ever prospered and gone forward because Christians had plenty of money and worldly power. The Gospel prospers when Christians really know Jesus, go deep with Him, and resolve to live their whole lives for His Glory, regardless of all else. If we are as concerned with spiritual riches and power as we are with material riches and power, we can be world-changers. Even a surface knowledge of the history of missions will reveal the wondrous

13

fact the Gospel has prospered through those who concerned themselves not with stuff, but with Christ.

Meet C.T. Studd (1860-1931). He was an English cricket star. For you 'Yanks', cricket is the Englishman's answer to baseball. (If you think baseball is slow...). He gave away a fortune and went on the mission field. He knew Jesus deeply. The spiritually shallow come out with sayings like, 'If only God would save the rich and famous, then we would see the Kingdom come'. But God just does not seem to work that way. Studd *was* rich and famous when Jesus grabbed him, and he made himself nothing so that Christ could be something in him. It would be like Patrick Mahomes or David Beckham giving up their fame and their riches, at the height of their physical powers, to go to some totally obscure place for the sake of the Gospel. Studd went to India and then Africa. People thought that was crazy, but God did not, and the history of Christian missions (far more important than the history of cricket or football) has vindicated him.

Hear him:

> How could I spend the best years of my life in living for the honours of this world, when thousands of souls are perishing every day? [1]

> Some want to live within the sound of church or chapel bell;
> I want to run a rescue shop within a yard of hell.[2]

Studd became a world-changer. I know we use that term a lot. But he really did. He founded WEC International, which has trained and sent out thousands into the mission field. Only eternity will reveal the true

---

[1] Grubb, N. (2014). *CT Studd: Cricketer and Pioneer*, p 179. The Lutterworth Press.

[2] Cited in many texts by many authors.

impact of his decision to do all things with his whole being, body and soul, big or small, to the Glory of God.

The history of Christian missions is loaded with amazing stories of nobodies who lived for the Glory of God and thus became world-shakers:

George Muller,

Hudson Taylor,

Amy Carmichael,

Henry Martyn,

Catherine Booth.

Spiritual giants. Spiritual billionaires. They lived for God's Glory, not their own.

Will *your* name be added to that list? Will *mine*?

Spiritual wealth is the currency of the Kingdom. By spiritual wealth I mean:

A true and genuine knowledge of Jesus Christ,

A heart for holiness,

A charitable spirit,

A love for the lost,

RESOLVED.

A hunger for truth,

A life lived for the Glory of God.

To be rich in such things is to be truly rich. It is to be powerful in the things that matter. God's way is so different than ours! To Him, a widow's two pennies are worth more than all the cash of the world's rich (Luke 21:2). God can do amazing things through the 'surrendered simple'.

When our young Jonathan resolves 'to do all things with my whole being, body, and soul, big or small, to the Glory of God, and, so far as possible, to avoid anything which offends God and His Glory', he is pursuing spiritual wealth; He is exercising spiritual muscle; He is purchasing shares in the Kingdom of God; He is choosing true riches over temporary riches.

This is a rich *Resolution*.

Captivated by Christ and His Gospel, wooed by things unseen, this young man - barely old enough to shave - brings to mind Moses, the young prince of Egypt:

By faith Moses, when he had grown up, refused to be known as the son of Pharaoh's daughter. He chose to be mistreated along with the people of God rather than to enjoy the fleeting pleasures of sin. He regarded disgrace for the sake of Christ as of greater value than the treasures of Egypt, because he was looking ahead to his reward. By faith he left Egypt, not fearing the king's anger; he persevered because he saw him who is invisible.
(Hebrews 11:24-27)

16

So, I say again, if we are as concerned with spiritual riches as we are with material, we will be world-changers. To resolve to live for the Glory of God, both in soul and body, that is, in the secret place of the heart, and the public place of the actions, is to embark upon a life of spiritual power and purpose. Go deep with Christ. Seek to become a giant in spiritual things. Determine that the currency of the Kingdom will be your treasure. In an age of material wealth at the price of spiritual poverty, by God's grace, determine that yours will be a life marked by something more than fleeting fancies. Determine that yours will be a life marked by the currency of the Kingdom.

Nothing can hinder the Lord from saving, whether by many or by few.
(1 Samuel 14:6)

'I sometimes think that the Lord was looking for
someone weak enough and small enough to use, so that
that all the glory would go to Him and not to a man,
and that He found me.'[3]
(Hudson Taylor)

---

[3] I heard this quote from the godly and manly Rev Geoffrey Sharp, Plymouth Methodist Central Hall, during a drive in his car to a prayer meeting in 1987. I recall it from memory as I have never found it in print.

Resolved 5

Resolved never to lose one moment of time but to use each moment in the most profitable way I possibly can.

Be very careful, then, how you live – not as unwise but as wise, making the most of every opportunity, because the days are evil. Therefore, do not be foolish, but understand what the Lord's will is.
(Ephesians 5:15-17)

Come to me, all you who are weary and burdened, and I will give you rest. Take my yoke upon you and learn from me, for I am gentle and humble in heart, and you will find rest for your souls. For my yoke is easy and my burden is light.
(Matthew 11:29-30)

Dear Friend in Jesus,

Before we *dare* venture farther down this *Resolutions* highway with Jonathan, I need to have a heart-to-heart with you. Stop what you are doing and lean in with me. I must ask you a question. It is the most urgent question I can ever ask you: Are you fully, totally, desperately, joyfully trusting in all that Jesus Christ is and all He has done for your salvation? Have you harboured your soul in Him and His Gospel? Do you rejoice that Jesus lived the sinless life that God required of you? Do you rejoice that He died the sinner's death that God required of you?

Yes?

Are you sure and certain that all your hope is in Christ and Christ *alone*?

OK! That being settled, we can proceed!

RESOLVED.

Why did I press you so? Why did I ask you the same question five different ways? Because unless we are living out of the fullness of Christ crucified for our sins and risen for our justification, this *Resolution* will produce legalistic despair in us. But from the position of security in Jesus, this *Resolution* has the power to deliver us from the tyranny of the urgent and unto the freedom of walking in God's daily purposes for us. Submitting our time - our moments and our days - to the Lordship of Jesus will actually set us free from bondage to our own agenda. *Our* timetable inevitably wearies and burdens. *His* timetable actually ensures our fruitfulness *and* provides rest for our souls – for He is gentle and humble.

So, from that place of safety in Jesus and His wonderful Gospel, here we go!

Oh, the brevity of life! Oh, the shortness of time! How soon our earthly days are over! How soon we will be called to give account to our Lord and Saviour for our lives, our years, our days, our hours, our minutes! I think here of the Psalmist's wise prayers:

Teach us to number our days, that we may gain a heart of wisdom ...
... Show me, Lord, my life's end, and the number of my days;
let me know how fleeting my life is.
(Psalm 90:12; Psalm 39:4)

I know Jonathan's words have a whiff of youthful zeal about them. I want to say, 'Learn to relax a bit, son! You resolve to "never lose one moment of time"? Really?' I feel the temptation to excuse Jonny for his overzealousness and thereby let us off the hook. But that would be too easy. Remember, he held himself to this *Resolution* for the next 35 years. It was not so much an expression of his youthful zeal as of his life-long resolve to not waste *any* of his earthly days.

RESOLVED.

So, let's take the medicine. Our generation is a wasteful (the Bible word for wasteful is *prodigal*) generation. We have more leisure than any culture has ever imagined. We have it so good *now* that rarely do we contemplate the fast approach of death and our day of account. *We are wasters.* We waste food, we waste stuff, but worst of all, we waste *time.* Would we not do well to live with life's end in view? Would we not benefit from living with an eye on Heaven? Would it not help us to 'make the most of every opportunity' if we remembered every day that life is brief and soon our wonderful Lord and Saviour will call us to give our account?

Oh, if I could have some days back! I mourn the days I spent being irritable instead of cheerful, selfish instead of giving, wallowing instead of worshipping! How often I have wasted grace! I need to press in here and - with repentance in my heart - ask Jesus to give me grace to 'make the most of every opportunity', or, as the King James Version says, to 'redeem the time'. And I need to be motivated by joy. I need to *want* to use my moments and my days for Jesus and for others; I need to *want* to not waste my time.

Our Bible passage at the top of this letter from Ephesians 5 reminds us of our great Gospel reason for being diligent with our time: 'because the days are evil'. We are in a war! How dare we play and snooze our way through the battle! Opportunities are abounding for us to spread the fame of Jesus for the joy of all peoples. These are *our days.* We should be as earnest – and excited - as a farmer at harvest or a fisherman before a bountiful sea. It is our time to grasp opportunities.

Not all of us are as gifted as Jonathan Edwards was. His output was profound. It was as though he packed two lifetimes into his 54 years. Not all of us can 'go' as hard as he did. (He usually spent 13 hours a day in study, counsel, teaching, preaching, and writing, on top of caring for his family of eleven children.) I am thankful for times of leisure that Jesus gives me. Sometimes resting and re-creating *is* the best use of my time. That is OK! But the challenge here is for us to live each day in the light of 'That Day' as accountable stewards of the life and gifts that God has given to us.

Jesus is not a slavedriver! He is actually easy to please. *His* yoke is easy and His burden is light. In fact, I am confident that we will find *His* Lordship over our time far more 'do-able' and pleasant than *our* lordship over our time.

So, in a spirit of Gospel joy, from one who has been redeemed from sin and slavery to safety in Jesus, here is my offering to you: Let's receive this challenge from Jonathan to bring, *deliberately, actively, and happily,* our days and moments – including our hobbies and leisure times – under the lordship of Jesus Christ. My best advice is that we begin each and every day by lifting our hearts to the Lord Jesus and *asking Him for grace* to live that day as He would have us live it – including our work, our rest, our play, our chores, our engagements. If we make this our life habit, we will find deliverance from the tyranny of the urgent into the freedom of the purposes of our good, gracious, and generous God.

For it is by grace you have been saved, through faith – and this is not from yourselves, it is the gift of God – not by works, so that no one can boast. For we are God's handiwork, created in Christ Jesus to do good works, which God prepared in advance for us to do.
(Ephesians 2:8-10)

'Time is given us to use in view of eternity.'[1] (Harry Ironside)

---

[1] Widely attributed to Harry Ironside.

RESOLVED.

Resolved 6

Resolved to live with all my might, for all of my life.

For Christ's love compels us.
(2 Corinthians 5:14)

Therefore, since we are surrounded by such a great cloud of witnesses, let us throw off everything that hinders and the sin that so easily entangles. And let us run with perseverance the race marked out for us, fixing our eyes on Jesus, the pioneer and perfecter of faith.
(Hebrews 12:1-2)

Friends,

Joe DiMaggio, from 1936 to 1951, excluding the three years that he spent in the U.S. Military during World War II, played more than 2000 Major League Baseball games for the New York Yankees. During that time, his team won the World Series nine times.

Known for his tenacious competitiveness and phenomenal skill, 'The Yankee Clipper' summed up his heart with these words: [1] 'I'm just a ballplayer with one ambition, and that is to give it all. I've got to help my ball club win. I've never played any other way'.

Late in his illustrious career, when his aging body was wearing out, and he could only play with great pain, 'Joltin' Joe' was asked why he still insisted upon giving it his all, every game, every play, no matter what, even if the effort would have no impact on the outcome of a particular

---

[1] The following two quotes are from the Joe DiMaggio Official Website: http://www.joedimaggio.com/the-legacy/quotes-from-joe/

game. His reply? 'Because there's always some kid who may be seeing me for the first or last time. I owe him my best'.

Such an attitude grips me. It challenges me! It judges me! Can I sum up my heart so clearly? Can I say of my dedication to Christ and His Gospel: 'I'm just a Jesus-follower with one ambition, and that is to give it all. I've got to help the cause of Christ win. I've never lived any other way'?

Can I say of my resolve to give my all for Christ, every moment, regardless of pain and discomfort: 'There's always some lost soul who may be seeing Christ in me for the first or last time. I owe him my best'?

Jonathan Edwards would understand Joe DiMaggio...at least in a sense. His resolve 'to live with all my might, for all of my life', resonates with Dimaggio's, only for Edwards the stakes are infinitely higher, the rewards forever more glorious, the cost of lethargy beyond estimation. He delivers a similar *Resolution* later on, adding the motive of wanting to leave this brief life with no regrets:

> I frequently hear persons in old age say how they would live, if they were to live their lives over again: Resolved that I will live just so as I can think I shall wish I had done, supposing I live to old age.

The thing that gets me is that we applaud such resolve in a ballplayer. We make a hero of him and induct him into our Hall of Fame. But, let a Christian show such heart-attitude for Things Eternal, and we deem him:

A fanatic,
Unbalanced,
Legalistic,

RESOLVED.

Weird...

Joltin' Joe knew he could never get a ball game back. We can never get back a meal with a friend, a talk over the garden fence with a neighbour, or an encounter with a lonesome soul on the bus. Richard Baxter looked upon every sermon preached as though it might be his last: 'I preach as a dying man to dying men'. Every day we receive 1440 minutes from the Lord. We can waste them or use them well. Every week we receive 168 hours from Jesus. We can give our best with them or squander them. But we can never get them back.

Solomon, reflecting upon a life largely wasted, urges us:

> *Whatever your hand finds to do, do it with all your might.*
> (Ecclesiastes 6:10)

Resting in Jesus and His finished work for our sins (a good thing) is not to be confused with becoming lazy or half-hearted (a bad thing). The quaint slogan, 'Let Go and Let God', might look sweet on a coffee cup, but its questionable theology might put you to sleep when you need to be on high alert. Perhaps you should put that cup back on the shelf, right between the ones that say, 'Don't Wrestle, Nestle', and 'Why Struggle When You Can Snuggle?' and leave it there.

How about some biblical descriptions of discipleship:

> Fight the Good Fight!
> I make my body a slave...
> Make every effort...
> Pursue holiness!
> Take up the cross and follow!
> I die daily...
> Count it all joy when you experience trials...

RESOLVED.

Spur one another on…
Awake! You sleeper…
The Love of Christ compels me!

It is hard to find a picture of DiMaggio in a baseball uniform without a smile on his face. Could it be that there is a direct link between being sold-out for something and joy? I think so! Could it be that the lot of the half-hearted is joylessness? I know so! Do you picture a lemon-faced Edwards, or a joy-filled, earnest, worshipping, delivered, focused, relieved, Heaven-bound, young life-grabber making this *Resolution*?

For Jonathan Edwards it is all or nothing, every day, for all of his days. Christ is worthy of nothing less. Joy demands nothing less. The 'team' deserves nothing less. The watching world needs nothing less.

> *I am greatly encouraged; in all our troubles my joy*
> *knows no bounds.*
> (2 Corinthians 7:4)

> *For the joy that was set before him Jesus endured the cross,*
> *scorning its shame.*
> (Hebrews 12:1)

Jim Elliot (1927-1956) knew the joy of giving his all for Jesus. What an impact his brief life had … and is having! Elliot prayed, 'I seek not a long life, but a full one, like you Lord Jesus'.[2] That is just what he received. Found dead in an Ecuadorean river with a spear in his back, his all-or-nothing life for Jesus not only resulted in an entire Amazonian people group coming to Christ, but in thousands of young people being motivated for missions (I was one of them!).

---

[2] Elliot, J. (1948) Diary entry.

RESOLVED.

Jim, Joe, and Jon would have had a bang-up time together. They were cut from the same bolt of cloth. If ever I could find them sitting around a fire, passionately and joyfully talking about giving life their all, I would have to crash the party. 'Hey Jonny, Joey, and Jimmy, move over! Let me squeeze in! I need a dose of what you have!'

I want to be a happy member of that exclusive but inviting club: The Fellowship of the Whole-Hearted.

Will you join me?

> *Jesus replied: 'Love the Lord your God with all*
> *your heart and with all your soul and with all your mind...'*
> (Matthew 22:37)

'Wherever you are, be all there! Live to the hilt every situation you
believe to be the will of God.'[3]
(Jim Elliot)

---

[3] Elliot, J. & Elliot, E. (1978). *The Journals of Jim Elliot*. Old Tappan: N.J: Revell Co.

RESOLVED.

Resolved 7

Resolved to never do anything which I would not do if I knew
I had but one hour left to live.

*You also must be ready because the Son of Man will come
at an hour when you do not expect him.*
(Luke 12:40)

*What is your life? You are a mist that appears for a
little while, and then vanishes.*
(James 4:14)

Dear Friends,

It might be helpful if we turn Jonathan's *Resolution* on its head and
formulate it positively:

Resolved to do always those things which I would do if I knew
I had just one hour left to live.

Too radical?

Before we write this *Resolution* off as 'impossible' or 'unreasonable',
let's take some time and consider the wisdom in it. It just might do us
(and those around us who are having to put up with us) the world
of *good.*

Part of our problem might be that we do not rejoice in the thought of
Heaven enough. Do we really believe that the Bible is right when it tells
us that to 'depart and be with Christ ... is ... better by far' (Philippians
1:23)? If we can anticipate Heaven - which we cannot gain without

dying first - like a child anticipates Christmas morning, Jonathan's *Resolution* suddenly makes obvious sense. *How else can I think?*
Do you ever ponder your final day? Students think about graduation; businessmen dream of their retirement; little girls joyfully imagine their wedding day. But when it comes thinking about, hoping for, living for, the sure-to-come day when we exchange these 'Shadowlands' for God's solid Heaven, we, strangely, push those thoughts away.

Forgetting that we are 'frail creatures of dust', we put up with no end of foolishness in our lives which we would never allow were it the last day of our lives, and we knew it to be.

It is not morbid to consider, often, the brevity of life, the nearness of death, and the wonders of Heaven. It is wise to do so. We live better *in* time when we realize that soon we will be *out* of time. In fact, the Jesus-Followers who have lived the best, most useful, lives have been those who have lived with their fast-approaching death in clear view.

What would *you* do if you knew that today was your last day this side of Heaven? How would you live differently? Would your attitudes and actions be different if you knew that this was to be your last day with your spouse, children, colleagues, friends, enemies? If you knew that tomorrow you would be with Jesus, would you live and witness differently today?

If you knew this to be your last hour, would you spend it looking at pornography? Gossiping? Complaining? Would you go shopping? Would you give in to lust, greed, envy and bitterness or would you battle for holiness, lift your head to Heaven, and summon supernatural strength for one more good sprint to the finish line?

RESOLVED.

Living each day in the light of our last day delivers us from selfish, surface living. Calvin Miller tells the story of a dying friend:

> I met one of my best friends on the day she learned that she had less than six months to live. No life should be lived without one such friend. For only when the edges of life are clearly marked, does friendship celebrate all its gifts with understanding...

> Her name was Anne, and while, by her own confession, her last months were far from morose, she spent her days 'sorting'. With Anne's short lifespan, we had time to contemplate and enjoy only the absolute essentials of our relationship. The dial of the clock's finality moved with hands so swift that things cheap and temporary held no fascination.

> Anne was physically beautiful. She had spent a great deal of her life maximizing her beauty with cosmetics. Her skin was ivory and warm. But things dermal and outward lose their importance when things visceral and inward go wrong. Down where creams and oils cannot penetrate, the body must sometimes reckon with strong judgments. Then the deep issues of life must hold sway over all things surface.[1]

'The deep issues of life', these are the very things we tend to ignore. Like that sick goldfish you had when you were a kid, our culture sucks from the surface, afraid, unwilling, unable to go deep. But find almost anyone who is knowingly living their last days and you will find a person who has moved beyond surface to depth, beyond image to substance. Our eighteen-year-old Jonathan is advising us to live *every* day this way.

---

[1] Miller, C. (2000). *Into the Depths of God,* p.13. Minneapolis: Bethany House.

RESOLVED.

Living with the end in view produces power and perseverance in us. Seeing the finish line emboldens us to call out to God for power to run well.

Eric Liddell (1902-45) was a follower of Jesus. He was also a very fast runner. The 'Flying Scotsman' ran for Great Britain in the 1924 Olympics. Having refused to run the 100 meter heat on a Sunday, he opted to run the mid-week 400 instead. It was not his best event. He won the race. He set a new Olympic record.

When asked how he managed to win a race which was not his forte, he revealed his simple strategy:

> I ran the first 200 as fast as I could, and then, with God's help,
> I ran the second 200 even faster.[2]

Friend! There is something about having the end in view that causes us to call out for God! There is something about knowing that you are rounding that last bend which focuses one's attention, spurs one on, and energizes one's efforts. Living with the end in sight encourages - forces - one to summon God's help ... and God gives us His help!

Now, here is the thing: We *never know* when we are rounding that last bend! You might be rounding it today! I might be on the home stretch. You might be 18 or 85, but you never know when God's ordained days for you are up. Only God knows.

> *All the days ordained for me*
> *were written in your book*
> *before one of them came to be.*
> (Psalm 139:16)

---

[2] https://www.truthforlife.org/resources/sermon/approved-god/

RESOLVED.

So, either we:

1) Ignore death. Live carelessly, with no thought of tomorrow, of our death, of eternity … only to die unprepared.

2) Fear death. Live a frightened life, hugging the shore, afraid venture out lest we perish … only to miss God's purposes for us.

3) Be ready for death. Recognizing our mortality and God's saving mercy, fix our eyes on the prize and live every day as though it could be our last … thereby discovering the freedom and joy of running this race with all our might.

Jonathan is wise beyond his years. I need to learn from this eighteen-year-old! Oh, to live *every day* with the conscious thought that soon, very soon, I shall be summoned by the King!

> What a tonic for the tired!
> What a boost for the bored!
> What a rebuke to the restless!
> What a jolt to the joyless!
> What a warning for the worldly!
> What a wonder for the weary!

Heaven! Being with Jesus! Soon!

Therefore, since we are surrounded by such a great cloud of witnesses, let us throw off everything that hinders and the sin that so easily entangles. And let us run with perseverance the race marked out for us, fixing our eyes on Jesus, the pioneer and perfecter of faith.
(Hebrews 12:1,2)

'When it comes time to die, make sure that all you have to do is die.'[3]
(Jim Elliott)

---

[3] Elliot, J., & Elliot, E. (1978). *The Journals of Jim Elliot.* Revell Co.

RESOLVED.

Resolved 8

Resolved, in my speaking and in my doing, to always remember that there is no-one more a sinner than I, to always remember that I have the same weaknesses and failings as others, and, when I see *others'* sin, to be reminded of my own sins, and use the failings of another to lead me to confess my own sins.

But the tax collector, standing some distance away, was even unwilling to lift up his eyes to heaven, but was beating his breast, saying, 'God, be merciful to me, the sinner!'
(Luke 18:13 NASB)

Why do you look at the speck of sawdust in your brother's eye and pay no attention to the plank in your own eye?
(Matthew 7:3)

Dear Friend in Jesus,

Jonathan is going hard after God! His earnestness over his own heart and life is at the same time inspiring and disturbing. Of course, it is inspiring to see a young man with such a sold-out heart for Jesus, but we need to admit that *his* singleness of heart for Jesus might reveal *our* divided heart. Disturbing!

So, before we proceed with Jonathan's eighth *Resolution,* let's pause a moment, catch our breath, stretch a bit, gulp some water, and then hit the track.

Running with Jonathan is, for me, like trying to keep up with Usain Bolt. 'Hey Jonny! Wait up!' I am not going to keep up with Jonathan stride for stride. But that does not mean that I cannot run the same race as well as *I* can and finish the course. It does not mean that I cannot

32

learn from Jonathan's stride. The more I see Jon sprinting ahead, the more I need to remember that this whole adventure with Jesus is a *grace adventure.* Jesus has saved me and apprehended me because *He* is wonderful, not because I am! And He will give me all the power I need to run well.

> *May our Lord Jesus Christ himself and God our Father,*
> *who loved us and by his grace gave us eternal encouragement*
> *and good hope, encourage your hearts, and strengthen you*
> *in every good deed and word.*
> (2 Thessalonians 2:16,17)

Jonathan would be the first to say that this entire enterprise of following Jesus is a *Gospel* endeavour. It is all from God. The will to run is from God. The ability to run is from God. Grace is there when we stumble and fall. Some of us will run with a firm, strong stride. Some of us will limp our way along. Some of us will have to be carried. But for each one of us it will be Jesus and His grace that enables us to start, to keep going, and to finish! I can imagine Jonny looking back over his shoulder at me - way back in his dust - having heard my faint, 'Wait up!' and shouting back, 'Don't look at me! Look at Jesus!' For it is Jesus, not Jonathan who gives all strength and all joy for this race.

It will be good here to recall Jonathan's preamble to his *Resolutions*, for it roots them in grace and the Gospel:

> Being sensible that I am unable to do anything without God's help, I do humbly entreat Him by his grace to enable me to keep these *Resolutions*, so far as they are agreeable to His will, for Christ's sake.

So, with gracious Jesus in full view, let's hit the track with Jonathan's next *Resolution.*

RESOLVED.

Read it again, if you will, at the top of this letter.

It is all about how we see and deal with our own sins.

How we view our own sin and failing says much about the true state of our souls. Many of us spend much of our time fussing over the sins of *others*, when what is needful is that we be diligent with our own hearts, and deal with our own sins.

Listen! We have a merciful God who is *always* ready to hear us when we confess and cleanse us when we cry to Him! So, you and I will do well to realize our sin and run to –not from - Jesus.

> *If we confess our sins, he is faithful and just and will forgive us*
> *our sins and purify us from all unrighteousness.*
> (1 John 1:9)

> *Godly sorrow brings repentance that leads to salvation and*
> *leaves no regret.*
> (2 Corinthians 7:10)

To view *myself* as 'the sinful one' is not morbid. It is reality. When I stop complaining to God about everyone else and instead humble myself before Him and deal with *my* sin, then my world actually changes. Do you remember the parable Jesus told of the two men who went to church? You can read the story in Luke 18. The 'good man' prayed, 'Lord, I thank you that I am better than others!' The 'bad man' simply beat his breast and – literally – prayed, 'God, remove your wrath from me *the* sinner!' *The* sinner! 'Lord! I am the problem! I thought it was my wife, or my kids, or the other person, but now I see that the problem is *me*!' Jesus said that *this* man, the 'bad man,' not the *other* man, the 'good man,' went home right with God.

34

RESOLVED.

What victory!

G. K. Chesterton (1874-1936) was a famous British author and Christian thinker. The story is told (it may be true, it may be an urban legend, but either way it bears truth) that *The Times* newspaper asked numerous famous authors to write an essay answering the question:

What is wrong with the world?

Chesterton's essay was the shortest ... and the most profound:

I am.[1]

Right on, G.K!

It is the testimony of almost any and every person who has walked long with Jesus that they see their sins more clearly than ever and Christ's mercy more wonderfully than ever. It was the aged and godly John Newton who said it so well:

My memory is nearly gone, but I remember two things: That I am a great sinner, and that Christ is a great Saviour.[2]

What if, as Jonathan resolved to do, *I* get to grips with *my* own sins before God and give grace to others for theirs? What if, as urged by Jonathan, when I see another's sin, *I* go to the Lord over *my own* instead of 'tut tut-ing' over theirs? *My reaction* to the sins of others is often *more sinful* than their sin was in the first place.

---

[1] https://www.theguardian.com/books/booksblog/2010/jan/08/gk-chesterton-world-whats-wrong see also Chesterton, G. K. (1912). *What's Wrong with the World*. London; Toronto: Cassell.

[2] Cited in Aitken, J. (2007). *John Newton: From Disgrace to Amazing Grace*, p.347. Wheaton, IL: Crossway.

RESOLVED.

Certainly, this is the 'speck vs. plank' issue that Jesus spoke of. Let's admit that we can feel a perverse pride over our brother's sin. We can gloat over his speck, all the while not seeing that our *attitude* toward his speck has become a log in our own eye! Fellowship is broken as our pride and self-deceit causes a barrier to be raised between us. How much better to use their sin as an occasion to examine our own hearts and lives!

This would be revolutionary, both in terms of my relationship with God and my relationship with others.

O Friend! Through the Gospel we have a merciful God and an open Heaven! Never be slow to repent and confess, for your cries will be heard, your sins will be cleansed, and your peace will be restored. Avoid like the plague seeing yourself as better, and others as the problem. You and I have jurisdiction over no hearts but our own.

Is this not the way to true revival? Do not wonders happen when we *go low* with God? *Anything* (including someone else's sin!) that brings me to the foot of the cross again, repenting, confessing, and being cleansed by the blood of Jesus is a *good* thing.

May we find our fellowship together on Calvary's hill, where we meet at the foot of the Cross.

In repentance and rest is your salvation ...
(Isaiah 30:15)

'Love will flow from one to another, when each is prepared to be known as the repentant sinner he is at the Cross of Jesus.' [3]
(Roy Hession)

---

[3] Hession, R. (2016). *The Calvary Road*, p.10. CLC Publications.

RESOLVED.

'Sinners are attractive because they are loved; they are not loved because they are attractive.'[4]
(Martin Luther)

---

[4] Martin Luther. Quoted in Reeves, M. (2021). *Overflow*.p.34. Moody Publishers.

RESOLVED.

Resolved 9

Resolved to think much on all occasions of my own dying, and of the common circumstances which attend death.

Show me, Lord, my life's end, and the number of my days;
let me know how fleeting my life is.
(Psalm 39:4)

... it is appointed unto men once to die...
(Hebrews 9:27 KJV)

Dear Friends,

Some years ago, my eye caught the headline of a British newspaper: British Death Rate Declines. Really? I know what the well-meaning journalist was *trying* to say – simply that people in the UK were living longer.

But the death rate hadn't declined. It was, is, and shall forever be ... 100%.

In the olden days, followers of Jesus prepared themselves for their dying day. They contemplated the brevity of life as a normal part of their devotion to Jesus. Christians wrote and read books about death. Preachers preached about how to die well. Pastors considered it their duty to prepare their flock to meet God.

In 1651, Jeremy Taylor published *The Rules and Exercises of Holy Dying*. Richard Baxter published *Dying Thoughts* in 1683. When John Wesley gathered his preachers together each year, he asked for accounts of 'triumphant deaths' amongst their people. The early Methodist were known for their 'good deaths'. A physician said to Charles Wesley

38

RESOLVED.

'Most people die for fear of dying, but I never met with such people as yours. They are none of them afraid of death!'[1]

Charles Spurgeon preached often about death. One of his most memorable sermons was entitled 'Precious Deaths', taken from Psalm 116:15:

Precious in the sight of the Lord is the death of his faithful servants.

Refusing to contemplate your death will not make you live one minute longer. Considering your life's end will not make you live longer, but it will make you live - and die - better.

Jonathan Edwards was not morbid to 'think much on all occasions' of his dying. Neither was Richard Baxter, who disciplined himself to think on Heaven for thirty minutes each day. Spurgeon was not perverse to preach on the preciousness of a Christian's death. These people lived in light of Eternity. They kept an eye on Heaven. They did not love *this life* more than they loved the thought of being with Jesus, and they knew and understood that in order to be with Jesus, they would have to die. So, they diligently prepared to die well.

As a great piece of music builds toward its finale, or a sports event moves toward a goal and a prize, so the aim of a Christian must be to finish well. We need to see that it is *normal* and *needful* for a Christian make all effort to do so. Listen to the Apostle Paul:

I am torn between the two [remaining here or dying and going to be with Jesus]: I desire to depart and be with Christ, which is better by far ... I press on towards the goal to win the prize for which God has called me heavenwards in Christ Jesus.

---

[1] https://www.seedbed.com/dying-well-according-to-john-wesley/

RESOLVED.

(Philippians 1:23; 3:14)

As followers of Jesus, we look at death through the lens of the Gospel. As believers in Jesus, we must have neither a morbid fascination with death nor a fanciful denial of death. Death has been defeated through the death of Jesus and his victorious resurrection. John Owen, a Puritan, actually wrote a book entitled *The Death of Death in the Death of Christ*![2] It no longer has power over us, and the grave will not have the final say over us.

Considering our death makes us wise for life. Psalm 90:12 invites us to ask God to '[t]each us to number our days, that we may gain a heart of wisdom'. We gain focus. We stop wasting time and energy on useless things. We love better. We endure better. Remembering our approaching death actually causes us to treasure this transient life while at the same time holding it with loose hands. The ordinary becomes sacred. Fleeting moments become valuable. Gospel opportunities become treasured moments not to be wasted. Family meals, church services, days at the office, happy times, hardships, feasts and fastings, all take on new value and proper perspective when we keep death in view.

Remembering our impending death humbles us. And it is *always* good for us to be humbled. We are safe when we are low. When we forget our death, we get careless in almost every category of life. We cease to cherish. We grow lax with sin. We boast and plan as though we were God.

> *Now listen, you who say, 'Today or tomorrow we will go to this or that city, spend a year there, carry on business and make money.' Why, you do not even know what will happen*

---

[2] Owen, J. (1799), Falkirk: printed and sold by Johnston, T.

*tomorrow. What is your life? You are a mist that appears
for a little while and then vanishes.*
(James 4:13,14)

Nothing is diminished when a Christian contemplates his death. Everything is enhanced.

Charles Spurgeon was once asked, 'If you knew a sermon was your last one, what would you preach?' He replied, 'I *always* preach as though it were my last sermon'. Richard Baxter proclaimed, 'I preach as a dying man to dying men!'

Change the context from sermons and preaching to the surroundings of your life. How would living with your end in view transform your living and your loving? Amy Carmichael (1867-1951), the fiery little Irish missionary to India said it so well: 'We have all eternity to celebrate the victories but only a few hours before sunset to win them'.

I have read endless biographies of believers who lived meaningful lives. I tell you, the best of them lived with a regular contemplation of the brevity of their lives, the fast approach of death, their being called to account by their Saviour, and the glories of Heaven ahead.

But Jonathan does not stop at thinking 'much on all occasions' about his death. He thinks also of 'the common circumstances which attend death'. In other words, what is typical about one's dying day? How do people actually die? It is foolish and brazen for believers to think that we will get a free pass from the trials which accompany dying. We too must embrace the 'common circumstances'. We get sick. Our bodies begin to fail. We have racking pain. Or we are suddenly taken without notice. We go to sleep one night, not to awaken in the morning. An accident overtakes us. A virus steals in and with a cough we are gone. The doctor's office phones, and it is not good news. These are 'common occurrences'.

As no one has power over the wind to contain it, so no one has power over the time of their death.
(Ecclesiastes 8:8)

As a pastor, over the years, I have seen many people die. Some have been ready, some have not. Not all Christians die well. I make this observation regarding the 'common circumstances which attend death'. No matter how death comes upon us, it is foolhardy to believe that we can wait until we are dying to put anything right. Sometimes a believer is privileged to see their death approaching and 'put their house in order', but often people are too sick to think, in too much pain to repent, to correct relationships, or to do anything meaningful. Sometimes death comes in an unexpected instant. The common circumstances which attend death will prevent most of us from making last-minute repairs. We need to live everyday with the accounts cleared, and the books balanced.

Now … Smile. I mean it. SMILE! We have a Saviour 'who has destroyed death and has brought life and immortality to light through the gospel' (2 Timothy 1:10). We will benefit in every area of our lives (I mean that) if we think often of our last day. We do not need to walk in fear. We do not need to pretend or ignore. We agree with God that life is brief and uncertain, that Jesus has conquered death, that we have conquered with Him, that the grave will not have the final say over us. So …

Prepare every day to die, and then get on and live for Jesus, the Gospel, and others!

We are Resurrection People!

42

RESOLVED.

My flesh and my heart may fail,
but God is the strength of my heart
and my portion forever.
(Psalm 73:26)

'Soar we now where Christ has led, Alleluia!
Following our exalted Head, Alleluia!
Made like him, like him we rise, Alleluia!
Ours the cross, the grave, the skies, Alleluia!'
(Charles Wesley)

RESOLVED.

Resolved 10

Resolved, when I feel pain, to think of the pains of martyrdom, and of hell.

At this they covered their ears and, yelling at the top of their voices, they all rushed at him, dragged him out of the city and began to stone him ... While they were stoning him, Stephen prayed, 'Lord Jesus, receive my spirit.' Then he fell on his knees and cried out, 'Lord, do not hold this sin against them.'

When he had said this, he fell asleep.
(Acts 7:57-60)

So, he called to him, 'Father Abraham, have pity on me and send Lazarus to dip the tip of his finger in water and cool my tongue, because I am in agony in this fire.'
(Luke 16:24)

Dear Friends,

In case we need reminding, the Big Story on planet earth today is *not* the Corona Virus. The Big Story is the Gospel, and the wonders of God's Grace through His Church, spreading through the entire world. Resurrection Sunday is ahead, and it is a great time to be alive and following Jesus.

The virus is not eternal. It will not endure. Jesus, the Gospel, and His Redeemed People are eternal and will endure. Of this we can be certain. But this is not to say that Christians will not suffer and die in these days, perhaps by this virus, perhaps by some other calamity.

44

RESOLVED.

Jonathan's *Resolution* is timely - very timely: It is about perspective; it is about context; it is about thinking deeply. It is a simple, plain, understandable and realistic statement. It has life-changing power.

When it came time for Jonathan Edwards to die, his was a most painful and horrible death. At the age of 54, with a wife and eleven children, a smallpox inoculation went wrong, and he contracted the dreaded disease. His death was excruciating. This *Resolution,* which we remember he would have read weekly for 35 years - some 1,800 times - must have been a strengthening elixir in his great hour of need.

Here is Jonathan's premise: Life has painful seasons; for some of us our lives are like a never-ending winter of pain, others know sunny days but storms loom. Pain is not polite. It does not form an orderly queue. It does not take a number. It does not wait its turn.

Here is Jonathan's strategy: While we must not make light of our pain, we can put pain in perspective. Many of us are experiencing profound pain. Indeed, our entire society – our world – is in a season of extraordinary pain. But Jonathan has wisdom for us here: My pain today is slight when placed alongside the pains that many have suffered, and are suffering, for Jesus' sake, and when compared to the pains that I deserve, but have been delivered from, in hell.

Consider the pain of our martyred sisters and brothers. Whenever Jonathan feels pain, he has resolved to consider it in the light of the myriad of brothers and sisters in Jesus who have been tortured and finally killed for their confession of Christ. He considers their separation from loved ones, their deprivations, their emotional and physical torture, their violent and vicious deaths.

The 20th century was the bloodiest century for Christians ever, with more dying for Christ in that century than in the previous 19

45

together. The Gordon-Conwell Seminary Center for the Study of Global Christianity estimates that about 90,000 believers in Jesus are martyred every year. That is one every six minutes. [1]

Jonathan takes his cue straight from the Bible when, in his own suffering, he remembers those who have paid with their lives. He is not being fanatical here, but biblical:

> *There were others who were tortured, refusing to be released so*
> *that they might gain an even better resurrection. Some faced jeers*
> *and flogging, and even chains and imprisonment. They were put*
> *to death by stoning; they were sawn in two; they were killed by*
> *the sword. They went about in sheepskins and goatskins, destitute,*
> *persecuted and ill-treated – the world was not worthy of them.*
> *They wandered in deserts and mountains, living in caves and in*
> *holes in the ground.... Consider him [Jesus] who endured such*
> *opposition from sinners, so that you will not grow weary and lose*
> *heart. In your struggle against sin, you have not yet resisted to the*
> *point of shedding your blood.*
> (Hebrews 11:35-38; 12:3,4)

In putting his pain into perspective, Jonathan is avoiding destructive self-pity. He is steeling himself against any ingress of bitterness or accusation toward God. He is drawing inspiration. While not making light of our present sufferings, considering our brothers and sisters imprisoned today in the cruellest of circumstances, and those who will die as we read this, is a great help for us. We are enabled retain a sweet heart of faith and thanksgiving. Whether your pain be physical, relational, emotional, financial, take his pastoral advice and apply it like a salve to your situation.

---

[1] https://www.christianpost.com/news/over-900000-christians-martyred-for-their-faith-in-last-10-years-report.html

RESOLVED.

Open before me is the remarkable old book, *Foxe's Book of Martyrs* (1563). I have just read the account of Roman persecution in the ancient city of Antioch, particularly of a little boy who freely confessed Christ before the Roman Prelate, only to have his head removed and handed to his mother. Thank you, Jonathan, for encouraging me to view my pain in light of that mother's.

Elyse M. Fitzpatrick reminds us that the comforts of martyrs are *Gospel* comforts. As the wonders of Christ crucified and risen sustain them in their trials, they surely will sustain us in ours.

> When those early [and present day] Christians faced the chains and the beatings and felt the lick of the flame, the humiliation of the stripping, the mocking and the persecution, they didn't assuage their breaking hearts through a rehearsal of their personal accomplishments. They remembered that God became a man; he died and rose again; he is ruling as the ascended Lord, and he is also dwelling within – their only hope of glory. What do you need to remember today? The same thing: the incarnation, the resurrection, the ascension. Believe the Gospel....[2]

And the pains of hell? Why should a Christian ever think of these? Considering these delivers us from the temptation to accuse God of being 'unfair' in regard to our pain. Let's admit, we can sometimes be tempted to lift a hand toward God in protest that 'we deserve better'. Oh friends! Let us be careful here! What I *deserve* is hell and judgment. What I *get* is forgiveness of sins and Life Eternal!

> *He does not treat us as our sins deserve*
> *or repay us according to our iniquities.*

---

[2] Elyse M. Fitzpatrick, (2015) *Comforts from the Cross,* p.114. Grand Rapids. Zondervan.

RESOLVED.

(Psalm 103:10)

Is God 'unfair'? You bet He is! If God were 'fair' to me, I would go to hell. He is *gracious*. He does *not* give me what I deserve. I need to remember the deserved pains of hell from which I have been saved – and the *un*deserved joys of Heaven which await me - when I am tempted to complain to God about my temporal pains. Doing so will deliver me from a bitter, accusing spirit, and bring a sweetness toward God into my present painful situation.

Oh, to have a well-instructed soul which learns to think and dwell upon solid truths! Solid truth will deliver solid comfort to our souls even through the deepest trials. Again, thank you, Jonathan.

I want to leave you with the First Question of the 1563 Heidelberg Catechism.[3] Moms and dads, boys and girls used to memorize such wonderful things. Perhaps you and yours can commit this to memory. We need such great thinking again in our day.

Question: What is your only comfort in life and death?

Answer: That I am not my own, but belong with body and soul, both in life and in death to my faithful Saviour, Jesus Christ. He has fully paid for all my sins with His precious blood and has set me free from all the power of the devil. He also preserves me in such a way that without the will of my heavenly Father not a hair can fall from my head; indeed, all things must work together for my salvation. Therefore, by His Holy Spirit He also assures me of eternal life and makes me heartily willing and ready from now on to live for Him.

---

[3] Ursinus, Z. (2012). *The Heidelberg Catechism*. Jazzybee Verlag.

RESOLVED.

Resolved 11

Resolved, as far as possible, when presented with something wonderful and puzzling about God and His ways, to not delay in opening my Bible and my heart to search and discover all that God has revealed to me about Himself.

But grow in the grace and knowledge of our Lord and Saviour Jesus Christ. To him be glory both now and forever! Amen.
(2 Peter 3:18)

Now this is eternal life: that they know you, the only true God, and Jesus Christ, whom you have sent.
(John 17:3)

The secret things belong to the Lord our God, but the things revealed belong to us and to our children forever.
(Deuteronomy 29:29)

Dear Friends,

Do you want to bless God? Pursue Him! Desire Him! Get to know Him who desires to be known!

Do you want to bless others? Pursue God! Desire Him! Get to know Him who desires to be known!

Do you want to bless yourself? Pursue God! Desire Him! Get to know Him who desires to be known!

We have been created to know God. Sin, having separated you, and me, from a true knowledge of God has been dealt with by Jesus, not simply so that we can 'go to Heaven', but so that we can *know God*. What makes Heaven heavenly is that that is where God is.

I can promise you that the greatest need in your life, the deepest desire of your heart (even if you do not know it) is to deepen your knowledge of God.

The same is true for me.

Now God is not hiding: *We* hide. *He* looks. He discloses Himself. He *wants* to be known. He speaks to us through His creation. But more, He has spoken conclusively to us through Jesus Christ, and given us the Bible as a faithful record of His self-disclosure.

Jesus said:
> *Everyone on the side of truth listens to me.*
> (John 18:37)

The Bible will give up its treasures - countless life transforming gems of Truth about God and His ways - to anyone who is dissatisfied with surface things and dares to dig. Knowing God is not the reserve of pastors and PhDs. No! Grandmothers and teens, moms and dads, mechanics and doctors, nurses, electricians and homemakers can, with an open Bible and the help of the Holy Spirit, know God truly and deeply.

Now, we cannot know God *exhaustively*. How could we? That would make us God! But just because we cannot know *everything* about God, that does not mean we cannot know *many things* about God. Because God has revealed Himself in the Bible, we can know God *truly* and *sufficiently*. The problem is that we often do not want to. We are content with a dim knowledge of Him who has created us to

be thrilled by Him. We end up fascinated by the frivolous and temporal and bored by the weighty and eternal.
Are you hungry to know God, or have you spoiled your appetite?

I am often spurred on in my pursuit of Jesus by the stories of those who have applied themselves in their life's endeavour:

George Washington Carver (1864-1943) was born into slavery. As a young black man in the Reconstruction South, life was stacked against him. Kidnapped, orphaned, unable to begin school until twelve, he nevertheless had a voracious appetite for learning. He finally entered college, having overcome no end of racial obstacles. He achieved his Bachelor's from Iowa Agricultural College (now Iowa State University), and his Master's in botany in 1897. These achievements for a man of colour in his day were testimony to his sheer dedication to learning.

Carver eventually taught at the Tuskegee Institute in Alabama. Faced with an agricultural crisis in the southern USA, through tireless research, he is credited with 'saving the South' by delivering it from the monocrop of cotton. He introduced the peanut as a cash crop and developed more than three hundred commercial uses for it, as well as hundreds more for soybeans and sweet potatoes.

George applied his mind to learning for the sake of others. He was offered huge salaries to leave the South and go and work for the likes of Thomas Edison and Henry Ford, but he declined, drawing a meagre $125 per month for more than forty years at Tuskegee. His calling was to discover; and as a devoted follower of Jesus Christ, he said of his endless discoveries, 'God gave them to me. How can I sell them to someone else?'

His tombstone bears the words:

RESOLVED.

He could have added fortune to fame, but caring for neither,
he found happiness and honour in being helpful to the world.

George wanted to learn all he could in the field of botany. As a Christian, this was for him an act of worship. He was provoked by mysteries and unanswered questions to a life of discovery: 'I wanted to know the name of every stone and flower and insect and bird and beast. I wanted to know where it got its colour, where it got its life'.[1] In the same way, Jonathan Edwards longed to learn all that he could of Christ and Christian Truth. Sadly, to the loss of all mankind, even Christians no longer hold theology, once called the 'Queen of the Sciences', in high regard. Few apply their minds to diligent, fascinating, study of Jesus, 'in whom are hidden all the treasures of wisdom and knowledge' (Colossians 2:3). We are satisfied with surface, elementary knowledge where the most important subject is concerned, while at the same time we apply all sorts of effort and diligence to lesser subjects, some important, some not.

But Carver's brilliant observation, 'If you love it enough, anything will talk with you',[2] applies to the Bible as surely as surely as it did to his peanuts!

Believing that God is a self-revealing God who has spoken truthfully, authoritatively, clearly and sufficiently in the Bible, Edwards set out to discover all that he could about Him this side of Heaven. He would have considered it ungrateful at best, downright sinful at worst to have had any other attitude. To leave God's gracious written Word gathering dust under a table all the while walking in comparative ignorance and

---

[1] McMurry, L. O., & Edwards, L. M. (1981). *George Washington Carver: Scientist and Symbol*, p.18. Oxford University Press.
[2] Widely attributed to Carver.

shallowness, trusting in wives-tales and silly notions, would have been a major sin to Edwards. What would he say to some of us these days?

The reason we have such an incredibly rich bank of theological truth in the many writings of Edwards is largely due to the attitude shown in this *Resolution*. His influence eclipsed many because his hunger for Truth eclipsed many.

Jon was not content to shrug his shoulders and mumble, 'I dunno', to theological chestnuts. He aimed to search the Scriptures, pray and ponder, study and beat on the door of Truth until he had answers...not to the 'secret things of God', but to those 'things revealed', to everything that God has given to us to know. Being determined to 'grow in the grace and knowledge of our Lord and Saviour Jesus Christ' (2 Peter 3:18), his writings and his sermons became rich tapestries, carefully woven displays of biblical Truth and real experience. They were not removed from life, not the products of sheltered study, but the products of a life lived in the warp and woof of authentic discipleship.

Like Carver, Jonathan Edwards was useful because he applied himself to learning. How we need such men and women today! How the work of God cries out for hungry students of Truth who will resolve to solve! Enough of laziness, shallowness, indifference, and ungratefulness! To our knees before God, asking Him to give us hearts to know Him in truth! Give yourself no option and give Him no rest until you have a genuine break-through, expressed in a diligent resolve to be a disciple (literally a 'learner') of Jesus.

In the end, we are as happy, holy, and useful as we want to be. There will never be an easier time to get serious with Jesus and Truth than right now.

RESOLVED.

*The law from your mouth is more precious to me than thousands
of pieces of silver and gold.*
(Psalm 119:72*)*

I want to know Christ...
(Philippians 3:10)

'Once you become aware that the main business that you are here
for is to know God, most of life's problems fall into
place of their own accord.'[3]
(J.I. Packer)

---

[3] Packer, J. I. (2021). *Knowing God*, p.34. InterVarsity Press.

RESOLVED.

Resolved 12

Resolved, that if I take delight in the discovery of a wonder of God because it makes me think highly of myself, or if I hope that others will see my accomplishment and think much of me, I will waste no time in laying that discovery aside until I can enjoy it only to the Glory of God, the betterment of myself, and the blessing of others.

*We all possess knowledge. But knowledge puffs up
while love builds up.*
(1 Corinthians 8:1)

Dear Ones,

As we continue in our journey through these *Resolutions*, we see what a wise young man our Jonathan is!

Remember his last *Resolution* with me: that he will diligently and avidly seek after a true knowledge of God and His ways. Not stopping at puzzles and mysteries, he will endeavour to discover all that God has revealed for him. But our young friend sees two deadly vipers hidden in the pathway of all discovery and knowledge: pride and vanity.

Pride: The tendency to think more highly of yourself than you ought.
Vanity: The desire to have others think more highly of you than they ought.

All true and genuine discovery of Jesus and His ways should humble the explorer. How can it not, when God is eternal, unchanging, holy and awesome while man is temporal, transient, sinful and pitiful?

And yet God gives us grace and means to discover *Him*. How can this do anything but humble us? I remember John Piper saying that no one

RESOLVED.

goes to the Grand Canyon to boost *their own* self-esteem. No! The vista humbles the observer. How much more *must* the beholding of the ineffable God produce reverent awe in the worshipper!

Two things should happen when wonderful things about God are discovered:

1. The proud should be reduced and broken.
2. The humble should be lifted up and healed.

In 1855, a 20-year-old Charles Spurgeon began a sermon with these words. Read them slowly:

The highest science, the loftiest speculation, the mightiest philosophy, which can ever engage the attention of a child of God, is the name, the nature, the person, the work, the goings and the existence of the great God whom he calls his Father.

There is something exceedingly improving to the mind in a contemplation of the Divinity. It is a subject so vast, that all our thoughts are lost in its immensity; so deep, that our pride is drowned in its infinity. Other subjects we can compass and grapple with; in them we feel a kind of self-content and go our way with the thought, 'Behold, I am wise'. But when we come to the master-science, finding that we cannot see its height, we turn away with the thought … 'I am but of yesterday and know nothing'. No subject of contemplation will tend more to humble the mind, than thoughts of God…

And … Oh, there is, in contemplating Christ, a balm for every wound; in musing on the Father, there is a quietus for every grief; and in the influence of the Holy Ghost, there is a balsam for every sore. Would you lose your sorrow? Would you drown your cares?

56

RESOLVED.

> Then go plunge yourself in [God's] deepest sea; be lost in his immensity, and you shall come forth as from a couch or rest … I know nothing which can comfort the soul … as a devout musing upon the subject of the Godhead…[1]

But sadly, and more often than not, a third thing happens: The discoverer becomes proud and puffed up. He feels himself superior because of what he knows. Having - in the midst of his Bible reading - forgotten that he is nothing and that God is everything, he has begun to think that he is something special and that his learning has placed him above others. He begins to look down upon those who have not read as much or prayed as much. He desires that others see his advancement. He hopes they notice his bookshelf or his fervency. He beams when he asks the Adult Class Sunday School teacher a question that cannot be answered and swells when he makes the point that draws the quiet gasp and admiration of the class.

All the while he is offending God, for, 'God opposes the proud' (James 4:6).

When we stop and think about it, little else can be as offensive - and as *silly* - as pride in one's knowledge of God – the God who made Himself nothing to save miserable offenders; the God of whom we would know *nothing at all* were He not gracious to show us Himself.

Now, Jonathan's *Resolution* requires him to know his own heart very well. To sense the approach of sin, especially pride - such a slithery, stealthy, slippery sin - requires a well-tuned inner life. It demands that we bring our hearts daily before the Lord, praying with the Psalmist:

---

[1] Spurgeon, C.H. (1855) The Immutability of God. Accessible at
https://www.spurgeon.org/resource-library/sermons/the-immutability-of-god/#flipbook/
See also J.I Packer, (1973), *Knowing God*, p.18. Downers Grove: IVP.

RESOLVED.

Lord ... you know me ... Search me, God, and know my heart;
test me and know my anxious thoughts. See if there is any
offensive way in me and lead me in the way everlasting.
(Psalm 139:1;23,24)

So, when Jon learns something wonderful about God, having searched some truth out of the Bible like an adventurer on a treasure-hunt, he is careful to see the fruit of *humility* attending his discovery. If, on the contrary, he somehow feels himself superior or desires for others to see his advancement, he quickly employs a simple soul-defending strategy: He lays that discovery aside like one would lay aside a razor-sharp knife, until such a time that he can hold it rightly and employ it only for the Glory of God, for the proper good of himself, and the good of others. He will not allow his spiritual knowledge to be an occasion for showing off.

Oh, how deadly is pride - especially when cloaked in spirituality! How destructive to one's own soul and to all others within range! It separates. It divides. It destroys peace. Pride is the very foundation of Satan's Kingdom while humility is the bedrock of Christ's. All sin, every war, each division is built upon that evil foundation of pride. And pride finds a home in 'religion' as certainly as it does in 'the world'. Indeed, entire churches and denominations have been founded upon ... *pride*! Pride often causes followers of Jesus to divide from other followers of Jesus. Being convinced that 'I am right' (and I might be) can lead me to no longer walk with a brother for whom Christ died. In that case, while my position might be right, my posture is certainly wrong. How the heart of Jesus must break! Pride of learning, pride of doctrine, pride of heritage, pride of accomplishment, pride of one's church, pride of one's prayer life, pride of one's giving, pride of one's particular position. Pride, pride, pride! It leads one down an increasingly narrow path until there is no room for anyone to walk alongside ... including Jesus!

RESOLVED.

Jonathan will have nothing of it. Neither must we.

Any true encounter with God and the truth of God will lead one *toward* other believers … especially weaker ones, especially ones who might differ from you … in a humble desire to serve them and walk in meaningful fellowship with them. True discovery, where Christ is concerned, brings joy and a humbling sense of how little one really knows. It should make one sweeter and easier to live with!

Sometimes I need to examine myself and ask: What is making me cross? Why is that brother bugging me? Why am I losing my peace? Why am I discouraged? Have I not been noticed? Have I been passed over? Have I not been applauded? Has someone been preferred before me? Has my pride been aroused?

Oh friends! May we seek God and His ways … but on our knees. And may every discovery, every step of growth, every book read, every jewel unearthed serve only to bring us to a new place of humble adoration of the wonders and goodness of our gracious God.

For by the grace given me I say to every one of you: Do not think
of yourself more highly than you ought, but rather think of
yourself with sober judgment, in accordance with the faith God
has distributed to each of you.
(Romans 12:3)

'Nothing sets a person so much out of
the devil's reach as humility.'[2]
(Jonathan Edwards)

---

[2] Edwards, J. (1829). *A Narrative of the Revival of Religion in New England: With Thoughts on that Revival,* (No. 48). W. Collins.

Resolved 13

Resolved to be eagerly seeking out those to whom I can be
generous and charitable.

*But when you give a banquet, invite the poor, the crippled, the
lame, the blind, and you will be blessed. Although they cannot
repay you, you will be repaid at the resurrection of the righteous.*
(Luke 14:13,14)

*You will be enriched in every way so that you can be generous on
every occasion, and ... your generosity will result in
thanksgiving to God.*
(2 Corinthians 9:11)

Dear Friends in Jesus,

What great Gospel days we are living in! What perfect times to reach
our culture with the love of Jesus! These are *our days of
opportunity*. We need to pray for, and receive, a spirit of abounding,
lavish generosity that we might lead a revolution of Jesus-empowered
love.

Jonathan Edwards' *Resolutions* cannot be contained in the small world
of private faith. They must spill over into the wide world of public
action. A heart that is extravagant for Jesus must be a heart that is
extravagant for others. Jonathan resolves to not begrudge giving, to not
give in a miserly way, but to 'eagerly seek out' objects of charity. This
reflects the very heart of God! After all, has not God eagerly sought us
out? Is He not extravagant in His grace towards us?

The same year that Jonathan was born in Connecticut, 1703, John
Wesley was born in Epworth, England. While the two never met, they

would certainly have known of each other through their mutual friend, George Whitefield. Wesley was not a perfect man. But the grace of God in his life spilled over into extravagant giving to others. For him, holiness could not remain private. He said:

There is no holiness that is not social holiness.

Bearing in mind that he had no children to support and no heirs to care for (for as Proverbs 13:22 says, 'A good person leaves an inheritance for their children's children'), his life's record of generosity bears remarkable testimony to the holiness of his heart. Over the course of his lifetime, he generated tremendous wealth through the selling of books and writings. Yet the more he made, the more he gave. Zach Van Zant, in his article *The Radical Budget of John Wesley*,[1] gives us the details:

His first year at Oxford, his income was 30 pounds a year (enough for a comfortable living for a single individual). Through budgeting, he found that he could live on 28, and gave away 2. In his second year, his income doubled to 60 pounds, but he kept his expenses the same, and thus gave away 32 pounds (more than he kept for himself). This process continued, even as his income vastly grew.

Eventually John Wesley was giving away 98% of his income.

This is what *Jesus does* when He gets a hold of a heart.

Has He gotten a hold of your heart?
Is He the sole owner of mine?

---

[1] https://www.zackvanzant.com/blog/john-wesley-budget

RESOLVED.

As our culture is gripped by a grave crisis, *we* need to be gripped by something greater: the grace of God. As others 'hunker down' it is time for us to 'break out'. We have a chance now to move against the spirit of our age. Our age has often been marked by selfish gain. A looming economic crisis is spreading a pandemic of fear. Before long, a spirit of 'looking out for number one' could be infecting people far and wide. How the people of Jesus need to demonstrate the values of the coming Kingdom right now!

The story is told of a little boy listening to his father's fervent prayer for the dire needs of a neighbour to be met. Immediately following that passionate prayer, the little boy approached his father with his little hand extended.

'What is it son?' asked the father.

'Well, dad, I heard your prayer for Mr. Jones, and ... if you give me your wallet, I can go answer that prayer right now.'

There is a fascinating look at the overwhelming, grace-fuelled generosity of the early Christians in Acts 11: 27-30:

> *During this time, some prophets came down from Jerusalem to Antioch. One of them, named Agabus, stood up and through the Spirit predicted that a severe famine would spread over the entire Roman world. (This happened during the reign of Claudius.) The disciples, as each one was able, decided to provide help for the brothers and sisters living in Judea. This they did, sending their gift to the elders by Barnabas and Saul.*

Do you see it? Go look again! A famine is prophesied ... for the entire Roman world. What is the response of the disciples? 'Let's take an offering for others!'

RESOLVED.

Question: Who thinks like this?
Answer: People who have become citizens of a New Kingdom.

I confess to you that I often betray a miserly spirit. My dear wife moves toward generosity far more readily than I do. I need to hear and heed the words of Jesus when He tells me to throw a feast for the poor, knowing that God will more than make it all up to me in the Age to come. I need to be convinced that it is His Father's happy pleasure to one day give me all that is His and to therefore be extravagant toward others now:

> *Do not be afraid, little flock, for your Father has been pleased to give you the kingdom. Sell your possessions and give to the poor. Provide purses for yourselves that will not wear out, a treasure in heaven that will never fail, where no thief comes near and no moth destroys. For where your treasure is, there your heart will be also.*
> (Luke 12:32-34)

For me, a spirit of radical, extravagant generosity finally boils down to how I view God (doesn't everything?). Do I really get that He has been wildly good to me? Do I really believe that He is my Portion, my Treasure, my Enough? Do I truly trust that He is good and will always outgive me, whatever I give to others? (I am not trying to abuse this like the 'prosperity preachers' do, but it is true that I can never outgive God.)

Generosity results in something even greater than people getting blessed. It results in God being blessed. His Father-heart must be so warmed as the generosity He has poured into us is poured out of us to others. And all of this rebounds in praise and thanksgiving back to the God who gave in the first place. The circle is completed:

63

RESOLVED.

This service ...is overflowing in many expressions of thanks to God.
(2 Corinthians 9:12)

Here is a plea to all happy citizens of a New Kingdom in these great days of Gospel opportunity: What if we – each and every one of us – deliberately and joyfully seek to simplify our lives so that we can give more freely to the cause of Jesus in our day? How about adopting a 'war-time' instead of a 'play-time' mentality to free up our (vast) resources for Kingdom-minded living and giving?

Lord Jesus! Work this in us! Cause us to be so sure of your ever-generous disposition towards us that we will become increasingly extravagant givers in this age of fear. Make us eager to seek out those in need and ever eager to seek to meet those needs. And may this all result in You being blessed and praised in endless expressions of thanks to You.

And God is able to make all grace abound to you, [so]that always
having all sufficiency in everything, you may have
an abundance for every good deed.
(2 Corinthians 9:6-8)

Jesus Christ ... gave himself for us to redeem us from all
wickedness and to purify for himself a people that are his very
own, eager to do what is good.
(Titus 2:14)

'A whole lot of what we call 'struggling' is simply
delayed obedience.'[2]
(Elizabeth Elliott)

---

[2] Elliot, E. (2013) Leaving Self behind. Radio Broadcast.

RESOLVED.

Resolved 14

Resolved never to allow any feelings or actions of anger towards irrational beings.

Better a patient person than a warrior, one with self-control than one who takes a city.
(Proverbs 16:32)

Everyone should be quick to listen, slow to speak and slow to become angry, because human anger does not produce the righteousness that God desires.
(James 1:19,20)

Friends in Jesus,

Have you ever kicked your dog? How about screaming at your computer? Do you always respond sweetly, in a Jesus-loving way, to the distant voice in those telemarketing calls you receive? You don't slam the phone down, do you?

A bit of road rage now and then?

Does your spouse 'get your hackles up' when he 'just doesn't get it'?

Slammed any doors lately?

Laid on that horn today?

How about those sharp words and angry tones?

Employing a bit of sarcasm, a splash of abusive speech?

65

RESOLVED.

The dog did not make me mad. He only gave occasion for the inner me - the *real* me - to come out.

Your anger is not your phone's fault. You are responsible for your response.

Your wife did not understand what you meant, but your sharp response says more about you than about her.

We might think Jonathan Edwards has gone too far. The popular taunt these days is to accuse him of overreach. But our young mentor is actually onto something here. He is taking us deep - to heart matters. Like a wise physician he is looking for the telltale evidence of deadly disease.

We might protest: 'Don't irrational beings deserve my wrath?'

No. Your wrath, like mine, is tainted with sin.

'Who cares anyway?'

God cares.

And I should care.

My little angers, my slam of the door, that irritated response to (what I deem to be) my wife's 'stupid question' all say something about me. They are indicators of a deep malady.

By 'irrational beings' Jonathan simply means creatures who don't know better. In Jonathan's day he probably thought of his horse. Today it might be the dog, your child in certain circumstances, the old lady who cannot back her car up straight, that snail-slow kid at the check-out counter. It could be your husband at times when he is out of his depth. (My wife once sent me to the cabinet to get her 'pink make-up' or something like that. At that point, *I* was certainly an 'irrational being' in need of mercy and not anger!)

I think we can fairly expand the *Resolution* to include inanimate objects: phones, lawn mowers, computers, - whatever gets on the end of our 'Why won't this stupid thing work?' exasperation. It will be helpful to stand back for a moment and remind ourselves of what God wants in our salvation. He is not just after outward obedience. He is wanting sons, not slaves. He wants to reproduce His character in us. And consider His character as He displays it toward us, who, compared to Him, are all at times 'irrational beings'. He (thankfully) is never short-tempered, capricious, or irritable. Since His aim is transformation not just reformation, He must deal with us at depth ... at heart level. Jesus cares about things which often – at least for a while – remain unseen by others: things like, peevishness, fault-finding and unwarranted anger. Jesus said,

You have heard that it was said of those of old, you shalt not murder; and whoever murders shall be in danger of the judgment: But I say to you that whoever is angry with his brother without a cause shall be in danger of the judgment.
(Matthew 5:21,22, NKJV)

As a doctor is concerned with hidden cancer cells, not just with full-grown tumours, so Jesus sees the telltale trouble spots that perhaps no-one else sees. That golf club I threw, that irked response to your wife, that irritability, that little fit over the lost T.V. remote; me being bothered because the barista did not make the coffee to my liking ('Can't a person just get a decent cup of coffee around here?') ... These things are *revealing*. And, left unchecked, if allowed to play out their natural course, left to grow and fester, they become destructive outward behaviour. They do not stay politely in their place. They break out. They grow. If unchecked, ungodly attitudes and angers can ruin lives and even generations.

The progression goes like this:

Sow a thought ... reap an *act.*
    Sow an act ... reap a *habit.*
        Sow a habit ... reap a *character.*
            Sow a character ... reap a *destiny.*

This is how *God* sees the little things. This is The Great Physician's take on the seemingly trifling attitudes and actions that we excuse and overlook. It is *not* that God is picky. It is not that He is impossible to please. It is that He is *loving.* He is *wise.* He is *thorough.* He really intends to get us through this dangerous life and safe into our Heavenly home. He really sees that the greatest dangers are not outward, but inward – right in our own hearts and in the secret places.

The root of all this is sinful self-righteousness, wanting my own way, and therefore being annoyed at others for not bowing to me and my agenda. God won't have it ... and neither should we.

God really intends to make us like Jesus. Entire transformation is His goal. It may not be yours, but it is His. We might be content with a little change in outward behaviour - giving up drunkenness or swearing. But God does not stop there. He will redo us all the way.

> *... He who began a good work in you will carry it on to*
> *completion until the day of Christ Jesus.*
> (Philippians 1:6)

RESOLVED.

C.S Lewis says it wonderfully in a word-picture:

> Imagine yourself as a living house. God comes in to rebuild that house. At first, perhaps, you can understand what He is doing. He is getting the drains right and stopping the leaks in the roof and so on: you knew that those jobs needed doing and so you are not surprised. But presently he starts knocking the house about in a way that hurts abominably and does not seem to make sense. What on earth is He up to? The explanation is that He is building quite a different house from the one you thought of: throwing out a new wing here, putting on an extra floor there, running up towers, making courtyards. You thought you were going to be made into a decent little cottage: but He is building a palace. He intends to come and live in it Himself. [1]

The make-over is to be complete. God will sweeten us all the way through. He will beautify to the core. He has no half-measures and no option B that we can choose which will leave us 'unbothered'. Why would we want that anyway? Why want a half-job? Why leave the cancer cells? Why paint over the cracks? Why not desire the beauty of Jesus to be found in us?

I once knew a good and godly pastor who would regularly pray, 'Lord, when somebody kicks me, let them get honey all over their foot!'

Invite God, the Holy Spirit, to bring a new sense of conviction to you regarding your attitudes, angers, and seemingly trifling irritations. Learn to abhor these as you would poison in the pot. And then, ask God to help you love the beauty and sweetness of a pure, love-filled heart. Long for it like a miner would long for gold, and eagerly seek after it. Learn to repent quickly of the 'little things'. Be glad to be able to say as a physician would, 'It was bad ... but we caught it early'.

---

[1] Lewis, C. S. (2016). *Mere Christianity*, p. 205. London: William Collins.

RESOLVED.

Let us not settle for less than all that God has for us in saving us from sin and unto Christ-like holiness, for,

The unfading beauty of a gentle and quiet spirit ...
is of great worth in God's sight.
(1 Peter 3:4)

'If a sudden jar can cause me to speak an impatient, unloving word, then I know nothing of Calvary love. For a cup brimful of sweet water cannot spill even one drop of bitter water, however suddenly jolted.'[2]
(Amy Carmichael)

---

[2] Carmichael, A. (2003). *If: What Do I Know of Calvary Love?* p. 35. CLC Publications.

RESOLVED.

Resolved 15

Resolved never to do anything out of revenge.

Do not take revenge, my dear friends, but leave room for God's wrath, for it is written: 'It is mine to avenge; I will repay,' says the Lord.
(Romans 12:9)

Then Peter came and said to Him, 'Lord, how often shall my brother sin against me and I forgive him? Up to seven times?' Jesus said to him, 'I do not say to you, up to seven times, but up to seventy times seven.'
(Matthew 18:21,22)

Dear Friends in Jesus,

Cain, Samson, Jezebel, Absalom, Herodias, Haman, Saul, Joab … The stories of men and women whose lives were driven by – and ruined by – a desire to get even are almost too many to count in the Bible.

They give warning to us that a vengeful spirit is a doomed spirit and that a desire to seek out one's own view of justice hews a path of destruction.

In exploring Jonathan Edwards' *Resolution* 'to never do anything out of revenge', we could write pages. But go for yourself and read some of the stories of the characters named above. See the ruin of revenge. Pray for a sensitive spirit to discern even the tiniest bitter root within and cultivate in its place a sweet, life-giving spirit.

Oh, to have a heart of simple, free, forgiving love for all!

RESOLVED.

Bitterness and vengefulness are never found alone. They bear many children. They have a large family. Just look at their names!

Get rid of all bitterness, rage and anger, brawling and slander,
along with every form of malice.
(Ephesians 4:31)

Rage! Anger! Brawling! Slander! Malice!

A revengeful spirit is like a storm-tossed sea. Even if one's revenge is not literally expressed – as it was in Absalom's tragic life – it will fester and rot you from within until it ruins you and those around you. A desire for revenge can become all-consuming. Do not let it be found in you in the smallest form. It can grow until it takes on a life of its own and ravages all in its path.

> Revenge ruins families.
> It poisons generations.
> It drives people to insanity.
> It makes nations war.
>
> A vengeful spirit divides churches.
> It degrades the cause of Christ.
> It separates and saddens.
> It sours and spoils.

Let's settle this right now: If I am going to live for Jesus, people will hurt me, misunderstand me, and take advantage of me. So be it. I have Jesus, and He understands. I will, by grace, seek a sweet spirit of forgiveness and refuse to nurse a vengeful heart. I will leave retribution to Him.

RESOLVED.

May the Lord judge between you and me. And may the
Lord avenge the wrongs you have done to me,
but my hand will not touch you.
(1 Samuel 24:12)

If it is possible, as far as it depends on you,
live at peace with everyone.
(Romans 12:18)

See to it that no one falls short of the grace of God and that no
bitter root grows up to cause trouble and defile many.
(Hebrews 12:15)

For me, there is one massive motive which spurs me to overcome a bitter spirit and to join with Jonathan in his resolve to 'never do anything out of revenge'. Simply this: If I am going to live a life that is effective for Jesus, if I am going to be useful to God, then,

I do not have the time or energy to have a bitter, vengeful heart.

A vengeful spirit is a drain on everything good. It consumes thought time (Have you ever spent time mulling over what you 'would say to so-and-so' if given the chance?). It ruins prayer time. It robs joy. It taxes strength. It side-tracks from good endeavours.

If I want my life to count (and I do), then I do not have the perverse luxury of expending my energy and efforts in 'trying to get even' or daydreaming about giving some offender a 'piece of my mind'. I am a servant of Jesus! I have a Kingdom to proclaim and a Saviour to live for! I have all Heaven ahead of me. I can endure a bit of abuse along the way.

RESOLVED.

Think about this with me: Seeking revenge is a very wicked thing. It is brazenly predicated upon the self-righteous thought that *I* occupy some moral high ground over another person. It cannot exist without the ridiculous notion that *I* have a clear understanding of all the facts, and *I* am in a position to justly punish.

What foolishness!

Am I not a sinner too? Is there no speck (or beam!) in my eye as well? Have I not been forgiven by our Holy God of infinite crimes against His Highness? Do I not stand by grace alone? Do I have complete knowledge of another's heart and motives? Is not my own heart enough for me to deal with? Has not Jesus already died for that very sin my brother committed against me? Dare I hold against him what Jesus has atoned for? Must I not freely forgive him?

My dear brothers and sisters, take note of this: everyone should
be quick to listen, slow to speak and slow to become
angry, because human anger does not produce
the righteousness that God desires.
(James 1:19,20)

God, and God alone, is able to rightly execute revenge. He alone occupies the office of Judge. He is righteous in all that He does and is moved by the pure motives of His Glory, the security of His redeemed, and the good of all creation. My revenge will inevitably be tainted by sin and selfishness. God is infinitely more patient and measured than I. I will take a sledgehammer to a nut. God's vengeance will be exact and never provoke an apology from Him. We can therefore leave our case and cause with Him, release people from their debt to us for pain caused, walk in forgiveness and peace with all men and women, *and go live for Jesus!*

RESOLVED.

For the Lord will vindicate his people and have compassion on his
servants... The Lord will vindicate me; your love, Lord, endures for
ever – do not abandon the works of your hands.
(Psalm 135:14; 138:8)

You and I will never walk through the abuse and mistreatment that
Jesus did. And yet we learn that '[w]hen they hurled their insults at him,
he did not retaliate; when he suffered, he made no threats. Instead, he
entrusted himself to him who judges justly' (1 Peter 2:23).

Consider Corrie ten Boom (1892-1983). How she suffered at the hands
of the Nazis in Ravensbruck concentration camp! Her sister, Betsie,
died in that camp. In 1947 she was preaching in Germany, when she
was approached by a man whom she recognized as one who had been a
cruel Ravensbruk guard. That man extended a hand to her, asking her
for her forgiveness:

> I stood there with ... coldness clutching my heart. But forgiveness
> is not an emotion. ... Forgiveness is an act of the will, and the will
> can function regardless of the temperature of the heart.

> 'Jesus, help me!' I prayed silently. 'I can lift my hand. I can do
> that much. You supply the feeling'.

> And so woodenly, mechanically, I thrust my hand into the one
> stretched out to me. And as I did, an incredible thing took place.
> The current started in my shoulder, raced down my arm, sprang
> into our joined hands.

> And then this healing warmth seemed to flood my whole being,
> bringing tears to my eyes. 'I forgive you, brother!' I cried. 'With
> all my heart!'[1]

RESOLVED.

The guarding of your heart against any hint of vengeance is of vital importance. Are you allowing a bitter pot to simmer toward your wife, your child, a church member? Perhaps it is on low, on the back burner. But why permit it at all? You are cooking a stew that will somehow, someday, boil over, poisoning many. Be rid of it! Give Jesus the pain that has come your way – for He will gladly take it from you (Isaiah 53:4) – and receive a sweetness of spirit of forgiveness from Him toward those who have hurt you. Then, get on living for something bigger than yourself: Jesus and His Kingdom.

Beloved! Let it go! Repent of any hint of a vengeful spirit. Renounce the self-righteousness that accompanies it. Pursue a heart of love for all, especially toward those who have hurt you. Walk in the freedom that comes in forgiving others. Deliberately move in an opposite spirit than the vengeful world around you.

If we will serve Jesus and His Gospel, then we have not the strength or time for anything less than free hearts of love toward all.

It is for freedom that Christ has set us free. Stand firm, then, and do not let yourselves be burdened again by a yoke of slavery.
(Galatians 5:1)

'Those who were able to forgive their former enemies were able
also to return to the outside world and rebuild their lives, no
matter what the physical scars. Those who nursed their bitterness
remained invalids. It was as simple and as horrible as that.' [2]
(Corrie ten Boom)

---

[1] ten Boom, C. (1974). *Tramp for the Lord: The Story that Begins Where The Hiding Place Ends*, p. 57. CLC Publications.
[2] ten Boom, C. (1974). *Tramp for the Lord: The Story that Begins Where The Hiding Place Ends.*, p.57. CLC Publications.

RESOLVED.

Resolved 16

Resolved never to speak with a motive to dishonour anyone, and, if
I speak negatively of anyone, to do so only if it is necessary
for their genuine good.

*What you have said in the dark will be heard in the daylight, and
what you have whispered in the ear in the inner rooms will be
proclaimed from the roofs.*
(Luke 12:3)

*Let your conversation be always full of grace, seasoned with salt,
so that you may know how to answer everyone.*
(Colossians 4:6)

*The King will reply, 'Truly I tell you, whatever you did for
one of the least of these brothers and sisters of mine,
you did for me.'*
(Matthew 25:40)

Dear Friends,

Oh, to be filled to overflowing with love and good-will toward all
people! Oh, to be delivered from every ounce of sourness, fault-finding,
and tale-bearing!

Do you take a perverse delight in discovering - and then discussing - the
faults and failures of another? Do you couch your 'concern' in a 'desire
to pray' for that person?

Jesus takes all of this terribly personally. His razor-sharp teaching in
Matthew 25, with the cutting edge being those words 'whatever you did
[for others] you did for me', apply not just to good works of charity, but

certainly as well to unkind words of gossip. He loves the people we are speaking unkindly about. Just think about that! How would you like it if someone was speaking in a cutting way about your dearest?

Christ died for that one - and their faults - whom we are delighting to criticise and to denigrate to others.

When we think of it that way ... What wickedness!

Personally, I need real help here. I confess to you and to all that I have broken Jesus' heart in this manner more times than can ever be counted. Oh, may His blood atone for my sins in this regard! That whisper, that 'tut-tut', those unkind words, that little bounce of glee over another's missteps are grievous sins which need to be confessed and cleansed by Jesus' blood.

The fact that my unkind words about another offend God is bad enough. But they also offend me, the offender. The one who shares the malicious morsel actually poisons his own soul in so doing. I cannot be walking intimately with Jesus and be breaking His heart at the same time. My *abiding* in Christ is interrupted, so my fruitfulness is diminished. Love, joy, peace, patience, kindness, goodness, gentleness, self-control, these precious fruits of God's Spirit, are stunted when I spoil my intimacy with my Saviour by my malicious attitude and speech.

But the poison spreads farther than God and myself. These unkind words do not stay put: they stray. What I whisper in the ear, what I say in private, if said from a motive to dishonour another, finds its way out. It is inevitable. Then fellowship is broken, people are hurt, secrecy becomes suspicion, teams are destroyed, the Gospel suffers, churches fracture.

RESOLVED.

But to replace these bitter, sour words with sweetness! To *abide* in Jesus and have His nature formed within us! To have hearts that are so transformed by grace that we are overflowing with love for all! To have a heart that is moved *only* by love for one another, that would not *dare* speak against one for whom Christ has suffered and died. God gives us language to build up, not to tear down: to encourage, not to hurt. Not only should we *not* hurt others with our words, but our words should also actually *help* our brothers and sisters. They should be 'full of grace' and 'seasoned with salt'.

The spiritual discipline of controlling one's words, of never speaking unkindly to or about anyone unless it is absolutely necessary for their well-being is a major battle for each of us. But fighting it is not optional.

> *Do not let any unwholesome talk come out of your mouths, but only what is helpful for building others up according to their needs, that it may benefit those who listen. And do not grieve the Holy Spirit of God, with whom you were sealed for the day of redemption. Get rid of all bitterness, rage and anger, brawling and slander, along with every form of malice. Be kind and compassionate to one another, forgiving each other, just as in Christ God forgave you.*
> (Ephesians 4:29-32)

Of course, sometimes we might have to share a painful word with or even about someone. Be careful here! Make sure that your heart is right before God before you venture a sound! Have you wept first? Has your heart broken first? Here are two preachers: Both find a need to speak a word of warning about some man's ministry. One is weeping as he speaks while the other is wagging his head and sounding off. Which is pleasing to Jesus? Which is helpful? I get terribly concerned when I find myself delighting in some one pointing out the faults of an aberrant preacher or politician. We dare not take delight in the faults of another. We should grieve, our hearts should break, and, if we *must* speak, we had better speak from a place of brokenness and sorrow, with no motive other than to bring help and healing.

Years ago, in a small English town where I pastored, I often walked by three gardens (U.S. 'lawns') whilst making my pastoral calls. One was full of weeds. That is, for us, a picture of the sick heart and its poisonous tongue. Another had not a weed to be found. It had been concreted over. While it had no poison, it offered no beauty either. This is a picture of a heart that will not properly share a grievance but hardens toward another. The third was lovingly and caringly filled with flowers. Someone was diligent over it. It offered beauty. That is for us the picture of the sanctified tongue. That is the goal! Not weeds, not concrete, but beauty and life in our words!

Lord Jesus! Make my heart sweet and my words life-giving!

> *With the tongue we praise our Lord and Father, and with it we curse human beings, who have been made in God's likeness. Out of the same mouth come praise and cursing. My brothers and sisters, this should not be. Can both fresh water and salt water flow from the same spring? My brothers and sisters, can a fig-tree bear olives, or a grapevine bear figs? Neither can a salt spring produce fresh water.*(James 3:9-12)

Gossip, in Romans 1, is listed alongside murder, and rightly so, for it kills spiritual life, relationships, missions, families, and so much more. And it is as much a sin to receive it as to give it! Avoid it as you would murder or theft. Look at the company we keep when we speak unkind words:

RESOLVED.

They have become filled with every kind of wickedness, evil, greed
and depravity. They are full of envy, murder, strife, deceit and
malice. They are gossips, slanderers, God-haters, insolent,
arrogant and boastful; they invent ways of doing evil; they
disobey their parents... (Romans 1:29,30)

I spread gossip not just by speaking unkind words, but by receiving
them as well. Here are three questions to ask a talebearer that will stop
gossip in its tracks:

1) Why are you telling me this?
2) Does Bill know that you are telling me this?
3) If I go to discuss this with Bill, can I quote you as my source?

Beloved, may we seek all grace (for God will give it) to be so filled
with the sweetness of Jesus that our words will ever and only be to
build one another up. May it be that we never take delight in the faults
of another. May we always and only bring honour to God as we speak
well and humbly about those for whom Jesus has died. May our hearts
and words be not a patch of noxious weeds, nor a hard block of
concrete, but like a beautiful garden, full of life and sweet fragrance.

Lord Jesus! May your love conquer me in every way!

If anyone speaks, they should do so as one who speaks the
very words of God ... so that in all things God may be praised
through Jesus Christ. (1 Peter 4:11)

'With the help of grace, the habit of saying kind words is very
quickly formed, and when once formed, it is not speedily lost.'[1]
(Fredrick W. Faber)

---

[1] Faber, F. (1901) *Kindness*, p.84. London: R. & T. Washburn.

RESOLVED.

Resolved 17

Resolved that I will live as I will wish I had done when I come to die.

Show me, Lord, my life's end and the number of my days;
let me know how fleeting my life is.
(Psalm 39:4)

By the grace God has given me, I laid a foundation as a wise
builder ... But each one should build with care.
(1 Corinthians 3:10)

Dear Pilgrim,

Many years ago, I heard a statement from a preacher that arrested me. I think the preacher was Stephen Olford.[1] If my memory fails me as to who the preacher was it does not fail me as to what the preacher said:

You had better build a good life because you are going
to spend eternity with it.

The story goes of a builder who was asked by a generous and kind man of means to build a fine house. The builder, not being given to diligence, cut many corners, hid many defects, and overall made a shoddy job of it.
'The owner will never know', he thought. Upon completion, the builder presented the house to the kind man as a 'job well done', only to have that generous man hand the keys right back to the shifty builder with the words, 'You did not know it, but you built this fine house for yourself, my friend, for I am giving it to you as a gift'.

---

[1] Stephen Olford was known as 'The Preachers' Preacher'. Billy Graham said he was the man who most influenced his ministry.

RESOLVED.

This brief life is valuable, not only for its own sake, but because it spills over into the next. As C.T. Studd said:

> Only one life, 'twill soon be past,
> Only what's done for Christ will last.
> And when I am dying, how happy I'll be,
> If the lamp of my life has burned bright for Thee. [2]

Jonathan Edwards lived with an eye on Heaven. Even as a young man he saw life as brief, and Eternity as near. How wise we will be to do the same! This *Resolution* carries with it both a *backward* glance and a *forward* gaze. Soon our precious, fleeting sojourn on Earth will end. To then look back and see our lives as having been lived for Jesus and His Eternal Kingdom should be in our thoughts every day.

How many backward glances bring regret and tears?

Many have deeply regretted their compromised lives.

Many hope to die well, but do not care to live well.

Many confuse grace as license for laziness instead of power for pursuing.

May it not be so with you and with me! May we not be like the man who climbed to the top of the ladder only to find he had it leaning against the wrong wall! Heaven is ahead. Joy unspeakable awaits every redeemed soul. Feet-dragging-following is sure to produce regret at the end. No man or woman ever got to the end of their days and

---

[2] Cited in Phillips, J. (1995) *Only One Life: The Biography of Stephen F. Olford.* Loizeaux Brothers.

RESOLVED.

regretted being sold-out for Jesus. No one has ever died, seen the glory of Jesus, and proclaimed, 'Dang! I should have been more worldly!' I remember the brief-lived William Borden (1887-1913). Six words were written in the back of his Bible, words that belong together. Perhaps you can write them not just in your Bible, but into your life's story:

No Retreats, No Reserves, No Regrets.

Grace frees us to choose Jesus over lesser things every day and those choices have eternal significance. God's grace is super abundant for us. Learn to keep 'short accounts' with God. Bring your life daily before His throne of grace, confessing your sins and receiving His cleansing. Don't allow unconfessed sin to build up in your soul like sludge in a pipe, for 'Godly sorrow brings repentance ... and leaves no regret' (2 Corinthians 7:10).

But what of the forward gaze? Ah friend! There is no greater motive for all-in following after Jesus than a bright hope of Heaven. Nothing steels the resolve like the knowledge that soon we will be with Jesus! What empowers simple believers to make otherwise impossible choices? What enables martyrs to face the flames? What strengthens women and men and boys and girls to fight sin and Satan and choose Jesus every day? What ennobles the soul to say 'yes' to God when it will cost one dearly to do so? What spurs on mission and service when ease and comfort beckon? What keeps a spouse faithful in the midst of a nearly impossible marriage? What strengthens one to praise and rejoice in the midst of agonizing illness with no happy ending in this life?

What is there like the hope of Heaven?

Living with a future hope is transformational. *Today* is transformed by my view of *tomorrow.* My view of the future shapes me right now. If I

84

want to 'live as I will wish I had done when I come to die', then a bright view of the joy that is ahead is the best nourishment for me today. Think about it: Even Jesus, as He anticipated the cross, was motivated by Heaven.

For the joy that was set before him he endured the cross, scorning its shame, and sat down at the right hand of the throne of God.
(Hebrews 12:2)

Do you see that? Jesus was enabled to do His Father's will – atone for our sins on the cross – because He focused on the *eternal joy* beyond the trial. The Bible over and over points us to future joy as a motive for present perseverance (see, for example, 2 Corinthians 4:17; 1 Peter 5:10; Romans 3:3-5).

Jonathan, in a sermon entitled *The Portion of the Righteous,* presents a beautiful picture of the joy and happiness of Heaven. I want this picture to spur you and me toward 'no reserves, no retreats, no regrets' living.
He imagines Heaven as a boundless sea of happiness, into which each believer is cast. Seeing each believer as a vessel (jar), each will be filled to the brim with the happiness of God. But some believers, *because of their responses to grace in this life* will have greater capacity than others:

For all shall be perfectly happy; every one shall be perfectly satisfied. Every vessel that is cast into this ocean of happiness is full, though there are some vessels far larger than others.[3]

Why settle for a thimble-sized capacity for joy when God would want to fill a gallon? There is no shortage of happiness in Christ!

---

[3] Jonathan Edwards. *The Portion of the Righteous. The Works of Jonathan Edwards,* p. 902. Edinburgh: The Banner of Truth Trust.

RESOLVED.

Is it wrong to be motivated by a reward? Not if Jesus was. And not if the reward is God Himself. Certainly, the Lord would have us choose Him over all joy-robbing sins and all lesser things today, knowing that each choice enlarges our eternal capacity to enjoy Him forever. To be motivated today by the sure hope of greater eternal joy in God is good and right.

And without faith it is impossible to please God, because anyone who comes to him must believe that he exists and that he rewards those who earnestly seek him.
(Hebrews 11:6)

Blessed are you when people insult you, persecute you and falsely say all kinds of evil against you because of me. Rejoice and be glad, because great is your reward in heaven.
(Matthew 5:11,12)

Do you want to live as you 'will wish [you] had done when [you] come to die'? Then, certainly, live with regard to your backward glance. By grace, make choices that will finally leave no regret. ...

But more, live with regard to your forward gaze.

There is such glory ahead! May it be that the bright hope of Heaven fashions our today toward Jesus-shaped living tomorrow.

To him who is able to keep you from stumbling and to present you before his glorious presence without fault and with great joy: to the only God our Saviour be glory, majesty, power and authority, through Jesus Christ our Lord, before all ages, now and for evermore! Amen.

86

RESOLVED.

(Jude 24,25)

Walk as if the next step would carry you across
the threshold of Heaven.[4]
(Jim Elliot)

---

[4] Elliot, E. (2008). *Shadow of the Almighty*. Hendrickson.

Resolved 18

Resolved to live on my worst days as I already have determined to live on my best days, when my heart was most devout, when my mind best understood God's truths, and my spirit most longed for Heaven.

> *Has God forgotten to be merciful?*
> *Has he in anger withheld his compassion?*
> *Then I thought, 'To this I will appeal:*
> *To the years when the Most High stretched out his right hand.*
> *I will remember the deeds of the Lord;*
> *yes, I will remember your miracles of long ago...*
> (Psalm 77:9-11)

Dear Friends,

Praise God for His special times of grace and favour! Those seasons when the Bible seems to open itself, when prayer flows without hindrance, when the truths of an unseen world are clearly visible, when the veil between earth and Heaven is paper thin, are all precious foretastes of a feast to come.

During such times we can make great spiritual progress. There are seasons when our heart's devotion is purest and our apprehension of eternal truth is clearest. At those times we can valiantly put off sin, change our course and make momentous life decisions. There are prayer times when it seems as though we can almost step through into Heaven. Such times of grace are precious and powerful times that need to mark our journey with Jesus.

There are beautiful times of spiritual discovery in a Christian's life. Truths about God – His nature and His ways – are taken hold of by the devout mind: Understanding increases, Bible passages unlock and open up. Great books are read. The brain works well and the heart warms in response to truth apprehended. The will makes great decisions. Directions are set and the stride lengthens.

Thank you, Jesus, for days when the wind is at my back and the sun is shining sweetly upon my pathway.

But ... there are also dark days: Clouds roll in, prayer seems cold and formal. Old sins, long dormant, awaken and seem to overwhelm. Sickness racks the body. Sorrow is our portion. Perhaps we bury a loved one. Exclamations marks are replaced by question marks. The Bible seems a complicated book. The brain grows dull. The heart goes cold. The stride becomes a shuffle and the course ahead seems fraught with confusion and danger.

There are seasons when, like Israel in the desert, '[w]e remember the fish we ate in Egypt...also the cucumbers, melons, leeks, onions and garlic' (Numbers 11:5). Former sins, which on better days we loathed, now seem strangely attractive again. Old habits, once repented of, come knocking, whispering, enticing. Repentance is hard and half-hearted. The battle seems impossible to win, if indeed it is worth fighting at all.

Lord Jesus! There are times when a gale blows right in my face and the path before me is dark and hidden!

Jonathan's *Resolution* is ripe with practical pastoral wisdom (was he really only *eighteen*?). He recognizes the ups and downs of following Jesus. He understands the seasons of discipleship. And he determines that it is the progress he has made with Jesus when the wind is at his back, not the slog through the mud when the storm is in his face, that will define him.

RESOLVED.

I have said many times before, but I need to say it again: What you think about when you think about Jesus Christ is the most important thing about you.

Theology - that is, your understanding of God - is all important. Those things you have learned about the Lord on the sure days, the things you have seen clearly in the sunshine, the decisions you have made for Christ when you have most clearly grasped spiritual realities, *need to sustain you in the fog, the wind, the gales of life.*

Horatio Spafford (1828-1888) understood the importance of good theology, of things learned in the light holding you in the dark. A deep Christian and very successful businessman, most of his holdings were destroyed in the Chicago fire of 1871. This was shortly after his four-year-old son had died of scarlet fever. Believing it best to take his wife and four daughters (aged 11, 9, 5, and 2) on a trip to Europe, he sent the five ahead of himself on the steamer, Ville du Havre.

On 22 November 1873, that ship was struck by another in the mid-Atlantic. It sank in twelve minutes and all four dear daughters perished. Upon rescue, his wife Anna telegraphed him with the solemn words, 'Saved alone'.

Spafford left at once for Ireland to join her. Mid-way across the Atlantic, the ship's captain called Horatio on deck as they approached the spot where his daughters had perished. At that very spot he penned the words which became a great hymn of comfort to so many:

> When peace, like a river, attendeth my way,
> When sorrows like sea billows roll;
> Whatever my lot, Thou hast taught me to say,
> It is well, it is well with my soul.

RESOLVED.

It is well with my soul,
It is well, it is well with my soul.

Though Satan should buffet, though trials should come,
Let this blest assurance control,
That Christ hath regarded my helpless estate,
And hath shed His own blood for my soul.

My sin—oh, the bliss of this glorious thought! —
My sin, not in part but the whole,
Is nailed to the cross, and I bear it no more,
Praise the Lord, praise the Lord, O my soul!

For me, be it Christ, be it Christ hence to live:
If Jordan above me shall roll,
No pang shall be mine, for, in death as in life,
Thou wilt whisper Thy peace to my soul.

But, Lord, 'tis for Thee, for Thy coming we wait.
The sky, not the grave, is our goal;
Oh, trump of the angel! Oh, voice of the Lord!
Blessed hope, blessed rest of my soul!

And Lord, haste the day when my faith shall be sight,
The clouds be rolled back as a scroll;
The trump shall resound, and the Lord shall descend,
Even so, it is well with my soul.

It is well with my soul,
It is well, it is well with my soul.

Do you see how theology matters? Do you see in this story that what
Spafford *believed* about Jesus, what he *learned* in the light, *kept him* in

the dark? If I waste my good days, trifling them away in all sorts of trivial pursuits, my spiritual poverty will be proven on my bad days. Conversely, if I 'make hay while the sun shines', my spiritual health will be evident when the storms hit (and they will hit).

> *Go to the ant, you sluggard;*
> *consider its ways and be wise!*
> *It stores its provisions in summer*
> *and gathers its food at harvest.*
> *How long will you lie there, you sluggard?*
> *When will you get up from your sleep?*
> (Proverbs 6:5-9)

So, Jonathan's resolve to live out of the abundance of his fair-weather harvest in the foul-weather trial really is in no way optional. We have no choice but to follow his lead if we are to endure in faith until the end.

I think here of William Cowper's (1731-1800) stanza from his famous hymn *God Moves in a Mysterious Way*:

> Judge not the Lord by feeble sense
> But trust Him for His grace.
> Behind a frowning providence,
> He hides a smiling face.

Let's expand it: *Judge not the Lord by feeble sense*: Don't rely on your weak and faulty feelings and hunches to figure out God's ways in the dark times. *But trust Him for His grace*: Go with what you know, with what you learned in the sunshine – God's grace, that is, the Gospel. *Behind a frowning providence*: God sometimes works in ways which seem hard. At such times, 'wives' tales' and guesses won't

92

RESOLVED.

do. *He hides a smiling face*: His character and disposition are always to do good to His children and you can trust that in the dark times.

Solid theology!

And solid theology - what you know about God - keeps you when everything else falls away.

> *Blessed is the one ...whose delight is in the law of the Lord,*
> *and who meditates on his law day and night.*
> *That person is like a tree planted by streams of water, which*
> *yields its fruit in season and whose leaf does not wither.*
> (Psalm 1:1-4)

> 'His purposes will ripen fast,
> unfolding ev'ry hour;
> the bud may have a bitter taste,
> but sweet will be the flow'r.'
> (William Cowper)

Resolved 19

Resolved never to do anything which I would be afraid to do if I expected it to be the very last hour before the trumpet sounded and Jesus returned.

Or, to put it in a positive light:

Resolved always to be doing what I would do if I knew that the trumpet was sounding and Jesus was returning within the hour.

Be dressed ready for service and keep your lamps burning, like servants waiting for their master to return from a wedding banquet ...
(Luke 12:35)

Therefore, my dear brothers and sisters, stand firm. Let nothing move you. Always give yourselves fully to the work of the Lord, because you know that your labour in the Lord is not in vain.
(1 Corinthians 15:58)

Dear Friends,

How is this for a name and title: 'Anthony Ashley Cooper, 7th Earl of Shaftesbury, Baron Cooper of Pawlett, Baron Ashley of Wimborne St. Giles'?

Anthony Ashley Cooper (1801-1885) was born into the British aristocracy. Raised by a cruel father and a social butterfly of a mother, he learned about Jesus and the Gospel from a family maid, Maria Millis (how wonderful is that!). She taught Anthony how to pray and trust Jesus and, in later life, Anthony, then the Seventh Earl of Shaftesbury, traced his life in Christ back to that dear household servant.

RESOLVED.

As an ardent follower of Jesus, Anthony Cooper, the Seventh Earl of Shaftesbury, served as a Member of Parliament for 50 years, beginning at the age of 25. During this time, Britain was in the midst of cataclysmic change as the Industrial Revolution rolled mercilessly forward. That revolution, coupled with a brutal class system of 'betters' and 'lessers', set the stage for unimagined oppression of the poor, including of children and of the physically and mentally infirm.

Because Anthony was a Jesus-follower, he could not stand idly by. He laboured tirelessly for the rights of the voiceless. He used his gifts and position in life to transform his society. Through child labour laws, factory reform, prison reform, education for the poor, Bible publication, empathy for the 'insane' (he secured the passage through parliament of the Lunacy Act in 1845), he led the charge in bringing compassion and Christian values into what was otherwise a cruel and heartless culture.

He was known as 'The Poor Man's Earl'. When he died in 1885 tens of thousands of London's poor lined the streets to pay respects to the man who had given his life on their behalf.

Anthony was motivated by an unusual love for Jesus, but especially by an unceasing moment-by-moment looking for the return of Jesus. He lived on his tiptoes, like a kid at Christmas, expecting and hoping for Jesus to show up any minute. He wanted to be found busy about his Master's work when his Master returned. Hear him:

> I do not think that in the last 40 years I have lived one conscious
> hour that was not influenced by the thought of our Lord's return.

It was said that whenever he heard the clock strike, he raised his thoughts heavenward, considered the brevity of life, the imminent return of Jesus, *and got to work.*

RESOLVED.

Look again at Jonathan's *Resolution* at the top of this letter. It is a double-edged sword. When looked at one way it is a strong inducement to *not* do certain things. Looked at another way it is a strong inducement *to do* certain things.

In the first way, recognizing that the King of Kings is at the door makes sin look unattractive: Will I want to be doing this, or saying that, or thinking this thought, when Jesus turns up? Fear is *not* a bad motive! It might not be the *best* motive, but if it pulls me away from sinful behaviour, then so be it. For a follower of Jesus to simply think 'I do not want Jesus to catch me doing this' is a good thing.

Do I want my last breath to be a sinful one?

Do I want my last words to be hurtful words?

Do I want my last actions to prove regrettable?

Whether we meet Jesus at His Second Coming or through death, He is at the door every moment and the desire to not be ashamed when He appears should jar us to reality when sin is wooing us:

And now, dear children, continue in him, so that when he appears, we may be confident and unashamed before him at his coming.
(1 John 2:28)

Our love for Jesus should expel our love for sin and our desire to not break His heart at His appearing should move us to battle stations.

But there is another way to look at this *Resolution*. The hope of seeing Jesus soon, whether it be via His visible return or Him calling us home, is a powerful inducement to *do* certain things. Soon, very soon, we will see our precious Lord and Saviour! Like a bride awaiting the return of her beloved, or a child excitedly expecting dad to appear any moment, *love* for our Lord Jesus spurs us to joyful work as we watch for His appearing.

How can I fritter away my days when I have been redeemed *from* sin and *for* purpose? Why would I want to? Christian history proves that those who have lived with an 'eye on the sky', ever watchful for Jesus' return, have been the most effective 'in time' for eternity. The taunt that we will be 'so heavenly minded that we will be of no earthly good' has proven itself to be false again and again. It is those most ready, most eager, most watchful for Jesus' appearing who labour most effectively. Witness Anthony Ashley Cooper, 7th Earl of Shaftesbury, Baron Cooper of Pawlett, Baron Ashley of Wimborne St. Giles as 'Exhibit A' of this fact!

Charles Wesley, ever mindful of the brevity of life and the nearness of Jesus wrote:

> I would the precious time redeem,
> and longer live for this alone,
> To spend and to be spent for them
> who have not yet my Saviour known;
> Fully on these my mission prove,
> and only breathe to breathe thy love.

Paul used the nearness of Jesus, the fact of the imminence of Jesus' appearing, to motivate a frightened young Timothy to action:

In the presence of God and of Christ Jesus, who will judge the living and the dead, and in view of his appearing and his kingdom, I give you this charge: preach the word; be prepared ...
(2 Timothy 4:1-2)

RESOLVED.

You might not be a pastor like Timothy was, but the wonderful fact of 'His appearing and His Kingdom' is as applicable to you and me today as it was to Timothy all those years ago.

Beloved! Live with 'an eye on the sky'. Learn to live with the conscious thought that soon - very soon - you will see Jesus.

What a tonic for the weary soul!

What an antidote for the poison of sin!

What a spur to the lazy labourer!

He who testifies to these things says, 'Yes, I am coming soon.'
Amen. Come, Lord Jesus.
The grace of the Lord Jesus be with God's people. Amen.
(Revelation 22:20,21)

'Preach [and live] as if Jesus was crucified yesterday, rose from the dead today, and is returning tomorrow.'[1]
(Martin Luther)

---

[1] Widely attributed to Martin Luther.

RESOLVED.

Resolved 20

Resolved to practice diligence and moderation in my
eating and drinking.

*'I have the right to do anything,' you say – but not everything is
beneficial. 'I have the right to do anything'– but I will
not be mastered by anything.*
(1 Corinthians 6:12)

Dear Friends,

I was surprised when I discovered that the great and godly evangelist, George Whitefield (1714-1770), kept slaves. Whitefield was a man who loved the Lord Jesus and his fellow man very deeply. His evangelistic efforts spanned racial boundaries, which was ground-breaking for his day. In most aspects, I count him a hero. Perhaps he was a 'solicitous' slave-holder. While that possibility might make the reality a little easier to take, it cannot erase the fact that slavery is evil and his keeping of slaves was wrong. Period.

Why did he do this? How could he justify it? I cannot give an answer for George, but I think this blot on his otherwise exemplary life highlights the fact that we can be blind in certain areas of our lives, especially areas where the prevailing culture is likewise blind. It takes a remarkable work of grace to open eyes where everyone is blind and does not even know it (double blindness).

When I first learned this fact about Whitefield, I remember asking myself:

'What are Christians in my culture blind to?'

RESOLVED.

'What are we justifying in our lives that Christians in other cultures and times would or do find shocking?'

'What are the 'respectable sins' in my life that more consecrated Christians or that a more consecrated conscience would disallow?'

The fact is that we, just like all Christians, at all times, in all cultures, have collective blind spots. We have areas where the surrounding culture has engulfed us not only as individuals, but as the Church of God.

Food and drink are just such an area.

It is a strange and sorry fact that many of us in the evangelical Christian world speak out loudly and often against homosexuality, abortion, drunkenness, racism, etc. (and we should engage well with these conversations) between mouthfuls, fork in hand, while on our way back up to the 'all you can eat' bar.

Once again, Jonny is timely and needs to be heard. But does he 'slice the cake' a bit too close for comfort?

Far from this *Resolution* being quaint, old fashioned, or outdated, it could not be more needful, relevant and hard-hitting. Beware of thinking Edwards to be some miserable austere character who scarcely ever smiled. We dare not take the all-too-common way out by crying 'legalism' whenever we encounter a disciple who is more earnest than we. Our Western culture is food mad. It is as though we have gone crazy with our super-abundance. Are we called to a life of bread and water, or is that just as extreme as gluttony but in the opposite direction? What are we to make of this young man's resolve?

RESOLVED.

Let's begin with a brief 'theology of food'.

First, the easy-to-chew part: We affirm that God is a jubilant God who invented food, flavours, and taste buds. He creates and calls all things 'very good' (Genesis 1:31). We rejoice in the fact that the Bible refers not only to fasting, but to feasting many times and in many different contexts (see Psalm 36:8). Indeed, the coming Kingdom of God is marked by feasting (Luke 13:29). We affirm that we are to receive all things, including food, with thankful and worshipful hearts (1 Corinthians 10:31).

Now, the hard-to-swallow part: We remember the concern of the Apostle Paul that a Christian is not to be mastered by anything (1 Corinthians 6:12), food being the first thing Paul is referring to. We remember that it is possible to make a 'god' of your stomach (Philippians 3:19), and idolatry in any form is wicked and destructive. We hear the repeated warnings in the Bible against gluttony (Proverbs 23:2) and remember that the Christian who chooses life over mere existence must view himself with the same attitude as an athlete who trains for a prize (1 Corinthians 9:24). Finally, we are mindful that our Lord Jesus Himself tells us that fasting is to be a normal part of the Christian's life (Matthew 6:17), though, sadly, it is not common practice.

OK, so what do we do with Edwards' *Resolution*? Rather than bite off more than we can chew, let's first remember that Jon has chosen life over mere existence. He wants to live a life which both maximizes the Glory of God and his own joy. He wants to live at full stretch. He is not running aimlessly, but with purpose.

His life can be likened to the disciplined life of an athlete. I have a casual acquaintance with a truly world-class, 'elite' athlete. He is in no doubt as to his goals. Truly, every aspect of his life, right down to his eating, is devoted to his aspirations. He has '[r]esolved, to practice diligence and moderation in [his] eating and drinking'.

And here is the thing: No one thinks him strange, legalistic, or austere. They admire him and understand that his resolve is a part of his determination to achieve his goals. Likewise, Jonathan Edwards is running for a prize. It is an eternal prize. He orders his life accordingly, right down to maintaining how and what he eats and drinks. He does not want to be sluggish. He does not want to love this life too much. He wants to sleep well, rise early, work hard. He actually reinforced this *Resolution* a few months later, adding a rider of constant vigilance:

> **Resolved** to ask myself every night before I go to bed, whether I have acted in the best way I possibly could with respect to eating and drinking.

Clearly, his resolve is not the passing fancy of a young zealot, but the considered decision of an earnest disciple.

Legalism? No. Commitment? Yes.

He does not want to be mastered by anything. We hear in him an echo of the apostle Paul before him:

> *I strike a blow to my body and make it my slave so that after I have preached to others, I myself will not be disqualified for the prize.*
> (1 Corinthians 9:27)

Jonathan Edwards' *Resolution* is right for our age. Martin Luther observed that the Christian is like the drunken man, who, having fallen off one side of his horse, remounts only to fall off the other side. We

RESOLVED.

move between unbalanced extremes. Insisting that we are not called to live on bread and water, we now want a feast at every meal. Edwards is balanced; 'diligence and moderation' does not mean never feasting. That is not even a remotely biblical notion. But it does mean choosing and maintaining a measured lifestyle, especially where eating is concerned, for the sake of the Gospel. He was not unique in this conviction; John Wesley and the early Methodists shared it, Hudson Taylor, Jim Elliott, George Verwer and John Piper too.

The best disciples have been measured, that is, careful, in all things, and it seems that *being measured in food and drink sets the pace in all other areas*. This fact is remarkable, but true. The overfed body tends towards spiritual laziness and becomes easy prey for sin and temptation. The temperate body maintains a vigilance that seems to help every other area of discipleship.

So, what are we going to do about this?

We have some choices:
1) Feel guilty and make a knee-jerk, impossible decision to live like a monk and never eat or drink anything nice again.
2) Ignore Edwards as being legalistic, quaint, and of no purpose for we more sophisticated disciples … and munch away.
3) See the deep relevance and wisdom of this *Resolution*, ask for grace to repent of our fork and spoon sin, and for wisdom and strength to begin to live like a disciple in this vital area of life.

Choice 3 is the wise, grace-way choice. Choice 3 will lead towards brighter eyes, a sharper mind, a humble sprit, and a thankful attitude. It will help you run so as to win the prize. Go to Jesus over this. Tell Him that you are serious about discipleship. Tell Him that you really want to prize Him above all things. Tell Him that you want your life to count, and that you do not want to be lazy, sluggish, or a poor steward of your brief life. Ask Him for grace to be as disciplined as an athlete in every area of your life, especially concerning food and drink. Ask Him for the resolve to make hard choices so that you can make a difference.

God will give us all grace to bring this battle-ground area into submission to His Lordship. Jesus really will help you. He wants to. He is more into your discipleship than you are!

> *So, whether you eat or drink or whatever you do,*
> *do it all for the glory of God.*
> (1 Corinthians 10:31)

'This is the secret of being content: to learn and accept that we live daily by God's unmerited favour given through Christ, and that we can respond to any and every situation by His divine enablement through the Holy Spirit.'[1]
(Jerry Bridges)

---

[1] Bridges, J. (1996). *The Practice of Godliness,* p.99. NavPress. Used by permission of NavPress-www.navpress.com

RESOLVED.

Resolved 21

Resolved never to do something, which, if I saw someone else doing it, would lead me to despise him or to think poorly of him.

Why do you look at the speck of sawdust in your brother's eye and pay no attention to the plank in your own eye?
(Matthew 7:3)

You, then, who teach others, do you not teach yourself? You who preach against stealing, do you steal? You who say that people should not commit adultery, do you commit adultery? You who abhor idols, do you rob temples? You who boast in the law, do you dishonour God by breaking the law?
(Romans 2:21-23)

Dear Ones,

Some may be asking, in these days of tremendous social and cultural upheaval, why I am writing pastoral letters based upon the centuries-old *Resolutions* of a teenager's relentless pursuit of holiness. Can I not find a more culturally relevant theme? Should I not be addressing the riots in the streets? Should we not be exploring race relations? Can we not discuss police reform and address political flaws? Surely, I should speak of social and structural injustices.

Here is my answer: While most certainly there is a right time and place for Christians to deal with issues such as those named above, there is nothing ... *nothing*, more culturally relevant and transformational than personal holiness. Personal holiness is never private holiness. It spills over into the public arena. History demonstrates that the Christian who affects his or her culture the most is the Christian who has pursued holiness of heart and life the most.

RESOLVED.

Godly men and women are mighty weapons for good in the hands of a holy God.

So, in these days of extreme social upheaval and need, I make no apology for our continued exploration of Jonathan's *Resolutions*. They could not be more timely. The more diligent I am with my own heart (the only heart I have any jurisdiction over), the more useful I will be in my Master's hands to effect changes so desperately needed in my world. History proves this in the lives of countless men and women whose deep rivers of personal holiness burst their banks into radical love for their neighbours.

The problem with the world is *systemic sin* and the answer to the world is the Gospel. And, as far as I am concerned, it has to begin with me - with my own heart and life. I remember being startled many years ago by these words from David Wilkerson:

> The Lord is more concerned with winning all of me for Christ than in me winning all of the world for Christ.[1]

For until I am truly won for Christ, I cannot be truly effective in my needy world.

Consider with me the *Resolution* at the top of this letter 'never to do something, which, if I saw someone else doing it, would lead me to despise him or to think poorly of him'. We live in an age of finger pointing. Ours is a generation of blaming and accusing. Being assured of our own righteousness and everyone else's wickedness, we watch

---

[1] Wilkerson, D. (1987). *Taking Hold of Christ*, World Challenge Pulpit Series, accessible at http://www.tscpulpitseries.org/english/1980s/ts870601.html. I heard David say this when at a conference with Tessa in Dallas in 1986. How his words found a home in my heart!

others' actions and quickly despise and think poorly of them. We focus on *their* speck, ignoring *our* plank.

But Jonathan's *Resolution* won't allow us to hide in our self-righteous corner. The fact of the matter is that, to one degree or another, we do the very things we hate seeing others do. We have in us, at least in seed form if not sprouted and growing, the very wickedness we condemn in others.

For example, here comes a middle aged, pick-up drivin', tobacco chewin', flag wavin', white guy in a baseball cap. In a moment I have him sized up. My subconscious has him pigeon-holed before he even opens his mouth. He must have a white sheet hanging in his closet, and a pistol somewhere under that belt-buckle.

He is a prejudiced, narrow-minded bigot. I am glad I am not like him!

Except, I am worse than him, for I have made my own savage heart judge and jury over him and am thereby every bit as prejudiced, narrow, and bigoted as I imagine him to be.

Or here are angry youths demonstrating. Spewing violence, some are throwing bricks and breaking windows. From my sofa I eat my nachos and silently curse them, forgetting that I spoke abusively to my wife earlier that day, slammed a door in anger, and have not spoken to my son in a week because I cannot abide his left-wing politics.

If only people were more like me.

Except, I am as sinful and diseased as the next man, only my sin is hidden under a paper-thin veneer of social respectability.

RESOLVED.

Seeing things we despise in others needs to lead us to self-examination, not to self-justification. Imagine how this would change our culture if we all simply practiced this today! Remembering that God looks upon our hearts and knows them in depth, what must He think when He sees us despising in others what we put up with, or even applaud, in ourselves?

The unexamined heart will too easily excuse in itself what it decries in others. A careless person will be blind toward his own faults while he glares at those of others:

He is hot-tempered. *I* am just passionate.

She is greedy. *I* am just appreciative of finer things.

He is lustful. *I* merely know beauty when I see it.

She is rude and offensive. *I* simply call things as I see them.

He is a glutton. *I* merely have a healthy appetite.

She covets. *I* admire.

Here is a thought that may make some mad at me: A youth sets fire to a building and my heart is set on fire with anger toward him. It might be that for me to be inflamed toward that riotous kid is just as wicked in God's eyes as that youth's behaviour ... or maybe more wicked, because people are more important than buildings.

How did Jesus put it?

> *For in the same way you judge others, you will be judged, and*
> *with the measure you use, it will be measured to you. Why do you*

RESOLVED.

look at the speck of sawdust in your brother's eye and pay no attention to the plank in your own eye? How can you say to your brother, 'Let me take the speck out of your eye,' when all the time there is a plank in your own eye?
(Matthew 7:2-4)

The godly response to someone else's despicable behaviour is to search my own heart for evidence of the same. A little searching will lead to grim discoveries of similar evils. These need to be repented of before they too burst forth. C.S. Lewis speaks of the first time that he, an educated, erudite Englishman began to truly examine his heart. What he discovered horrified him:

For the first time I examined myself with a seriously practical purpose. And there I found what appalled me: a zoo of lusts, a bedlam of ambitions, a nursery of fears, a harem of fondled hatreds. My name was legion. [2]

These are days when repentance is needed more than accusation, where humility needs to supplant haughtiness.

True holiness of heart and life – what Jonathan is going hard after – will without fail result in not only personal, but social transformation. To seek social change without going first for heart change will be to dress a wound lightly.

For it is from within, out of a person's heart, that evil thoughts come – sexual immorality, theft, murder, adultery, greed, malice, deceit, lewdness, envy, slander, arrogance and folly.
(Mark 7:21,22)

---

[2] C.S. Lewis, (1955). *Surprised by Joy, p.181.* Glasgow: Collins, 1955.

RESOLVED.

The best thing I can do for my world is to become more like Jesus. The second-best thing I can do is to urge and encourage you to do the same. That is why we are 'hanging' with Jonathan. He is addressing causes, not symptoms.

I will give you a new heart and put a new spirit in you; I will remove from you your heart of stone and give you a heart of flesh. And I will put my Spirit in you and move you to follow my decrees and be careful to keep my laws.
(Ezekiel 36:26-27)

'May God enable me to have a single eye and a simple heart, desiring to please God, to do good to my fellow creatures, and testify [to] my gratitude to my adorable Redeemer.' [3]
(William Wilberforce)

---

[3] Wilberforce, R. I., & Wilberforce, S. (1839). *The Life of William Wilberforce*, Vol 3, p. 295. London: J. Murray.

RESOLVED.

Resolved 22

Resolved to seek, with all my might, to be as eternally happy as I possibly can be. By God's grace I will let nothing hinder me from pursuing eternal joy in Jesus. With all the power of my mind, body, and will, I will battle for joy that will last in Heaven forever.

You make known to me the path of life; you will fill me with joy in your presence, with eternal pleasures at your right hand.
(Psalm 16:11)

But you have come to Mount Zion, to the city of the living God, the heavenly Jerusalem. You have come to thousands upon thousands of angels in joyful assembly...
(Hebrews 12:22)

Whatever you do, work at it with all your heart, as working for the Lord ... since you know that you will receive an inheritance from the Lord as a reward.
(Colossians 3:23)

Dear Friends,

Jonathan Edwards' *Resolutions* relentlessly point us to eternity. Indeed, the Bible relentlessly points us to eternity. God motivates us during our brief journey here toward Jesus-glorifying living by constantly presenting to us the wonders of His Heaven.

God speaks of pleasures and joys and rewards. He gives us word pictures of feasts and gardens, rivers and fruitful trees. We read of a glorious city whose citizens are countless redeemed people from every race and tongue. We hear of a wedding celebration, and of crowns and

111

thrones. We are told that we will be in the very presence of the God of all Glory.

I fear we often view salvation in a very sterile way. We believe certain doctrines, then God is obliged to remove our sins, then we do not go to Hell when we die but go to Heaven where everything is OK forever.

It is a sort of business deal.

But I do not think that is what God has in mind at all. It is not a business deal. It is a song. It is a dance. It is a romance. It is a feast. It is a consummation. And it expands into eternity.

Now, as our young Jonathan wants to be as happy in Heaven as he possibly can be, this *Resolution* provokes a number of questions:

Will we all be the same in Heaven?

What does the Bible mean by *rewards*?

Is it OK to want to be as happy as you can possibly be?

Does what Christian do in this life affect their eternity?

First, we need to grasp the fact that the Bible unashamedly speaks of rewards in Heaven. Jesus Himself does. The word *reward* is found 27 times in the New Testament, half of those times it is found on the lips of Jesus:

Rejoice in that day [the day of your persecution] and leap for joy,
because great is your reward in heaven.
(Luke 6:23)

RESOLVED.

*Truly I tell you, anyone who gives you a cup of water in my name
because you belong to the Messiah will certainly
not lose their reward.*
(Mark 9:41)

*For the Son of Man is going to come in his Father's glory with his
angels, and then he will reward each person
according to what they have done.*
(Matthew 16:27)

Now friends, let us not try to be more 'spiritual' than God designed us
to be! If God wants to motivate us with rewards, so be it. But let's be
vitally clear about two things:

1) Do not confuse rewards with salvation. Salvation is by grace and
not by works. We do not in any way merit salvation through our human
works or efforts (Ephesians 2:8,9).
2) Rewards involve nothing other than God Himself, not stuff. There
is no pleasure apart from Him: 'I am your shield, your very
great reward' (Genesis 15:1).

But God, who from His unbounded, free goodness to us, sent His Son to
be a sin-bearing Saviour, does not stop at forgiveness. He continues to
empower us to live a life that honours Him and serves His purposes in
this needy world. And it is at this point that the Bible speaks of God
rewarding us. We - who deserved nothing but wrath - are justified by
grace alone. Then we are empowered by *more* grace to live lives of
service and purpose in His Kingdom. And then... we are rewarded with
eternal joy in Him. Amazing God!

Our reward is God - Father, Son and Holy Spirit - and our capacity for
joy in Him. The fact of a coming reward, or rewards, presumes that we
will not all be the same in Heaven. Salvation is not a factory. The

RESOLVED.

Gospel is not an assembly line. This is a marriage. This is a love song. This is a relationship. The story is told, and believed to be true, of a friend of George Whitefield stating that John Wesley would not be seen in Heaven (Wesley and Whitefield had had a sharp and painful dispute) to which Whitefield replied, 'Yes, you're right, we won't see him in heaven. He will be so close to the Throne of God and we will be so far away, that we won't be able to see him!'

Let me speak to you for moment from my personal experience: There is a real sense in which I will be as happy into eternity as I want to be. There is never any shortage on God's side, nor any hesitancy with Him. Now, I know that my sins are forgiven by the wonder of the death of Jesus on the cross. I know that I am saved and safe forever. But I also know that I am called to a relationship with God, not just to a legal agreement. I know that I can squander my days or use them well. I can hunger after God or allow the junk of the world to spoil my desire for Him. I can be diligent with my heart or careless with it. I can waste grace or use grace. I can freely choose Jesus today as my Satisfier or seek satisfaction in the things around me.

I face these choices every day, and my response to these choices matters not only in time, but into eternity. The grave has no power to sanctify me. Is it not presumptuous to think that I will suddenly be after death what I had little desire to be during life? The choices I make here and now will ring into eternity. Jesus says:

Do not be afraid, little flock, for your Father has been pleased to give you the kingdom. Sell your possessions and give to the poor. Provide purses for yourselves that will not wear out, a treasure in heaven that will never fail, where no thief comes near and no moth destroys. For where your treasure is, there your heart will be also.
(Luke 12:34)

114

Do you see Him telling us to 'provide … a treasure in Heaven that will never fail'? Clearly, will not some Christians invest more in the solid things of eternity while others are investing much in the transient things of time?

It is not only OK for me to want to be as happy as I can be, but it also honours God supremely when I pursue my happiness in Him. As John Piper famously said, 'God is most glorified when we are most satisfied in Him'.[1]

Jonathan wants treasure in heaven. He wants abundant joy in Jesus… forever. He does not want to waste grace. Like an athlete running for a prize, or a farmer labouring in hope for a crop, he is applying himself toward a future reward. He is thinking beyond the weekend (quite something for an eighteen-year-old!) and into forever.

Are you? Am I?

What I am in time, I will, by the grace of God in a glorified reality, be in eternity.

> *But by the grace of God, I am what I am, and his grace to me was not without effect. No, I worked harder than all of them—yet not I, but the grace of God that was with me. … Now there is in store for me the crown of righteousness, which the Lord, the righteous Judge, will award to me on that day—and not only to me, but also to all who have longed for his appearing.*
> (1 Corinthians 15:10; 2 Timothy 4:8)

---

[1] https://www.desiringgod.org/messages/god-is-most-glorified-in-us-when-we-are-most-satisfied-in-him

RESOLVED.

Therefore, my dear brothers and sisters, stand firm. Let nothing move you. Always give yourselves fully to the work of the Lord, because you know that your labour in the Lord is not in vain.
(1 Corinthians 15:58)

'He is no fool who gives what he cannot keep, to gain what he cannot lose.'[2]
(Jim Elliot)

---

[2] Elliot, J. (1949) Journal: Entry for October 28.

116

RESOLVED.

Resolved 23

Resolved to venture out often, to do new and unexpected things for God's Glory, but always to examine the motive behind those deeds, and if, upon reflection, a deed was not done for the Glory of God, to repent and not repeat that deed.

Live as children of light (for the fruit of the light consists in all goodness, righteousness and truth) and find out what pleases the Lord.
(Ephesians 5:8-10)

Dear Friends,

I puzzled for some time over this *Resolution*, and then, in a moment, I saw Jonathan's genius behind it. Most of us live our Christian lives on the defensive. Our goal is to not make too many mistakes. We define ourselves not so much by our purpose in Christ as by what we do not do.

We do not smoke.

We do not gamble.

We avoid certain places and people.

We tend to hug the frigid shore of life, afraid to venture into the deep lest we capsize. Failing to understand the wonders and freedom of a life lived under the grace of God, fear of failure and fear of 'getting it wrong' freezes us.

Jonathan is taking exactly the opposite course. He is setting his compass for adventure. He is taking risks. He is pushing out from

RESOLVED.

shore. Rather than choosing the safe option, he is daring to discover God's deeper purposes for his life. He realizes that when one lives under the banner of grace, one can risk, and even fail, and not be cast aside by the God who takes endless pleasure in His children.

Fear freezes. Grace frees us!

So, our young hero resolves to venture often into new areas with Jesus, testing the water, stepping out on the ledge, cutting a new trail. Why not? Jesus is His Saviour! His grace is sufficient! His mercies are sure! Like a child learning to ride a bike, the father's smile and encouragements make the skinned knees worth it. God is pleased when we understand His redemptive love so fully that we dare the adventure of faith. God is grieved when we have such a miserly view of Him that we cower in the safe shallows of familiarity. Jonathan's advice is simple, faith-filled, grace aware and daring.

Go for it! Give it a try! Write that next chapter of your life! By all means, examine your heart along the way and if you find that your motives are self-glory, instead of God's Glory (perhaps that is why there is so little joy in the effort!), adjust your motives or leave the thing alone altogether. But don't quit living the adventure of faith!

Does not Jesus encourage just this strategy? Remember his story of the servants who were given money to invest (Matthew 25:14-30)? In that story, three different servants (us) were given money to invest for their master (talents and abilities to use for God's Kingdom purposes). Not all had the same amount of money to invest (not all of us have the same number of gifts from God to develop). But all were expected to get on with it (all of us are expected to take steps of faith and invest what we have in furthering God's Kingdom).

RESOLVED.

You know the story: One man was so afraid of his master and so afraid of failure that he did nothing:

Then the man who had received one bag of gold came. 'Master,'
he said, 'I knew that you are a hard man, harvesting where you
have not sown and gathering where you have not scattered
seed. So, I was afraid and went out and hid your gold in the
ground. See, here is what belongs to you.'

His master replied, 'You wicked, lazy servant!'

Big point: God is *not* like the master in this parable. But some of us think He is! We view Him as a 'hard man' instead of a loving father, and we bury our gifts instead of risking them for our joy and His Glory. Yet because He is a loving, grace filled father and not a 'hard man', He would far rather us try and fail than sit stuck fast in inaction because of fear of failure.

Go on!

Write that book!
Explore that yet hidden talent!
Visit that needy neighbour!
Make that mission trip!
Play that instrument and sing that song!
Start that class!
Pursue that ministry!
Make that move!

Yes, of course, keep watch over your intentions and motives, and if you find that your motives are suspect, change them, or change course. But don't become a wallflower when Jesus has asked you to start dancing with Him. Don't settle for being a shore-hugger when Jesus has called you to go deeper and let your nets down.

119

RESOLVED.

Of course, I want to be wise in my adventures and not arrogantly rush head-long into disaster. But if I wait until I am guaranteed success in *everything,* I will never do *anything.* Sure, I want good, God honouring motives in all that I do. But I also know that if I wait until my motives are perfect before I do *something*, I will end up doing *nothing.* I have a living Saviour who has embraced me in His love and empowered me with His Holy Spirit for action. He can handle my failures, and He can even deal with my suspect motives. What He does not want to see is me cowering in fear and doing nothing.

Our view of God is of paramount importance here. Is He a scowling headmaster ready to punish you for your next mistake, or a welcoming father bidding you to learn to ride? Is he selfish and stingy and impossible to please, or is He generous and giving and eager to help us succeed? Here are a few Scriptures that may answer this vital question for us. Linger over them until they transform your view of God:

> *With this in mind, we constantly pray for you, that our God may*
> *make you worthy of his calling, and that by his power he may*
> *bring to fruition your every desire for goodness and*
> *your every deed prompted by faith.*
> (2 Thessalonians 1:11)

> *You, Lord, keep my lamp burning;*
> *my God turns my darkness into light.*
> *With your help I can advance against a troop;*
> *with my God I can scale a wall.*
> (Psalm 18:28,29)

> *And God is able to bless you abundantly, so that in all things at*
> *all times, having all that you need, you will abound*
> *in every good work.*

RESOLVED.

(2 Corinthians 9:8)
For God hath not given us the spirit of fear; but of power,
and of love, and of a sound mind.
(2 Timothy 1:7 KJV)

It is God who arms me with strength
and keeps my way secure.
He makes my feet like the feet of a deer;
he causes me to stand on the heights.
He trains my hands for battle;
my arms can bend a bow of bronze.
(Psalm 18:32-34)

He said to Simon, 'Put out into deep water, and let down
the nets for a catch.'
(Luke 5:4)

Where would the Kingdom be without those who have displayed a spirit of risky faith in the face of fear and discouragement? When, in 1786, an English shoemaker named William Carey told his church leaders he wanted to take Jesus' Gospel to the people of India, he was scolded, 'Young man sit down! When God pleases to convert the heathen, He will do it without your aid or mine!' He went anyway, telling his praying friends, 'You hold the rope and I will go down into the hole'.

Way to go, William!

Way to go, Jonathan, for reminding me to get on and live the adventure!

For we are God's handiwork, created in Christ Jesus to do good
works, which God prepared in advance for us to do.
(Ephesians 2:10)

121

RESOLVED.

'You cannot swim for new horizons until you have courage
to lose sight of the shore.'[1]
(William Faulkner)

---

[1] Widely attributed to William Faulkner.

RESOLVED.

Resolved 24

Resolved, whenever I commit an obvious sin, to explore it back to its root cause, so that I can be wise against it, so as not to repeat the act, and so to destroy the very origins of it.

For it is from within, out of a person's heart, that evil thoughts come – sexual immorality, theft, murder, adultery, greed, malice, deceit, lewdness, envy, slander, arrogance and folly. All these evils come from inside and defile a person.
(Mark 7:21-23)

Above all else, guard your heart, for everything you do flows from it.
(Proverbs 4:23)

Dear Ones,

Sixty-thousand people were on their feet. It was the 1929 Rose Bowl in Pasadena California. The University of California Golden Bears were head-to-head with the Georgia Tech Yellow Jackets. The game was being broadcast across the entire continent, a remarkable feat for radio in that day. Roy Riegels, the stand-out California linebacker, had just picked up a Georgia fumble. With the ball firmly in his hands, he spun around and sprinted the length of the field towards the end-zone. The crowd was cheering as the player was running with all his might, sixty yards, towards the goal. Nobody was going to catch him. ... Not even his own team-mate Benny Lomm, who was running behind him shouting at the top of his lungs....

Something was wrong.

Was the crowd cheering or laughing?

RESOLVED.

Roy Riegels was running...the wrong way. Benny Lomm finally caught up with him and pulled him down just before the Georgia Tech goal line. But it was too late. The mistake cost California two vital points and they went on to lose that great game 8-7. Roy Riegels has gone down in football history as 'Wrong Way Riegels'.

After the game, a chastened Riegels said, 'I was running toward the sidelines when I picked up the ball. I started to turn to my left toward Tech's goal. Somebody shoved me and I bounded right off into a tackler. In pivoting to get away from him, I completely lost my bearings...

I surely thought I was going the right way'. [2]

Roy could tell you the exact second, and point to the exact spot, where he got it all wrong. You can actually see it on the ancient film footage. 'Somebody shoved me and I bounded right off into a tackler. In pivoting to get away from him, I completely lost my bearings'. If he could have rolled back time, he would have gone to that spot and moment when he 'pivoted to get away from him' and turned the other way!

Our young Jonathan is wanting to go to the root of his sin. He wants to trace the error of his ways back to the seminal issue, the vital moment, the pivotal decision, and deal with things there. He wants to go to the viper's nest and destroy sin at its source. Rather than endlessly brush at webs, he wants to kill the spiders. Rather than clip the dandelion flowers, he is aiming for the deep roots. He is not interested in simply dressing a wound, he wants to deal with the deeper disease.

---

[2] http://en.wikipedia.org/wiki/Roy_Riegels

RESOLVED.

Long before the affair hits the headlines, the telltale, deadly signs become evident: the wink, the word, the flirt. Even before these are the wandering thoughts and the careless imaginings. But even before these we find the dusty Bible, and the missed prayer time … evidence of a vacant heart toward God and of idols taking up residence.

True repentance goes deep and deals with problems at their source. It is surgical, not cosmetic. It heeds the prophet's warning:

> *They dress the wound of my people as though it were not serious.*
> (Jeremiah 6:14)

Upon reflection (essentially a moment of repentance) Riegels could recount just how and where he went wrong. He posts blame on no-one else. He owns the calamity as his own. An initial error, an early wrong step, brought about an inevitably costly result. Little errors, small sins, can produce tragic results. That affair began with a wink, but behind the wink was an adulterous heart. Now homes are shattered and generations ruined. That dubious business deal began with a whisper, but behind it was a greedy heart. Now crimes have been committed and reputations ruined.

When sin is recognized, Edwards resolves to run it down and deal with it at source. I would not be surprised if he had been reading Psalm 139 when he wrote this *Resolution*:

> *Search me, God, and know my heart*
> *test me and know my anxious thoughts.*
> *See if there is any offensive way in me*
> *and lead me in the way everlasting.*
> (vss. 23,24)

125

RESOLVED.

Shallow repentance produces shallow results. It cannot deliver joy and peace and freedom. In reality, shallow repentance is no repentance. True repentance recognizes the wickedness of the seemingly innocent first step, the wink, the whisper. The kind of repentance we are dealing with here asks searching questions of the soul:

> Why am I irritable?
> What is behind this lust?
> Why does that person bug me?
> Where did this attitude come from?
> When did I lose my peace?
> Who am I truly serving?

When we are careless with our hearts, we take wrong first steps without thinking about where these early steps will lead us. The Bible is full of the sad stories of those who, being slack with their hearts, allowed little indiscretions to lead them to disasters: Lot, Samson, David, Saul, Judas. We could fill volumes with their miserable tales. I just this week finished reading *Moby Dick* (I am sure I was supposed to have read it in high school). In its essence the book is about a man who has been careless with his heart. Captain Ahab allows vengeance to take root and eventually to control all that he is and does. He fails to nip it early. Vengeance comes to define him. His drive to avenge himself results in his - and his crew's - destruction.

Good repenting goes back to these early steps and deals with the heart sins that caused them: the arrogance, the pride, the lust, the laziness, the greed, the envy, the carelessness, the anger.

Finally, it goes to the root of all sin and resulting joylessness, the pivoting of the heart away from God as its first - and final - treasure.

RESOLVED.

Real repentance looks for the inner idols and, once they are found, it is ruthless with them. It is violent against the trickling rills because it knows that they become raging rivers. It resolves to wage irreconcilable war against heart sins - sin in any form. As a skilled doctor hears the cancer in the cough, so the diligent disciple sees the infidelity in the flirt, smells the death in the compromise. It knows that the game may be ultimately lost on a wrong first step. False repentance swats flies but never closes the door. It regrets but does not reform. It is always sorry, but never ceasing. It is forever apologizing, but never changing. It wallows in misery, but never washes in God's mercy.

Godly sorrow brings repentance that leads to salvation and leaves no regret, but worldly sorrow brings death.
(2 Corinthians 7:10)

Our young mentor has chosen true life over mere existence. He refuses permission to anything that will stand between himself, joy, Jesus, and Heaven. Therefore, when he sins, he is determined to find the origin of that sin, excise the tumour, cauterize the wound, and have done with it. Painful it may be, but such is the price if one's choice is Jesus above all.

However difficult thorough, diligent repentance may be, failure to do so will, in the end, be infinitely more painful.

That first step might well be the most important.

Just ask Roy.

There is a way that appears to be right, but in the end it leads to death.
(Proverbs 14:12)

127

RESOLVED.

'Be a consistent Christian, live above the world …and underneath you shall be God's everlasting arms.'[3]
(George Whitefield)

---

[3] Geldstone, James P. (1871) *The Life and Travels of George Whitefield,*. London, Longmans, Green, and Co., p.406

RESOLVED.

Resolved 25

Resolved to search my heart often, looking for that one thing within
that is causing me to question God's perfect and true love for me,
and then to wage war against it.

*But God demonstrates his own love for us in this: while we
were still sinners, Christ died for us.*
(Romans 5:8)

*This is how God showed his love among us: he sent his one and
only Son into the world that we might live through him.*
(1 John 4:9)

Dear Friends,

Jonathan Edwards was just eighteen years old when he wrote the first
thirty-four of his seventy *Resolutions*. He then over the next year and a
half conceived the next thirty-six. Then he committed himself to
appraise himself prayerfully by them once a week. As far as we know,
he did this for the next thirty-five years until his untimely death in 1758.
That means he would have prayerfully considered the above *Resolution*
over one thousand eight hundred times.

Imagine with me this young man, soon to be a husband, then a father
(of eleven children), then a middle-aged pastor, then an aging
missionary to Native Americans on the harsh frontier, then a college
president (the first president of what would become Princeton
University), searching his heart every week for any telltale evidence of
doubt regarding God's perfect and wonderful love for him! Then see
him go to war against whatever it was that caused that doubt to
rise. Imagine his continued victories as doubt-causing intruders were
regularly discovered and exiled and Gospel assurance continually

flooded in! Is it any wonder that Jonathan Edwards, in the midst of the trials and hardships of eighteenth-century frontier life, lived so remarkably well for Jesus?

Gospel assurance - being sure and certain that we are eternally loved by God through Jesus Christ, and that our sins are *gone* by virtue of His death on the cross - is the precious birthright of every child of God.

Gospel assurance:

Liberates us from our past,

Empowers us for our present,

Secures us for our future.

Jonathan does not want anything to diminish his assurance that God loves him with a perfect and true love.

Now we must understand that God's love is not proven through circumstances going well for us. God's love is proven through one thing and only one thing: that He sent His Son to suffer and die for us.

Here *alone* is the infallible proof that God loves us. This is plainly stated in the Bible:

You see, at just the right time, when we were still powerless,
Christ died for the ungodly. Very rarely will anyone die for a
righteous person, though for a good person someone might
*possibly dare to die. But God **demonstrates** his own love for us*
in this: while we were still sinners, Christ died for us.
(Romans 5:6-8 emphasis mine)

RESOLVED.

Do you see that word *demonstrates*? It is a very important word where our assurance is concerned! It means 'to exhibit', 'to show', 'to prove'. This tells us that God has already displayed and presented the proof of His astounding love for us. It happened while we were still His *enemies*, on a hill outside of Jerusalem.

John says the same thing:

> *This is how God showed his love among us: he sent his one and only Son into the world that we might live through him. This is love: not that we loved God, but that he loved us and sent his Son as an atoning sacrifice for our sins.*
> (1 John 4:9,10)

This tells me that if I look anywhere else for *proof* that God loves me with a true and perfect love, I am looking in the wrong place. My search will lead to confusion and not to confidence. For instance, here is a dear saint, a precious follower of Jesus, and he is sick. He has prayed, but God has not healed him. Jesus has instead chosen to walk with him through a season of suffering. But our friend takes this unanswered prayer as evidence that God may not love him with a perfect and true love. Others have been healed! His assurance is jolted and his faith is wobbling. What is the problem? Simply that our friend has taken his eyes off the cross. He is looking in the wrong place for proof of God's love for him. Now not only is his body suffering, but his soul is in turmoil.

Or there is a sister in Christ. How she has prayed for her wayward child! Yet the battle for that child's soul has now lasted decades. Her friends' children are all following Jesus. Our sister is wondering about God's love. She is questioning God's goodness. She is now not only concerned for her child but is in her own crisis of faith! The problem is simple, but profound: she has misplaced her confidence. Instead of

131

RESOLVED.

confiding totally in the finished work of Jesus, dying for her sins while she was still an enemy of God, she is looking at the battle for her wayward one and wondering about God's love for her.

Both these dear ones are sidelined from the battle… just as Satan wants them to be.

But ah! Here is one who has just received that raise at work! He was not sure if God truly loved him, but now he has proof! He has confused his boss's smile with God's smile. What will then happen when his earthly boss frowns? A faith crisis is in his future, for his eyes are on the wrong thing. His testimony is not Gospel-centred, but circumstance-centred.

He too is therefore sidelined from the battle… just as Satan wants him to be.

The wise saint will tell you that the one thing which time and again causes believers to question God's perfect and true love for them is looking for assurance in circumstances or experiences rather than in the Atonement.

We know that God loves us because Jesus died for our sins.

Period.

Come with me now to a scene in Heaven. Here we find a picture of victory for the often-tormented follower of Jesus. Satan has been 'hurled down'!

> *For the accuser of our brothers and sisters,*
> *who accuses them before our God day and night,*
> *has been hurled down.*

132

RESOLVED.

They triumphed over him by the blood of the Lamb
and by the word of their testimony;
they did not love their lives so much
as to shrink from death.
(Revelation 12: 10,11)

The 'accuser' has been silenced! How? By the pleasant circumstances and experiences of the brothers and sisters? No! But 'by the blood of the Lamb and by the word of their testimony'. What and who silences Satan? A simple follower of Jesus does when he proclaims, 'Jesus loved me and shed His blood to redeem me from sin and I place all my confidence in Him!' Satan has no answer, no higher card to play, for the finished work of Christ on the cross and the believer's testimony that he trusts solely in that, trumps all the accusations of the enemy.

But, if I am looking elsewhere to discover the love of God, I will wobble and not worship, I will tumble and not triumph, I will know confusion, not confidence.

I have recently watched a famous TV preacher here in the USA. His entire message is, 'Your pay raise is coming! That break-through in your situation is just around the corner! Your bank account is soon to be filled!' No! Point me to the cross and keep me there! Tell me over and over that God *loves us and has sent his Son as an atoning sacrifice for our sins.*

Friend, do not let anything or anyone rob you of Gospel joy and assurance. Plant your faith-flag on Calvary's hill and there make your stand. If you find yourself doubting the perfect and true love of God for you, a little self-examination will most certainly reveal that your eyes have moved from the cross to something else.

Put your hope back where it belongs.

RESOLVED.

And I pray that you, being rooted and established in love, may
have power, together with all the Lord's holy people, to grasp
how wide and long and high and deep is the love of Christ, and to
know this love that surpasses knowledge – that you may be filled
to the measure of all the fullness of God.
(Ephesians 3:17-19)

'Sometimes I go to God and say, "God, if Thou dost never answer
another prayer while I live on this earth, I will still worship Thee
as long as I live, and in the ages to come, for
what Thou hast done already."'[4]
(A. W. Tozer)

---

[4] Tozer, A.W. (1961) *Worship: The Missing Jewel of the Evangelical Church.* Camp
Hill, PA: Christian Publications.

134

RESOLVED.

Resolved 26

Resolved to rid myself of anything that lessens my assurance that I am saved, safe, and walking in love with Jesus.

I write these things to you who believe in the name of the Son of God so that you may know that you have eternal life.
(1 John 5:13)

Dear Ones,

Assurance is the birthright of every precious child of God. By *assurance* I mean the simple confidence that one is safe in Jesus forever – the past forgiven, the future secure. Assurance is possible because our salvation is warranted by the blood of Jesus shed once on the Cross for our sins:

God made him who had no sin to be sin for us, so that in him we might become the righteousness of God.
(2 Corinthians 5:21)

Assurance brings with it the precious peace that comes from knowing that our sins have been conclusively dealt with by God. Assurance has nothing to do with our performance, but all to do with God's promise:

But when the kindness and love of God our Saviour appeared, he saved us, not because of righteous things we had done, but because of his mercy. He saved us through the washing of rebirth and renewal by the Holy Spirit, whom he poured out on us generously through Jesus Christ our Saviour, so that, having been justified by his grace, we might become heirs having the hope of eternal life.
(Titus 3:4-7)

RESOLVED.

Assurance, of pardon – sins forgiven, of peace – relationship with God restored, and of position – standing secure in the place of grace, empowers the believer to live valiantly for Christ in the midst of a hostile world. Assurance makes mopers into missionaries and turns worriers into warriors:

> *We constantly pray for you, that our God may make you worthy of*
> *his calling, and that by his power he may bring to fruition your*
> *every desire for goodness and your every deed prompted by faith.*
> *We pray this so that the name of our Lord Jesus may be glorified*
> *in you, and you in him, according to the grace of our God*
> *and the Lord Jesus Christ.*
> (2 Thessalonians 1:11,12)

The simple believer can - and *must* - be totally confident that the work Jesus accomplished upon the Cross has finished the job in pardoning his past, promising his future and positioning him in the family of God forever.

Our young Jonathan does not want *anything* to abate his assurance that he is saved and safe in Jesus. We saw previously that taking one's eyes off the Cross and onto one's performance is sure to affect one's confidence in the finished work of Christ. To look anywhere but to the atonement for our proof of God's love is sure to lead one away from security and assurance.

But there is another deadly enemy of assurance: flirting with sin.

Shallow repentance, carelessness with one's heart, loving what God hates, walking in disobedience, all such will bring the child of God into desert lands. Being 'saved' has a 'to' as well as a 'from' aspect. We are not only saved *from* sin, but we are saved *to* holiness, *from* loving the

136

world supremely *to* loving Jesus supremely. That is why old Paul said to young Timothy:

> *Flee the evil desires of youth and pursue righteousness, faith, love*
> *and peace, along with those who call on the Lord*
> *out of a pure heart.*
> (2 Timothy 2:22)

But when a child of God plays around with sin, sailing too close to the wind, wondering 'how worldly can I be and still get to Heaven?', joy, peace, and assurance are chased off. The times in my life when I look to the sinful world for my satisfaction are the times when I am not able to rejoice in the wonders of my salvation. How can I? When I am loving the world that hates my Saviour, there is a civil war within me between the 'old me' and the 'new me'.

I am not saying that God casts me off on those bad days when sin and temptation overwhelm me. Not in any way! But I am saying that when I am careless with my heart, *I know* that I am not walking in a manner consistent with who I am as a new person in Jesus. All the wonders of my salvation, including the assurance that I am saved and safe in Jesus forever, are *experientially* under threat when I cuddle rather than crucify sin.

> *When I kept silent, my bones wasted away*
> *through my groaning all day long.*
> *For day and night your hand was heavy on me;*
> *my strength was sapped as in the heat of summer.*
> (Psalm 32:3,4)

There is nothing, *nothing,* more precious and necessary to a believer than his walk with Jesus. Salvation is not just some legal contract between God and me. It is a relationship, a friendship, a romance.

RESOLVED.

Consider a marriage, a good marriage. Consider *my* marriage. I am officially and legally married to Tessa. That bond is permanent and secure. Good ... but not enough! It is the daily *relationship* that the legal bond enables and exists for. And that daily relationship is dependent upon me constantly guarding my heart and my mind, my actions and my words. I cannot ruin the legal bond. I can ruin the daily romance. In order for the friendship to flourish, there need to be many repentances, many earnest corrections, many humble apologies. There needs to be active pursuit. There needs to be diligent prioritizing. Otherwise, my *experiential* assurance is under threat. The joy evaporates and the happy acts of love become chores. Before long we are wondering, 'Where has the love gone?' Maybe one of us even wonders, 'Does my spouse still really *love* me?'

The assurance - experientially - has been knocked.

This is exactly what happens with our daily relationship with Jesus. ... Our *justification before God* is a legal and secure declaration. But the point of it is to bring us into a *relationship with God,* and that relationship can be tarnished and dulled if not guarded and polished.

Friend, let nothing threaten your assurance! Let nothing inhibit your joy in Jesus! Treat sin as a cancer and do not let it abide in the slightest form ... not because you are insecure in Christ, but because you know that you have been saved from sin ... *for* Him. The dear, simple believer who *abides* ... which implies many repentances and cleansings ... is the believer who becomes a fruit-bearing, joy-filled, assured, friend of Jesus.

Don't settle for anything less!

> *May our God strengthen your hearts*
> *so that you will be blameless and holy*

138

RESOLVED.

in the presence of our God and Father when our Lord Jesus
comes with all his holy ones.
(1 Thessalonians 3:13)

'We weren't meant to be somebody - we were meant to
know Somebody.'[1]
(John Piper)

---

[1] https://sermonquotes.com/identity/10833-we-werent-meant-to-be-somebody.html

RESOLVED.

Resolved 27

Resolved to never purposely neglect to do what I should do, unless somehow it be for the greater Glory of God, and to regularly examine my motives for not doing something.

Jesus Christ .... gave himself for us to redeem us from all wickedness and to purify for himself a people that are his very own, eager to do what is good.
(Titus 2:14)

Then they said to each other, 'What we're doing is not right. This is a day of good news and we are keeping it to ourselves.'
(2 Kings 7:9)

Dear Friends in Jesus,

Oh, to be eager to do good!

As we have already noted, following Jesus is often felt to be a matter of *avoidance* – staying away from certain places and people and actions. Certainly, there is truth to this. We are *not* to do certain things, go to some places where those things take place, or hang around those who go to those places and do those things. The sad life of Samson, as detailed in the Bible, bears testimony to the danger of habitually being in the wrong place and with the wrong people.

But too often we followers of Jesus have allowed ourselves to be *defined* by what we do not do, where we do not go and whom we avoid.

RESOLVED.

Can we flip this on its head? Can we make it our goal to be defined by our nearness to the One who healed the sick, fed the hungry, preached the good news of the Kingdom, and loved the lost?

God anointed Jesus of Nazareth with the Holy Ghost and with power: who went about doing good and healing all that were oppressed of the devil; for God was with him.
(Acts 10:38)

God is desirous for us to do good. He likes to see us walk in His will and excel in the gifts he has given us:

The Lord be exalted, who delights in the well-being of his servant.
(Psalm 35:27)

And so, God is as concerned with the good that we fail to do as with bad that we do. We have been redeemed for good works as surely as we have been saved from bad works. True saving faith, by which the helpless sinner looks to his merciful and sufficient Saviour, is evidenced not only by turning from sin, but equally by a new desire to do good.

For we are God's handiwork, created in Christ Jesus to do good works, which God prepared in advance for us to do.
(Ephesians 2:10)

As the body without the spirit is dead, so faith without deeds is dead.
(James 2:26)

Here is a joyous piece of news for you: God is easy to please. He is impossible to impress, but easy to please. He is not against us but for us and He:

141

RESOLVED.

- Saves solely by His grace, and then
- Gifts and equips us to do good works, and then
- Prepares those works for us to do, and then
- Rewards us when we do those works!

What a God!

As in everything, our view of God is the determining factor. If I see God as harsh, difficult, contrary, capricious, and impossible to please, I will be reluctant to do anything. But if I see Him as He really is - generous, willing, enabling, steady, and easy to please - I will be eager and ready to do His welcome bidding.

In light of this, to be lazy and faithless, to be a timewaster or to fill our day with *our* agenda, to neglect the good that we can do out of a fear of failure or a simple lack of concern, is as offensive to our good and wonderful God as is obvious outward sin. We need to see that 'sins of *omission*' are just as grievous to God as 'sins of *commission*'.

Now to sharpen our focus: I am convinced that of all the 'good works' we can fail to do, the most grievous, the most obvious, the most hurtful to God and people is ...

Our Neglect to Tell Others about Jesus.

Is this not our greatest duty? If you had a vaccine against cancer or COVID, and held it to yourself, would this not be a grievous crime? Here we have the greatest news for mankind. Here we have the cure for the broken and poisoned heart. Here we have a chance to make our wonderful Saviour famous and people happy, and we sit in silence.

RESOLVED.

Certainly, our reluctance to bear happy witness to Christ to a needy world is our greatest sin of omission. Do you recall, in John's gospel, these words of Jesus?

Very truly I tell you, whoever believes in me will do the works I have been doing, and they will do even greater things than these, because I am going to the Father.
(John 14:12)

Have you ever puzzled over these words, Jesus telling us that we will do 'even greater things' than He did? How can we ever do 'greater things' than He did? Why, He raised the dead! How can *we* beat *that*?

Well, there is *one thing* that we can do that Jesus did very little of - and we can do it because He has returned to His Father and sent us His Holy Spirit- and that is *evangelism*. Jesus spent almost all of His ministry pouring Himself into a few people, and then tasked and empowered them … now *us* … to do what He did not do: take the Gospel to 'all creation' (Mark 16:15).

Could it be that the 'greater things' we are intended and enabled to do all involve loving our neighbours, crossing boundaries of unbelief, engaging our culture with the Gospel, and going near and far with the Good News of Jesus?

I think so.

Could it be that our reluctance to do so is the greatest crime of the Church?

I fear so.

RESOLVED.

Could the greatest injustice in the world be that millions have yet to hear of Jesus while Christians 'sit at ease in Zion' (Amos 6:1).

I know so.

We all speak freely about what we love. We cannot help but 'evangelize' about our favourite sports team and our kids. Our hearts are full to over-flowing about such things! Does our reluctance to speak freely about Jesus reveal a heart-love problem? If the greatest joy possible is to know Jesus, then certainly to help others know Jesus is that joy multiplied! It is a simple fact that the vast majority of people who turn to new life in Jesus do so *because a friend shared Jesus with them*, not because some hot evangelist came to town.

We can take a good Gospel lesson from the lepers in Samaria who came upon a feast in the middle of a famine. What evangelists they became!

> *Then they said to each other, 'What we're doing is not right. This is a day of good news and we are keeping it to ourselves.'*
> (2 Kings 7:9)

Friends, may we lift our hearts to God and repent of this great sin of omission: our reluctance and failure to share Jesus! All we need to be is beggars telling other beggars where we found bread ... *the* Bread of Life!

It need not be more complicated than that.

Lord Jesus! Forgive us deep, and then fill us up, and then fling us out!

RESOLVED.

You are the light of the world. A town built on a hill cannot be hidden. Neither do people light a lamp and put it under a bowl. Instead, they put it on its stand, and it gives light to everyone in the house. In the same way, let your light shine before others, that they may see your good deeds and glorify your Father in heaven.
(Matthew 5:14-16)

'Let us not glide through this world and then slip quietly into heaven, without having blown the trumpet loud and long for our Redeemer, Jesus Christ.'[1]
(C.T. Studd)

---

[1] Widely attributed to C.T. Studd.

RESOLVED.

Resolved 28

Resolved to keep up the good habit of faithfully studying the
Scriptures, so that I can clearly see myself growing
in the knowledge of God's Truth.

*But grow in the grace and knowledge of our Lord and Saviour Jesus
Christ. To him be glory both now and forever! Amen.*
(2 Peter 3:18)

Dear Friends,

The Bible is given that we might *know* God. It is not just given to
satisfy curiosity or to fill us with a range of facts. To read it only
intellectually is to miss the point. Jonathan wants to encourage us to
reverent Bible reading ... reading with an aim to *know God in truth.*

Christians do not hold séances to discover the unknown, they read the
Bible to discover God! We have a God who wants to be
known! Wonder of wonders! He is not hiding. He does not play
games with us. He is *self-disclosing.* And we, being created in God's
image, and being redeemed from sin by His grace and gifted with the
indwelling Holy Spirit, have the capacity to know Him.

*Now this is eternal life: that they know you, the only true God,
and Jesus Christ, whom you have sent.*
(John 17:3)

We do not - we cannot - know God through our own intuition, or via
our own efforts and searching. It is not as though we are brave
explorers and God is some mythological land we are seeking to
discover. It is *God* who is the explorer. *He* is the one who
condescends. We are the hiding rebels.

146

RESOLVED.

He has revealed Himself in all that is around us, for, 'The heavens declare the Glory of God; the skies proclaim the work of His hands. Day after day they pour forth speech: night after night they reveal knowledge
(Psalm 19:1,2).

This is what theologians call God's 'general revelation'. Through creation He has spoken and speaks to every human who has ever gazed upon a night sky or heard the sound of the wind rushing by.

But more, He has revealed Himself in Jesus Christ, the ultimate self-disclosure. As Charles Wesley said:

> Our God contracted to a span,
> Incomprehensibly made man.

And then, He has given us a faithful record of this revelation of Himself in Jesus by overseeing and shepherding the writing of the Bible. You and I can reverently open our Bible and read – not just *about* God, but the very inspired revelation of God's heart to ours!

> *In the past God spoke to our ancestors through the prophets at*
> *many times and in various ways, but in these last days he has*
> *spoken to us by his Son, whom he appointed heir of all things, and*
> *through whom also he made the universe...*
> (Hebrews 1:1)

This is what theologians call God's 'special revelation'. For in Christ and through the Bible, God has displayed the wonders of His redeeming love.

With the help of the Holy Spirit, every child of God, be she or he simple or educated, can understand their Bible and, in it, can discover

147

RESOLVED.

God and His ways. It is *not* a book locked up and reserved for the doctors and cloistered few! William Tyndale (1494 -1536) laboured to give England a Bible in her own tongue … until burned at the stake for doing so. Although he himself could speak seven languages and was fluent in Hebrew and Greek (the original languages of the Bible), he wanted the Bible in English for all. He famously said to the bishops of his day, 'If God spare my life, 'ere many years I will cause a boy who drives a plough to know more of the scriptures than you do'.[1]

But friend, does your Bible gather dust? It is not to be kept in a box as a keepsake, nor lost under a pile of magazines under the coffee table. It is to be *reverently read*. God will help you. Imagine receiving a letter from someone you love dearly, but never opening it. Imagine carelessly tossing it to the side. Your dear friend has revealed their heart to you in the letter! So, you open it! You read it! You cherish it!

How much more your Bible! Here is God's heart opened to you. How sad to leave it unread! How strange to have 'Bible believers' who cannot remember when they last read their Bibles or where they left them! But happy are those who – with hearts lifted to Heaven – read and learn of Jesus and His saving ways. Simply, if you prayerfully read your Bible for 10 minutes every day, you can read through the Bible in an entire year. Spending 30 minutes a day in the Word allows you to read it three times a year. In doing so, you will grow wise in your salvation and rich in your knowledge of God.

Bible-reading Jesus-followers become happy, healthy, and useful. They become stable and solid amidst life's storms. They cease to be gullible and find themselves powerful in spiritual battle. The more they read, the more treasures they find in the rich mine of God's truth. They increasingly think God's thoughts as their minds are renewed. Their words become wise, and they become helpers to others.

---

[1] Cited at https://www.desiringgod.org/articles/the-underground-translator

RESOLVED.

Blessed are those who read their Bibles! Do you read yours? Will you? God the Father wants you to read all about His Son and God the Holy Spirit will help you.

I leave you with a Scripture to encourage you and then two long quotes from two of my Bible-reading heroes, George Muller (1805-1898) of Bristol orphanage fame and John Wesley (1703-1791) the great revival preacher.

> *This book of the law shall not depart from your mouth, but you shall meditate on it day and night, so that you may be careful to do according to all that is written in it, for then you will make your way prosperous, and then you will have success.*
> (Joshua 1:8)

Above all things see to it that your souls are happy in the Lord. Other things may press upon you, the Lord's work may even have urgent claims upon your attention, but I deliberately repeat, it is of supreme and paramount importance that you should seek above all things to have your souls truly happy in God Himself! Day by day seek to make this the most important business of your life … But in what way shall we attain to this settled happiness of soul? How shall we learn to enjoy God? How obtain such an all-sufficient, soul-satisfying portion in him as shall enable us to let go the things of this world as vain and worthless in comparison? I answer, 'This happiness is to be obtained through the study of the Holy Scriptures. God has therein revealed Himself unto us in the face of Jesus Christ'.[2]

---

[2] Mueller, G. (2003) *A Narrative of Some of the Lord's Dealings with George Mueller, Written by Himself*, pp. 730-73. Muskegon, Mich.: Dust and Ashes Publications.

RESOLVED.

I am a creature of a day, passing through life as an arrow through the air. I am a spirit come from God and returning to God: just hovering over the great gulf till, a few moments hence, I am no more seen: I drop into an unchangeable eternity!

I want to know one thing - the way to heaven: how to land safe on that happy shore. God himself has condescended to teach me the way. For this very end He came from heaven. He hath written it down in a book. O give me that book! At any price, give me the book of God! I have it: here is knowledge enough for me. Let me be homo unius libri [a man of one book]. Here then I am, far from the busy ways of men. I sit down alone; only God is here. In His presence I open, I read His book for this end, to find the way to heaven'.[3]

---

[3] Wesley, J. *A Man of One Book*, in English Prose Vol IV Eighteenth Century edited by Craik, H, (1916): see https://www.bartleby.com/209/750.html

RESOLVED.

Resolved 29

Resolved to not pray frivolous prayers and shallow confessions that I
do not really mean and that I cannot offer in faith that
God will accept and answer.

For the Lord your God is among you, a mighty God and terrible.
(Deuteronomy 7:21 KJV)

*May these words of my mouth and this meditation of my heart
be pleasing in your sight, Lord, my Rock and my Redeemer.*
(Psalm 19:14)

Dear Friends,

There is a great difference between *familiarity* and *frivolity*. We are
invited to be familiar with God. We dare not be frivolous with
Him. We can be familiar because He is Abba, Father. We cannot be
frivolous because He is holy and awesome and – in the old English
sense – terrible.

I think we tend toward being a frivolous generation, and that is a
dangerous thing. I want to be very careful here. I can easily overstate
my case (Jonathan's case!) and misrepresent God as being stern and
austere. I do not want to do that.

I think I have to take you back to my boyhood for a minute, for my
earthly father very well represented our Heavenly Father. As a small
child I could climb onto the lap of my father, always assured of a
welcome. As a teen I often knew his embrace. I could be myself – with
all my attendant flaws – in his presence. He worked downtown in a big
skyscraper. As a young man I could gain access to him anytime, when
others could not, by phone or in person, with a big problem or just to

151

talk. He was always ready to listen (he really was). He was ready and willing to fix whatever mess I had made.

> But I dared not waste his time.
>> I dared not disrespect him.
>>> I could not slouch in his presence.
>>>> I could not approach with a swagger,
>>>>> Nor answer him with a 'yeah'.

I had to knock first and take my hat off when I entered his office.

Respect.

He was both 'daddy' and 'sir' to me. And that was good.

He was never 'my old man'. He was always 'my father'. And that was good.

I have said all this, giving you a peek into a sacred part of me, just to illustrate that our Heavenly Father, though Holy and 'terrible' (the modern word is 'awesome'), is One with whom we can be wonderfully familiar. Indeed, because of Jesus we can 'approach God's throne of grace with confidence, so that we may receive mercy and find grace to help us in our time of need' (Hebrews 4:16).

But I have also said all this to try to illustrate that this wonderful warm Father is One with whom we cannot be flippant, frivolous, and foolish.

Think about some of your prayers and confessions:

> - Do you not sometimes forget that you are dealing with a *Holy* Father, and that there is an immeasurable distance between you as a sinner and Him as God?

RESOLVED.

- Do you not sometimes 'say your prayers' but not really pray?

-Do you not sometimes forget that your sins are *crimes* and *catastrophes,* and that your confessions should be dead earnest and not mere shoulder shrugs?

- Are you too casual too often where God and your relationship to Him is concerned?

The Psalmist got it right:

> *But there is forgiveness with you, that you may be feared.*
> (Psalm 130:4 NKJV)

James got it:

> *The earnest prayer of a righteous person has much power*
> *and produces wonderful results.*
> (James 5:16 NLT)

Take some time and ponder the difference between *fervent* and *flippant*, between *familiar* and *frivolous,* between *boldness* and *brazenness.*
Consider the gulf between you and God that has been bridged by Jesus. Tremble at the wonder of it. Ponder the wonder of being able to approach God anywhere, at any time, with anything, great or small, good or bad. But dwell as well on the gravity of true prayer and confession, and the calamity of being careless in God's presence.

We are welcome into His throne room -
> but should we put our boots on His sofa?

He will listen to our simplest words –
> but should we check our phones in the middle of a conversation?

153

RESOLVED.

He does not require us to stand on ceremony –
but should we yawn while He is speaking?

Do we forget with whom we are dealing when we engage in the miracle of prayer? Think about this: If our prayers and confessions are bland when they need to be bold, if they are formal when they ought to be fervent, if they are wandering when they should be wondering, if they drift off when they need to drive in … in short, if we cannot take our prayers seriously, *why should God*?

Enough lecture.

Let me draw to a close with some encouragement toward simple, believing, fervent, familiar prayer and confession. The Bible is full of episodes and examples of simple believers who prayed simple, but earnest prayers and gained the ear of God with them. May we be encouraged to do likewise.

> - Childless Hannah: 'Hannah was praying in her heart, and her lips were moving but her voice was not heard' (1 Samuel 1:13).

> - The sinful man at church: 'But the tax collector stood at a distance. He would not even look up to heaven, but beat his breast and said, "God, have mercy on me, a sinner"' (Luke 18:13).

> - The blind man on the road: 'He called out,
> "Jesus, Son of David, have mercy on me!"' (Luke 18:38).

> - Lazarus' family: 'So the sisters sent word to Jesus, "Lord, the one you love is ill"' (John 11:3).

RESOLVED.

- The dying thief: 'Then he said, "Jesus, remember me when you come into your kingdom"' (Luke 23:42).

- Jabez, the child of pain: 'Jabez cried out to the God of Israel, "Oh, that you would bless me and enlarge my territory! Let your hand be with me and keep me from harm so that I will be free from pain." And God granted his request' (1 Chronicles 4:10).

These dear simple praying saints show us that we need not be *eloquent,* but we must be *earnest* in our praying. They show us that God is blessed by the *boldness* of His children. God is not impressed by words, but His heart is opened to the desperate. We dare not waste His time with pagan babble, but we will never waste His time with a desire for simple fellowship or the presentation of a desperate genuine need.

Where God is concerned, better one good groan than a thousand empty words.

And when you pray, do not keep on babbling like pagans, for they think
they will be heard because of their many words.
(Matthew 6:7)

'You are before the Lord; let your words be few,
but let your heart be fervent.'[1]
(Charles Spurgeon)

---

[1] Spurgeon, C. *Effective Prayer*: see https://www.spurgeongems.org/chs_prayer.htm

RESOLVED.

Resolved 30

Resolved to give my best every week to grow in the grace of God and
to be brought to a new and higher place with Jesus than
I was the week before.

*But grow in the grace and knowledge of our Lord and Saviour Jesus
Christ. To him be glory both now and forever! Amen.*
(2 Peter 3:18)

Abide in me ... for without me you can do nothing.
(John 15:4,5 NKJV)

Dear Friends,

In the Christian life, you must go 'down' in order to go 'up'. It is as we
humble ourselves before the Lord Jesus that we grow and become more
like Jesus. Many of us complain of an 'up and down' experience in our
Christian journey. You might want to try going 'down and up' instead!
Our young Jonathan wants to grow in grace. He wants to live life on a
higher plane. He wants to mature. He wants to grow up. He wants to
become more like Jesus.

Now at this point I want to make an assumption about Jonathan
Edwards. Remember that he was a young man of eighteen when he
first presented this and sixty-nine other *Resolutions* to himself. As we
have learned, he held himself to this – and the other sixty-nine – every
month for the next thirty-five years. I figure that he understood this
Resolution differently as a mature man than as a young man. (I'll
confirm with Jonathan when I see him in Heaven.) I am making this
assumption from examining my own growth toward maturity as well as
from understanding the stories of many others as they have grown in
grace.

RESOLVED.

I can imagine a young Jonathan *determined* to grow, climbing the mountain of spiritual advancement, striving to be more like Jesus. I have been in that place! Going *up*! And ... how weary we become when we think our growth is a matter of our grit!

Now I imagine an older Jonathan. He still wants to be more like Jesus. He still wants to grow in grace. But... he no longer is going up! He is going *down*. He has discovered that Jesus is always found in the low place. He meets us in the low place.

The way *up* is to go *down* where becoming like Jesus is concerned!

He has learned the way of humility. He has discovered (what a relief!) that growing comes not by striving, but by abiding. We too learn this by tumbling down the mountain of our own effort, often landing with a 'thump'. Lo and behold ... there we find Jesus! And *He* lifts us up!

> *Humble yourselves before the Lord, and he will lift you up.*
> (James 4:10)

So, are we simply passive in all of this?

Have we nothing to do?

How do we 'give our best' and yet not 'strive' in our own strength and efforts?

Let's explore.

First, let's agree that every genuine believer wants to grow in his knowledge of God. Every follower of Jesus wants to become more like

Jesus. Every child of grace is weary of their sin, wishes to be rid of it, and wants to say with the Psalmist:

> *I waited patiently for the Lord; he turned to me and heard my cry.*
> *He lifted me out of the slimy pit, out of the mud and mire; he set*
> *my feet on a rock and gave me a firm place to stand.*
> *He put a new song in my mouth,*
> *a hymn of praise to our God.*
> (Psalm 40:1-3)

Some will strive with their own might to grow 'up' thinking that it is all up to them and that they can do it. Some will be so passive as to do nothing at all, thinking Jesus will work some magic over and in them. But between the extremes of 1) *striving* and, 2) *being passive,* we have *abiding.* There is a vast difference between striving and abiding. And there is a great difference between abiding and doing nothing.

Striving says, 'I am determined to be a better Christian! And I can do it in my own strength! My own grit and determination will get me to a higher place! I am not like those lazy (so-called) Christians! I pray more! I read more! I am a go-getter for Jesus! I've got this!'

Passivity says, 'I don't have to do anything at all. I just let go and let God. I need make no effort. Why wrestle when I can nestle? God is faithful, so I don't have to be. I need not pray. I need not read. I need not pursue. No matter what I do, Jesus will take care of everything'.

I cannot quite imagine young Jonathan as a passive follower, but I certainly can picture him as a striver. Both are extremes, and neither is a proper picture of abiding. Abiding says, 'My one great concern is to walk with Jesus. He will be faithful to me, but I need to respond to His grace. My growth in Christ is dependent upon His love and power working in me, but I must avail myself of all that He has for me even as a branch avails itself of the vine. It is not up to me but up to Him, but He must have all of me. My *job* is daily surrender'.

I said earlier that we 'go down' in order to 'go up'. What does *abiding* have to do with this? Very simply: Jesus is always in the low place. He dwells with sinners. You do not find Him hanging out with the self-assured and successful but with the underdogs. Martin Luther, in a letter to his friend, George Spenlein, put it this way:

> Beware, my dear George, of pretending to such purity as no longer to confess yourself a sinner: for Christ dwells only with sinners. He came down from heaven, where He was living among the righteous, in order to live also among sinners. Meditate carefully upon this love of Christ, and you will taste all its unspeakable consolation. If our labours and afflictions could give peace to the conscience, why should Christ have died? You will not find peace, save in Him, by despairing of yourself and of your works, and in learning with what love He opens His arms to you, taking all your sins upon Himself, and giving you all His righteousness.[1]

It is when we learn to repent quickly (that is, going to the low place), hungrily feed on His Word like a starving man would a loaf of bread (that is, staying in the low place), and pray for grace and help to live the supernatural life of a Christian (that is, going to a lower place!) that we meet Jesus afresh. He is always there, for He is the friend of sinners! It is as you and I learn to dwell there that we actually 'abide' with Jesus, and *He* brings us 'up'.

---

[1] Luther, M. (2003). *Luther: Letters of Spiritual Counsel* (Vol. 18). Regent College Publishing, cited in Gillespie, J. (2013) *Beholding Jesus – Letters to my Children*, p.125. Overland Park, Kansas: Myrrh Books.

RESOLVED.

The beautiful little Old Testament love story, Song of Solomon, is a picture of Jesus, the willing and able one, and you and me, the needy and unable ones. It gives so many scenes of the needy, wandering, fickle sinner and the steady, willing, loving Saviour. Near the end, the Beloved (Jesus) is seen rescuing the wandering, resisting, fickle one (us), bringing her from the low, dry place to the high, green place. Their friends, seeing the rescue, joyfully ask,

> *Who is this coming up from the wilderness*
> *leaning on her beloved?*
> (Song of Solomon 8:5)

The striving is over, there is no more resisting, squirming, wandering, no more hiding. There is a readiness in the needy one that is met by an ability and a willingness in the Strong One. It is as we lean on our Beloved that we are brought up.

Would you grow in grace?
> Would you become more like Jesus?
> > Would you be brought to a higher place of grace?

There is only one way, and it is not by striving, and it is not my snoozing: Get low. Be ever ready to humble yourself with repentance. Be always wanting to learn of Him. Be constantly in a place of need. And there you will be sure to find a ready, able, and willing Jesus …

And He will bring you up.

> *Humble yourselves, therefore, under God's mighty*
> *hand, that he may lift you up in due time.*
> (1 Peter 5:6)

RESOLVED.

'When I try to change myself and patch myself up I can't do it…But if I surrender myself to Him who made me, I experience miracles.'[2]
(Corrie ten Boom)

---

[2] ten Boom, C. (1999) *Reflections of God's Glory,* p.25. Grand Rapids, Michigan: Zondervan Publishing House.

RESOLVED.

Resolved 31

Resolved never to say anything against anyone unless the Golden Rule demands that I do so. And if I must, to do so only out of love to others, in a way that honours Christ, and with a sense of my own faults and failures. And, when I have said anything against anyone, to bring it to the judgment of this *Resolution.*

Do to others as you would have them do to you.
The 'Golden Rule' (Luke 6:31)

Let your conversation be always full of grace, seasoned with salt ...
(Colossians 4:6)

Those who guard their mouths and their tongues
keep themselves from calamity.
(Proverbs 21:23)

Friends,

One of the key aspects of being divine image bearers is the ability to speak and communicate through words. This separates us from the animals and marks us as unique in all of God's creation.

God is a speaking God, and He has made us, the crown of His creation, likewise able to communicate our innermost thoughts outwardly through words. Should it then surprise us that in our present fallen state we should often use this glorious 'god-like' ability in perverse and destructive ways? Throw in a real devil who comes to 'kill, steal and destroy' (John 10:10), and it becomes obvious that speech can be a mighty weapon for good – to build up, or for evil – to tear down.

RESOLVED.

With the tongue we praise our Lord and Father, and with it we curse human beings, who have been made in God's likeness. Out of the same mouth come praise and cursing. My brothers and sisters, this should not be.
(James 3:9,10)

Beloved, God has gifted us with speech to build others up and not to tear them down, warning us against its misuse:

But I tell you that everyone will have to give account on the day of judgment for every empty word they have spoken.
(Matthew 12:36)

And yet today it seems that we fling barbed words this way and that with little or no thought of the damage they do, the offense they cause to God, and the judgment we bring upon ourselves.

So much venom is found in speech these days and it is so easy to enter the fray. Self-righteousness rules and accusation is the order of the day. What if we feared God before we flung our fierce words? What if our words were filled with love instead of inflamed with self-righteous judgment? What if we remembered that others, those at whom we are aiming our arrows, are divine image bearers - those for whom Christ bled and died?

Jonathan's *Resolution* - to never speak against anyone unless the Golden Rule demands it - would be revolutionary if employed in our lives and in our culture. Perhaps you are one of the rare, sanctified souls who actually controls his or her tongue. If so, then you are a blessing to God and to all around you. But for many of us, our undisciplined tongues are instruments of hurt rather than healing.

163

RESOLVED.

They make their tongues as sharp as a serpent's:
the poison of vipers is on their lips.
(Psalm 140:3)

Do we realize that we do the devil's work for him when we tear another down with our words? We fling his fiery darts for him with our tongues. Do we realize that God hears, and God's heart is offended? God loves the person we are shooting arrows towards! He cherishes them. He sent His Son to redeem them. He sings over them. He delights to do them good. He is sanctifying them. He is keeping them daily in His love. He has covenanted with them to never leave or lose them. He is preparing a place for them. He is endlessly patient with them. He wants them to be with Him in Paradise.

And here we come, with destructive, impatient, judgmental words. Over there is a person for whom Jesus died and here am I filled with self-righteousness toward them, looking at them with a critical spirit, assuming evil of them, speaking poorly of them to others, and perhaps harshly to their face.

We can break a person when we speak harsh, rash words to them. And, when we speak these venom-words to a third party and not directly to the person in question, we are gossiping. In so doing we are spreading a bad report, and sowing discord among people. And *God hates that*! In fact, Proverbs 6:16-19 states that God does not just hate the *words* that cause discord, but He hates the *heart* that speaks those words! As J.C Ryle, the nineteenth century Bishop of Liverpool, said, 'When a [person's] tongue is generally wrong, it is absurd, no less than unscriptural, to say that [their] heart is right'.[1]

---

[1] Ryle, J.C. (1859) *Expository Thoughts on the Gospels: St Luke Vol 1*, p.193. New York: Robert Carter and Brothers.

RESOLVED.

We sin against God when we speak against His beloved child.

Lord Jesus! Have mercy on us!

Yes, there are times when love demands that we speak against another. There are times when to be silent is a sin. But how we should tremble at such times! The Bible gives us good counsel for such times:

> *Brothers and sisters, if someone is caught in a sin, you who live*
> *by the Spirit should restore that person gently. But watch*
> *yourselves, or you also may be tempted.*
> (Galatians 6:1)

> *Be merciful to those who doubt; save others by snatching them*
> *from the fire; to others show mercy, mixed with fear – hating even*
> *the clothing stained by corrupted flesh.*
> (Jude 22,23)

To bring a difficult word to or about another should be done only after one brings that word to God first ... 'Lord. I must speak a word against one for whom You died. I tremble at the thought, Lord. They are precious to You, and I must remember this as I speak to them. Also, Lord, I have no righteousness of my own! I am as needy and sinful as they. May I not fool myself that I occupy some "higher ground". May I not look down upon them and come with a harsh tongue or attitude, for I too am a sinner. May my entire motive be their redemption and happiness, and Your Glory'.

Again:

Lord Jesus! Have mercy on me!

RESOLVED.

Let's go on the offensive here. Rather than just resolving to not say anything against another, let's make it our goal to actually be channels of grace to all through our speech. How transformational if we earnestly and deliberately believe the best about others, seeking to see them as God sees them, and using our words to *build up* rather than *tear down*! Let us move against the vitriolic spirit of our age. Remembering our own sinfulness and need of grace, let us seek grace to make our words sweet and life-giving to all who hear us!

> *Gracious words are a honeycomb, sweet to the soul*
> *and healing to the bones.*
> (Proverbs 16:24)

Lord Jesus! Fill me with sweetness towards all! May my words be full of grace and a source of life to all who hear them!

> *Let the words of my mouth, and the meditation of my heart, be*
> *acceptable in your sight, O Lord, my strength, and my Redeemer.*
> (Psalm 19:14 NKJV)

> 'While I disparage the exercise of 'building one's self-esteem', I
> indulge in it every time I imagine myself free from the
> defects I perceive in someone else.'[2]
> (Elisabeth Eliot)

---

[2] Elliot, E. (1999) *The Vice of Self-Esteem.* Newsletters: Sept 1st, p 1. See
https://elisabethelliot.org/resource-library/newsletters/the-vice-of-self-esteem-2/

Resolved 32

Resolved to be ever diligent to be faithful to whatever has been entrusted to me, that the Proverb, 'A faithful man who can find?' may in no way be true of me.

Whatever you do, work at it with all your heart, as working for the Lord, not for human masters.
(Colossians 3:23)

Many claim to have unfailing love, but a faithful person who can find?
(Proverbs 20:6)

Dear Ones,

Jesus Christ is to be Lord of all or not at all. Jesus is Lord over my cleaning of the toilet just as certainly as He is over my prayer life. We cannot reverently read our Bibles and then irreverently do a half job at work. Faithfulness is as important on Monday as it is on Sunday, in things public as in things private, for *everything* is sacred to the Christian, because *everything* is sacred to Jesus. Jesus sees no 'sacred / secular divide', and neither must we. For the follower of Jesus there is no compartment of life, not the least aspect of existence, over which Jesus does not say, 'Mine!'

We sometimes over-spiritualize what it means to be a Jesus-person. We make it more complicated than God intends for it to be. The story is told of a brand-new Christian who asked Martin Luther how he, as a new follower of Christ, should now serve Jesus. 'And what is your trade?' asked Martin. 'I am a cobbler. I make shoes,' replied the new Jesus-follower. 'Then in that case,' answered Luther, 'if you would serve Jesus, *make a good shoe and sell it at a fair price.*'

RESOLVED.

It is a fact of Christian history that the eighteenth-century Methodists became, under the Lordship of Jesus, such good and faithful workers that they ended up being business owners and leaders in their communities, simply because they applied the Kingship of Christ to every aspect of their lives. In this way Christian virtue infiltrated and transformed an otherwise corrupt and rotten society. These simple but consecrated Christians truly became salt in their world. Of them the proverb was true:

> *Do you see someone skilled in their work?*
> *They will serve before kings.*
> (Proverbs 22:29)

This is *not* to say that every hard-working Jesus-follower is destined to become a boss, and experience 'success' in the workplace. It *is* to say that God will be honoured in the diligence of a Christian's entire life, and that life will inevitably be a blessing to many.

If I am a Christian, I must be able to offer any and everything I do as an act of worship to the Lord. At the very same time, this life has become for me both insignificant, for it is passing away, and profoundly significant, for it is a gift from our gracious Father to be offered back to Him in true worship and reverence. If I cannot genuinely offer something to Jesus, then I should not do it, and if I can offer it to Jesus, be it reading my Bible or walking in the woods or preaching a sermon or cutting my grass or going to work, then it deserves my very best effort.

Simple.

Oh, but these days! As Christian virtue disappears, so does common diligence and the goodness and the satisfaction of a job well done. Age-old Christian-forged values such as 'a man is as good as his

168

word', or a handshake being as binding as a contract, are relics of a former day. Corruption, shoddiness, cutting corners, and showing up late for work are the trademarks of paganism and its corresponding culture, not of Christianity and the world the Bible shapes. But, as our culture moves ever farther away from its biblical moorings, these are becoming the trademarks of our day. Perhaps we now mock the idea of the 'Protestant work ethic', but we do so to our own detriment. It is, in fact, a beautiful and powerful transformational principle. Simply stated, it reinforces the biblical insistence that a person's faith in Jesus is proven in the workplace as surely as in the church pew. When practiced, it honours God and leads to blessing far and wide. (Please don't think I am advocating the modern perversion of this, the 'Prosperity Gospel'.)

Simple and powerful.

For a person today to give their best at any and every endeavour - precisely because Jesus is their Lord - is a powerful witness in a 'post-Christian', corner- cutting culture. Conversely, a person who dares to name Jesus as Lord and yet does not give a fair day's work or his finest effort for his earthly boss, is dishonouring his Saviour and presents a tragic and poor witness to the watching world.

Slaves, obey your earthly masters in everything; and do it, not only when their eye is on you and to curry their favour, but with sincerity of heart and reverence for the Lord.
(Colossians 3:22)

Jesus sees! Jesus sees when and what people do not see. And He rewards! Perhaps an earthly boss overlooks you. Know that Jesus does not. Keep giving that earthly boss the best because Jesus will make it right. Likewise, He knows when we time-out early, or cut that corner, or fake it. He sees the *back* of the toilet that no one else sees, and

RESOLVED.

(wonderful!) when we are faithful in the little thing, Jesus knows it and will bring us into greater things. Perhaps the recognition will not take place until Heaven, and perhaps no one will ever know except Jesus, but that is enough for the simple follower of Jesus.

> *His master replied, 'Well done, good and faithful servant! You have been faithful with a few things; I will put you in charge of many things. Come and share your master's happiness!*
> (Matthew 25:23)

Diligence in all matters is not optional for the people of Jesus. It is a key part of our worship and our witness. It can be a stark and striking point of departure from the self-seeking 'that'll do' culture around us. Know this: Grace is not a license for laziness. Grace is power for service. Grace is not God shrugging His shoulders at our sloppy second best. Grace is God infusing us with ability to do what we naturally cannot do. Grace is not God excusing our half-heartedness. Grace is God empowering us for whole-heartedness.

We are not, ever, for one minute, saved from sin though our efforts, our achievements, or our abilities. We must be totally clear on this! But, being saved from sin by grace through faith alone does not mean that Jesus' followers are an entitled bunch of lackadaisical lay-abouts. The exact opposite is to be true of us. With God's power in our lives, all excuses are gone, and our daily desire should and must be to honour God in all that we think, say, and do.

Friends, these are great days for us to shine with the light of Christ into a dark world! But we do it not just with a Bible, but also with a shovel, or a mop, or a pen, or a truck, or a computer, or a diaper.

I need to ask myself often, 'Is the wonderful Lordship of Jesus plainly seen in my daily doings ... from coming to work on time, to washing

the dishes, to keeping my word, to finishing a task, to fulfilling whatever has been entrusted to me?'
The world is waiting for ME to give my best.

A sluggard's appetite is never filled, but the desires of the diligent are fully satisfied.
(Proverbs 13:4)

'No work of art is more important than the Christian's life, and every Christian is called to be an artist in this sense... The Christian's life is to be a thing of truth and also a thing of beauty in the midst of a lost and despairing world.'[1]
(Francis Schaeffer)

There is not a square inch in the whole domain of our human existence over which Christ, who is Sovereign over all, does not cry 'Mine!'[2]
(Abraham Kuyper)

[1] Schaeffer, F. (1973). *Art and the Bible,* p.94. L'Abri Fellowship: IVP.
[2] Kuyper, A. https://intersectproject.org/faith-and-culture/abraham-kuyper-quotes-on-faith-and-culture/

RESOLVED.

Resolved 33

Resolved to be always active in making and preserving peace,
unless love requires otherwise.

*Blessed are the peacemakers, for they will be
called children of God.*
(Matthew 5:9)

*If it is possible, as far as it depends on you, live at
peace with everyone.*
(Romans 12:18)

*Peacemakers who sow in peace reap a harvest
of righteousness.*
(James 3:18)

Dear Ones,

Never confuse peace with appeasement. Ask Neville Chamberlain, the
befuddled British Prime Minister who in 1938 returned to Britain from
Munich having met with Hitler. 'We can work with him,' he
pronounced … to the doom of Europe. A savvy Winston Churchill saw
through Chamberlain's foolishness and, knowing that true peace can
never come via appeasement with evil, armed Britain for war.

Jonathan's *Resolution* urges us to pursue peace, but not at all costs. Not
at the cost of appeasement with sin and wrongdoing.

When Jesus was preparing His first disciples for His departure, He
bequeathed to them, and to us, something which this world can never
give us: peace. Peace with God, peace within, peace with others.

172

RESOLVED.

Peace I leave with you; my peace I give you. I do not give to you
as the world gives. Do not let your hearts be troubled
and do not be afraid.
(John 14:27)

Peace with God is the direct result of the atoning death of Jesus Christ.
On the cross, God's beloved Son averted His Father's righteous wrath
away from us by absorbing it for us. Through Jesus being
a propitiation - a wrath bearer - we who have
fled *to* God *for* refuge *from* God (think about that! See Psalm 2:12) are
now standing in the grace of God and have peace with God. The biggest
question in all the universe (no exaggeration), 'How can a sinner find
peace with an offended God?', is answered through the crucified man-
God on a cross.

Therefore, since we have been justified through faith, we have
peace with God through our Lord Jesus Christ, through whom we
have gained access by faith into this grace in which we now
stand. And we boast in the hope of the glory of God.
(Romans 5:1,2)

War is over. Conflict has ended. This is not a tenuous cease-fire. It is
total reconciliation between God and the believing sinner.

Peace with God!

A direct blessing of peace with God is peace within. The turmoil, the
civil conflict within the heart of the believer can and must end as a
result of peace with God having been established by Jesus. The
thinking goes like this: if the biggest problem in my life - me being
under the deserved wrath of an offended God - has been conclusively
solved through Jesus and the Gospel, then my inner conflict born of

RESOLVED.

guilt, shame, and regret - a lesser problem - must come to a peaceful resolution as I lay down all weapons of rebellion and surrender to Jesus. *... [L]et us draw near to God with a sincere heart and with the full assurance that faith brings, having our hearts sprinkled to cleanse us from a guilty conscience and having our bodies washed with pure water. Let us hold unswervingly to the hope we profess, for he who promised is faithful.* (Hebrews 10:22,23)

Conscience cleansed and peace within!

But then – oh yes – it *must* follow that we have peace with one another.

Peace with God, peace within, peace with others.

But how difficult can be the building and maintaining of this peace! Our young Jonathan sees the necessary connection between what the Gospel has accomplished between himself and God, and within himself, and what it must accomplish in regard to those around him.

Now, we can talk easily about peace with people that we will never meet. We can go on about international peace and building bridges between nations. It can all sound very good and, of course, it has its necessary place. But I need to bring this home…literally *home,* to my wife, children, brothers and sisters in my church family, and people in my neighbourhood … real people who might think and look and vote differently than I. It makes little sense if a person jets the world spreading 'peace' in distant lands if he despises his neighbour or cannot work to get along with his own wife.

RESOLVED.

Relationships are where discipleship gets real. The Bible insists that the acid test for my relationship with God is looking at my relationships with those around me who are made in His image:

Whoever claims to love God yet hates a brother or sister is a liar.
For whoever does not love their brother and sister, whom they
have seen, cannot love God, whom they have not seen.
(1 John 4:20)

How do we promote peace toward those with whom we actually share life? How do we become not simply passive appeasers - 'Chamberlains' - but active peacemakers and peace protectors - 'Churchills'?

Before we see a simple, practical, profound key to peacemaking and peacekeeping, let's notice the caveat in Jonathan's *Resolution*: *unless love requires otherwise.* There can be times when genuine love and concern for the greater good requires one to break the peace. Perhaps sin needs to be confronted and doing so will cause – at least in the short term – a war to break out. False peace is an enemy of true peace and a peacemaker does not want to preserve false peace. Meaningful peace comes sometimes at a high price, and true peacemakers may have to sacrifice 'comfortable peace' in the hope of establishing a meaningful peace.

So ... how do we promote, make, and preserve true peace among our fellows? The answer is profoundly simple but living it out can sometimes be profoundly difficult: We make peace with those around us the same way that God has made peace with us: via the wonders of the Gospel. Never forgetting the wonders of mercy and grace that have been lavished upon us, we in turn live a lifestyle of lavishing grace upon others. This does not mean we are soft on sin. It does not mean we do not confront difficulties that need to be faced. Quite the opposite: armed with redemptive love, and the Good News of Jesus, we

175

are bold to speak, refusing to dodge issues that we know will only lead to conflict and destroy peace (think Churchill vs. Chamberlain again).

But it also means that, as those who have received lavish grace from God, we cease to be critical and judgmental. We refuse to be peace-destroying faultfinders. We relentlessly pursue redemption because that is how God deals with us. We do not 'write people off' as the world does and settle for fracture and brokenness because God did not write us off and settle for fracture and brokenness. He came and made peace through the cross and so we work tirelessly to apply that cross-shaped peace to the real people all around us.

We love the sinner in front of us, and battle for peace with him, because we love the One behind us who first made peace with us and then sent us to love the sinner who stands before us. As God has reconciled us to Himself in Christ, so He has now made us to be ambassadors of reconciliation. He has committed this message to us, and our portfolio contains nothing but the Gospel.

Period.

We are the ambassadors of the glorious Heaven-sent Gospel of Peace. But we start right where we live. We do not have the option not to.

> *So, from now on we regard no one from a worldly point of view.*
> *... Therefore, if anyone is in Christ, the new creation has*
> *come: the old has gone, the new is here! All this is from God,*
> *who reconciled us to himself through Christ and gave us the*
> *ministry of reconciliation that God was reconciling the world to*
> *himself in Christ, not counting people's sins against them. And*
> *he has committed to us the message of reconciliation. We are*
> *therefore Christ's ambassadors, as though God were*

RESOLVED.

making his appeal through us.
(2 Corinthians 5:16-20)

'The true soldier fights not because he hates what is in front of him, but because he loves what is behind him.'[3]
(G.K. Chesterton)

---

[3] Chesterton, G.K. (1911) *Illustrated London News: January 14.*

RESOLVED.

Resolved 34

Resolved to speak the plain and pure truth, without
exaggeration, at all times.

Many words mark the speech of a fool.
(Ecclesiastes 5:2)

All you need to say is simply 'yes' or 'no';
anything beyond this comes from the evil one.
(Matthew 5:37)

But I tell you that everyone will have to give account on the
day of judgment for every empty word they have spoken.
(Matthew 12:36)

Dear Friends,

Where is truth these days? It is a rare commodity, more precious than
gold! 'Buy the truth and do not sell it', advises the wise man (Proverbs
23:23). In ancient Israel, Isaiah came with the sad proclamation, 'Truth
has stumbled in the streets!' (Isaiah 59:14). It has in our day as well.

As we find ourselves in an election year, I find myself weary in my
search for truth. Where is it? One politician says one thing; another
claims the opposite. And then there are advertisements. Products are
embellished: this one is 'the biggest' 'the newest' 'the fastest' and so
on. And then there is COVID! So many voices telling us 'the truth'
about this invisible foe! Who do we believe? Then, need I mention all
the differing reports on racial tension, police issues, international
calamities, climate concerns ...

Who is telling the truth?

RESOLVED.

Into this suffocating, stale, toxic atmosphere blows the fresh wind of a godly eighteen-year-old who has resolved 'to speak the plain and pure truth, without exaggeration, at all times'. Ah ... take a deep breath and let that feel good. I need to let it impact me personally. I can change a culture by letting God change me. I do not have to be infected by the viral spiral of lies and manipulation and spin.

I can - and must - resolve to be a simple man of truth.

Let's step back and survey things from God's perspective for a minute. Let's remember a few things about *God*. Oh, how we need to have God, not man, as our standard in these compromised times!

Let us remember:

That God is a God of Truth.

> *He is the Rock; his work is perfect: for all his ways are judgment:*
> *a God of truth and without injustice, righteous and upright is he.*
> (Deuteronomy 32:4 NKJV)

That God hates lying, lies, and ... lying lips (which are attached to people with lying hearts).

> *The Lord detests lying lips, but he delights in people*
> *who are trustworthy.*
> (Proverbs 12:22)

That God will punish all liars eternally:

> *All liars ... will be consigned to the fiery lake of burning sulphur.*
> (Revelation 21:8)

179

RESOLVED.

Consider how transformed our families, our business dealings, our political systems might be if, in every communication, we remembered that *God loves truth, hates lies, and lying lips, and will punish all liars forever in hell.*

Make that part of the oath of public office!

But it is too easy to point to politicians and movie stars to find our lies and liars. It is more necessary that we look at ourselves. There are numerous ways in which genuine Christians fail to tell the simple, plain, unembellished truth.

One is through the use of sarcasm (and teasing). This is all too common amongst we followers of the One who only and always speaks truthfully, and we need to see it as an ungodly form of communication. Sarcasm actually conveys contempt toward the object. It is a cowardly way to tell someone that we have a problem with them. The Bible teaches us to speak honestly with those with whom we have a problem:

> *If your brother or sister sins, go and point out their fault,*
> *just between the two of you.*
> (Matthew 18:15)

Jonathan would have us see sarcasm as a sin. That is how God sees it. I have a life-long habit of being sarcastic, teasing, and poking fun. I have been truly convicted that these are sinful forms of communication which do not simply speak the truth. I have for many years now been trying to break a habit of communication which fails to honour God and others.

Help me Jesus!

Exaggeration and embellishment are other forms of sinful communication. To overstate a case is to lie. Oh my! Who does not do this? Our whole world of commerce seems to overstate, puff up, mislead, garnish, etc. The old trope of the horse-trader who oversells his animal or the buyer who coyly grumbles at the purchase to haggle down the price are examples of dishonesty:

> *'It's no good, it's no good!' says the buyer –*
> *then goes off and boasts about the purchase.*
> (Proverbs 20:14)

Exaggeration is a culturally acceptable form of lying. But it is not acceptable to God! I have struggled with this sin (I am the biggest exaggerator in the whole history of the world), largely because it is so acceptable. It becomes habitual. But Jonathan's *Resolution* will not allow for it.

Flattery is an abuse of truth. Flattery praises another, but for ulterior and selfish motives. It is therefore dishonest. The Apostle Paul could say plainly, 'You know we never used flattery …' (1 Thessalonians 2:5) and Job warned, '… if I were skilled in flattery, my Maker would soon take me away' (Job 32:22).

Making excuses is another form of lying. Many of us do it all the time. We do it so much we do not even notice the sinister nature of it. 'I forgot', can be just an excuse. So can, 'I do not feel well', when the real truth is that we do not want to do something.

Apologizing when we do not really mean it is lying: 'Sorry I was late'.

'I'll pray for you', is often a convenient Christian way to close out a conversation. We should not say it if we do not truly intend to pray as promised.

RESOLVED.

How about 'I'm doing fine', in response to 'How are you?' when in fact our heart is broken over something?

How about asking 'How are you?' when you really do not want an honest answer?

'I'll call you',
        'Let's meet up sometime',
                'Leave it to me',

can either be meaningful statements of intent or cheap throw-away words that amount to … lies.

And (oh dear!) what about our singing! Do we sing lies? I fear so! It was the good and godly Mr. Tozer who boldly asserted, 'Christians don't tell lies they just go to church and sing them'.

    Take my silver and my gold, not a mite do I withhold!

Really? Not a mite?

(By the way, the best Christian hymns boast about the character and ways of God and the Gospel, not about us and our fickle following. The best hymns help us confess our sins, not declare our strengths.)

So, dare we resolve with our young hero 'to speak the plain and pure truth, without exaggeration, at all times'? How can we not? But by all means let's accept this challenge with a sigh of relief! Being a person of simple truth makes life vastly easier. You don't need a good memory if you never have anything to cover up. Relationships are kept strong and steady when truthfulness binds them. Your conscience can rest when you have not assaulted it with lies and deceptions. May the

RESOLVED.

Lord Jesus forgive us our lying ways and make us simple, truth-telling, guile-free, non-manipulating, God-fearing, truth-loving followers of Him whose very words are Truth.

Lord, who may dwell in your sacred tent?
Who may live on your holy mountain?
The one ... who speaks the truth from their heart;
whose tongue utters no slander...
and casts no slur on others...
(Psalm 15:1-3)

'A person who is fundamentally honest doesn't need a code of ethics. The Ten Commandments and the Sermon on the Mount are all the ethical code anybody needs.'[1]
(Harry Truman)

'One man who stopped lying could bring down a tyranny.'[2]
(Aleksandr Solzhenitsyn)

---

[1] Widely attributed to Harry Truman.

[2] Aleksandr Solzhenitsyn, *The Gulag Archipelago 1918-1956.*

RESOLVED.

Resolved 35

Resolved, when I am not sure if I have done as the Lord willed in a
situation, and my peace is therefore disturbed, to not just ignore it,
but to take note of it, and to also pay attention to
how the matter was resolved.

Let the peace of Christ rule in your hearts...
(Colossians 3:15)

*And the peace of God, which transcends all understanding,
will guard your hearts and your minds in Christ Jesus.*
(Philippians 4:7)

*When I kept silent, my bones wasted away
through my groaning all day long.
For day and night your hand was heavy on me;
my strength was sapped as in the heat of summer.*
(Psalm 32:3,4)

Dear Followers,

We are, and will be, as holy - and therefore as happy – as we want to
be.

It is hard to overstate the value of a healthy and peaceful
conscience. The best and most useful saints of old were men and
women who were careful with their consciences, their inner selves, their
hearts. They could feel the approach of sin. They could tell when they
were 'out of sorts'. They were aware of times when they crossed
boundaries and trespassed into forbidden territory ... even in the secret
places of their hearts. They walked closely with their God and therefore
could tell when they had fallen out of step with Him.

184

RESOLVED.

Many of us, by comparison, form a clumsy bunch. We run rough-shod over our consciences, bruising and battering our hearts. Having 'asked Jesus into our hearts', therefore considering ourselves to have settled the matter of our eternal destiny, we carelessly get on with doing what we really like to do: pursuing our own agenda with little thought of God. The idea of:

- daily fellowshipping with God,
- being watchful over our hearts,
- crucifying our flesh,
- keeping in step with the Holy Spirit,
- listening to God umpiring our consciences,
- being watchful for the slithering approaches of sin,
- knowing the deep secret chambers of our hearts,
- feeling the loss of tender peace,
- sensing when sin has gained a foothold in us …

… such things (which our Jesus-following grand parents took as basic to their spiritual well-being and walk with Jesus) we see as optional, advanced and perhaps even excessive.

Jonathan watches over his heart as a banker would his books or a gardener his flowers. Knowing that his heart – his real self – has been purchased by the blood of Jesus to be God's sanctuary, he is careful to notice when sin has disturbed his peace.

Jonathan cultivated a listening, aware heart, one that was attentive to God. His conscience was healthy and alive. He heeded the Psalmists warning:

I will instruct you and teach you in the way you should go;
I will counsel you with my loving eye on you.

185

RESOLVED.

Do not be like the horse or the mule,
which have no understanding
but must be controlled by bit and bridle
or they will not come to you.
(Psalm 32:8,9)

Rather than having to be yanked around like a mule, Jonathan urges us to be instructed by our loving heavenly Father, who will use His own peace within us as a guide and check to our attitudes and actions. Roy Hession, in his remarkable book *The Calvary Road,* invites us to allow God's peace to act like a referee in our hearts:

> There is one simple but all-inclusive guide the Word of God gives to regulate our walk with Jesus and to make us to know when sin has come in. Colossians 3:15 says, 'Let the peace of God rule in your hearts'. Everything that disturbs the peace of God in our hearts is sin, no matter how small it is, and no matter how little like sin it may at first appear to be. This peace is to 'rule' our hearts, or (a more literal translation) 'be the referee' in our hearts. When the referee blows his whistle at a football match, the game has to stop, a foul has been committed. When we lose our peace, God's referee in our hearts has blown his whistle! Let us stop immediately, ask God to show us what is wrong, put, by faith, the sin He shows us under the Blood of Jesus, and then peace will be restored and we shall go on our way with our cups running over.[1]

Do you see the diligence in this *Resolution*? In comparison, are not most of us terribly careless with our hearts? Jonathan tells us that when he loses his peace, rather than just shrugging it off or masking it over, he will actually 'take note of it'. He will write it down. He will journal it. He wants to be able to refer to the experience in the future. He will

---

[1] Hession, R. (1950) *The Calvary Road*, p.8. Roy Hession Book Trust, England.

not forget the experience. His walk with his Saviour is of paramount importance to him, and therefore if some action or attitude has diminished his peace, he wants to know it, understand it, and not allow it to gain a foothold in his life.

Likewise, he wants to note how he resolved the matter. When did he first notice his peace had vanished? What did he do to restore his peace? What did repentance look like in that instance? What did he learn from not only the misstep, but from the recovery?

I really want us to be gripped by the motive here of this young man. We need to make his resolve ours. Desiring Christ above all, pursuing holiness of heart and life, wanting continued fellowship with Jesus, seeking first to be shaped into God's likeness ... *is not fanaticism*! It is what we have been redeemed for.

I mentioned a gardener earlier. I have known diligent gardeners. My wife is one. A successful gardener takes notes. They write things down: 'This worked. I'll do that again! This did not work. I won't do that again!' No one thinks them strange when the beautiful fruit is borne! But ah! That fruit was not borne by accident. It was the result of deliberate, diligent, decisive direction!

And...Jonathan is not unique in this diligent attitude toward his inner life. Humble saints, known and unknown, have shared this governing concern, this overriding obsession, to let nothing rob them of their peace with God. Listen to Charles Wesley pray, through a hymn, for his heart:

> O for a heart to praise my God,
> a heart from sin set free;
> a heart that's sprinkled with the blood
> so freely shed for me.

RESOLVED.

A heart resigned, submissive, meek,
my great Redeemer's throne;
where only Christ is heard to speak,
where Jesus reigns alone.

Hear Fanny Crosby say the same thing about the peace of God guiding her heart:

Thy perfect peace Thou givest me,
My ever-present guide.
Thy perfect peace Thou leavest me,
What can I ask beside?

Friend, will you be like a horse or a mule, uncontrollable and in need of a heavy hand? Or will you be one controlled in the heart by the gentle and wonderful peace of God? Will your walk with Jesus be so important to you that you will allow nothing - *nothing* - to destroy your abiding fellowship with your dear Saviour?

Oh, let us learn to cultivate that listening heart, that tender conscience, that hears the referee's whistle!

Peace I leave with you; my peace I give you. I do not give to you
as the world gives. Do not let your hearts be troubled
and do not be afraid.
(John 14:27)

'Blessed are the single-hearted, for they shall enjoy much peace. '[2]
(Amy Carmichael)

---

[2] Carmichael, A. (1981). *Candles in the Dark: Letters of Hope and Encouragement,* p. 56. Fort Washington, PA: CLC Publications.

RESOLVED.

Resolved 36

Resolved never to speak against anybody, except I have some good and necessary reason to do so.

So, the people grumbled against Moses... They grumbled in their tents and did not obey the Lord.
(Exodus 15:24; Psalm 106:25)

Whoever slanders his neighbour in secret,
Him will I put to silence.
(Psalm 101:5)

Dear Friends,

This is now the third time our young Jonathan has checked himself in regard to speaking words against another.

Why?

Is it that Jonathan is aware of a particular proneness on his part to be critical of others? Could be. That is a very real danger for those who want to live rightly in a world gone wrong.

Is it that Jonathan is acutely aware of the sin attached to a muttering and grumbling spirit? Could be. That is an all-too-common fault among those of us who get our eyes off Jesus and onto one another.

Is it that Jonathan knows that speaking against another for whom Christ has died and whom Christ deeply loves, personally offends God? Could be. When we carelessly speak against a dear child of grace, we grieve the heart of the One who bled and died to redeem them.

RESOLVED.

Notice that Jonathan is not saying that we must *never* speak against another. His caveat is that there must be a good and necessary reason to do so. Speaking against someone must be motivated by love. There must be a true and genuine desire before God and people to bring about a greater good.

Look with me at the Bible passages given at the top of this letter. I have blended two passages into one because they refer to the same event. Exodus 15 narrates the grumbling of Israel against Moses, and Psalm 106 – written centuries later – gives an interesting commentary on that grumbling. I could have cited many occasions in the story of the Exodus when Israel grumbled, because grumbling had become habitual among them. But Psalm 106 gives a vital insight. 'They grumbled in their tents …' In other words, they sat around, in what they thought was private, and complained about Moses. And here is the stinger: *God heard them and judged them.* They no doubt were thinking that no one heard. 'We are in the privacy of our own tents,' they thought. But they had not factored *God* in! Major mistake!

*So, He swore to them with an uplifted hand that He would
make them fall in the desert.*
(Psalm 106:26)

Yikes!

Clearly there are multiple reasons why Jonathan repeats and repeats this *Resolution*. To speak against another without just cause is a grievous, pernicious sin. The offense caused to God and the hurt caused to man is massive. I think that we today habitually speak against brothers and sisters in Christ. We find ourselves taking delight in the folly of others and we sometimes take perverse pleasure in re-telling the stories of others' failings and flaws.

RESOLVED.

How God is grieved!

Moreover, in our current cultural climate, venom flies between politicians at a furious pace and it is all too easy to enter in. Be careful lest you find yourself sucked into the swirling vortex - like refuse in a toilet - of fault-finding. Delighting in the gaffs of public figures and then spreading bad reports is surely as sinful as doing so to members of your church or family. It is one thing to speak your mind plainly and with a humble heart, it is another thing to speak hatefully and with a haughty heart against another ... even a politician. Remember that, while politicians are accountable to the voting public and should be held to account, they are made in God's image and Jesus loves them too.

So, I want to venture out on a limb for a moment in an effort to give real wisdom as to *how* and *when* it is right to speak against another.

I will begin with *how*, for the how to speak against another is very simple: with tears and in the conscious fear of God. If I can speak against another without a broken heart and being forgetful of the fact that God hears every word I speak (see Matthew 12:36), then I am part of the problem and not part of the solution. In such a situation I am better off, and all around me are better off, if I simply keep silent.

As for the *when,* I am going to borrow wisdom from Bishop Augustine (354-430). This good and godly genius forged for us what has been called *The Just War Theory.* Augustine has given us guidelines for when it is right for a Christian to go to war. So, I am venturing out on this limb where I will attempt to amend his *Just War Theory* into a *Just Speaking-Against-Another Theory,* thereby hoping to answer the question, 'When is it right and necessary to speak against another?'

RESOLVED.

Ready?

When speaking against another (assuming my heart is right before God), I must be certain that:

1) I have the *authority* to do so. My relationship to the person or the situation puts me in a position whereby I am not merely meddling or sticking my nose into someone else's business.
2) There is a *just cause* which compels me to speak. Something has happened, is happening or might happen which will offend God or harm people if I do not speak.
3) I have the *right intention.* My desire is not just to 'be right' but to genuinely promote good and avert evil.
4) Speaking against another must be *a last resort.* I have prayed. I have approached the person first, if possible, and I see no other course of action but to speak.
5) I must have a *reasonable hope of helping.* If I do not genuinely think that speaking will help, then there is no reason to do so and I must keep quiet.

With these five principles in mind, now my words must be:

1) *Proportional:* as few as possible and absolutely no more than needed to clarify, help, rescue, avert evil, and promote good.
2) *Discriminating:* not scattered carelessly but spoken only to those who must hear them and to no others.
3) *Responsible: I* am responsible for the words I say including the pain they may cause to others.

Thank you, Bishop Augustine!

RESOLVED.

Words are deadly serious. They can be life-giving or death-delivering. Jesus expects us to use the amazing, divine-image-bearing gift of speech to help and heal, and not to hinder and hurt.

Perhaps you will pray these words with me:

Lord! I want my words to be sweet and healing! I do not want to be a grumbling, gossiping, fault-finding, part of the problem! I sanctify my tongue, as an expression of my heart, to You, Lord Jesus. 'Set a guard over my mouth, Lord; keep watch over the door of my lips. Do not let my heart be drawn to what is evil so that I take part in wicked deeds' (Psalm 141:3,4).

May the Lord Jesus cause us to sanctify our words to His greater purposes.

But I tell you that everyone will have to give account on the day of judgment for every empty word they have spoken.
(Matthew 12:36)

'Be careful what you say. Be careful how you say it. Be careful that you send the right message, that you send it to the right person, and that you do so with the right motive. '[1]
(Chuck Swindoll)

---

[1] Swindoll, C.R. (2005) *Great Days With Great Lives: Daily Insight From Great Lives of the Bible*, p. 201. Nashville, Tennessee: Thomas Nelson, Inc.

Resolved 37

Resolved, each night at bedtime, to take an account of my day, asking myself, 'In what ways did I fail to do God's will for my life today? What sins have I committed that I need to confess? In what ways have I done well, denying myself and living for Christ?' I also resolved to take such account weekly, monthly, and yearly.

We want each of you to show this same diligence to the very end, so that what you hope for may be fully realized.
(Hebrews 6:11)

Be diligent in these matters; give yourself wholly to them, so that everyone may see your progress.
(1 Timothy 4:15)

A sluggard's appetite is never filled, but the desires of the diligent are fully satisfied.
(Proverbs 13:4)

Dear Friends in Jesus,

I have said it before and it is worth saying again: each of us will be as holy - and therefore as happy - as we want to be. There is no shortage of grace available on God's part. Those who avail themselves of the abundant provision of God will grow in holiness of heart and life. Every child of grace can know the joy and purpose that comes with being diligent over one's heart.

I like stories of men and women who give their best and in return become excellent in their endeavours. Golfer Gary Player is just such a person for me. Gary was born in South Africa in 1935 and his mother died when he was just eight years old. His father worked away in the

gold mines. The family didn't have much. Little Gary (he is only 5'6")
excelled in sports ... especially golf. Gary dedicated himself to
becoming the best golfer he could be. He would go on to win more
professional tournaments than any man in history ... 160! He and
Vivienne, his wife of 63 years, raised their six children in a Christian
home. To this day his Gary Player Foundation has raised and given
over $65 million to children's charities around the world.

Gary, otherwise known as 'Mr. Fitness,' is famous for many slogans
and sayings but perhaps for none more (when being referred to as
'having good luck') than the response, 'The harder I practice, the
luckier I get!'

No man, no woman, no person ever has achieved their potential without
hard work and deliberate intention. Diligence! Focus! Purpose!
Perseverance!

So, we shift from a young golfer in South Africa to a young Jesus-
follower in early America. The stakes for Jonathan Edwards are vastly
higher than those for Gary Player, but the attitude and intention that we
find in one are to be found in the other. Jonathan has a goal as sure as
Gary does, but Jonathan's embraces both time and Eternity. Jonathan
wants to be all that he can be for Jesus. He has already resolved to live
with all of his might for Jesus, to waste not a day, to live with intention
and purpose. And ... *he knows his goals will not be achieved by
accident, by luck.*

We can look with envy upon those who have pressed in with Jesus. We
can wish that we too had discovered Him in all the wonderful ways in
which He has revealed Himself to them. We can dream that we had
their peace, their power, their purity. But the fact is that they have run
after God! They have yearned while we have yawned! They have

worshipped while we have wandered! They have been diligent while we have been delinquent!

Nothing happens without discipline and diligence. Diligence and discipline are *not* opposed to grace. Grace is not opposed to effort. Grace is not a license for leisure, but a power for purpose.

Picture Jonathan at bedtime. His day is over. Like a careful accountant or an earnest shopkeeper, he takes stock. He goes over things. He considers, he tallies, he reckons. He leaves nothing to chance. His investigations are vital to the achieving of his goal. His goal is to be more like Jesus and to be useful in His hands. So, he asks himself vital questions:

- How did I do today as a Jesus-follower?
- Did I put myself to doing what Jesus had for me to do?
- In what ways did I shirk my duties?
- Were my attitudes and words and thoughts God honouring?
- Did I live to please myself or my Saviour today?
- Did I say 'no' to self and 'yes' to Jesus today?
- Did I seek to serve or to be served?
- Did I employ the abundant grace of God for His Glory and my growth today?

What might I need to confess to my wonderful Lord before I close the books on this day?

Such questions are not toilsome to a Jesus-follower who has a clear aim in view. They are helpful. Many (most?) of us end our days with a bleary-eyed T.V. show or a scrolling aimlessly through our phones. How might our spirits benefit from some earnest time of reflection with Jesus?

RESOLVED.

Having observed people who excel in their passion, you cannot escape spotting their diligence. They track their progress. They go back over their weak points. It is the musician who practices her scales with the metronome ticking who becomes the virtuosa. It is the guy in the gym who trains with the notebook in hand, charting his progress, who becomes the strongman. Every person who has achieved some purpose or reached a goal has learned to chart and journal, to examine and adjust, saying 'yes' to what is truly important and 'no' to a thousand lesser rivals. Nobody thinks them strange or unbalanced when they become the envy of their peers.

Israel's David, who knew what it was like to be careless with his spirit, learned the hard way to be careful over it. He prayed a prayer we can join in:

Search me, God, and know my heart;
test me and know my anxious thoughts.
See if there is any offensive way in me,
and lead me in the way everlasting.
(Psalm 139:23,24)

I present to you a happy challenge: learn the skill of self-examination. Jonathan did. Jonathan became a spiritual giant. Don't leave your growth in Jesus to luck or happenstance. Ask Jesus to help you become diligent over your inner life the way (I am assuming) you are over your business and hobbies. Don't be afraid to ask yourself hard questions. Don't be slow to make adjustments. Be willing to say 'no' to the lesser so that you can say 'yes' to the greater. And remember: God is for you!

His divine power has given us everything we need for a godly life through our knowledge of him who called us by his own glory and goodness. Through these he has given us his very great and precious promises, so that through them you may participate in

197

the divine nature, having escaped the corruption in the world caused by evil desires.

For this very reason, make every effort to add to your faith goodness; and to goodness, knowledge; and to knowledge, self-control; and to self-control, perseverance; and to perseverance, godliness; and to godliness, mutual affection; and to mutual affection, love. For if you possess these qualities in increasing measure, they will keep you from being ineffective and unproductive in your knowledge of our Lord Jesus Christ.
(2 Peter 1:3-8)

'In a very real sense, a diligent person must learn to be neglectful. There are myriad clamouring and demanding temptations and lesser priorities a diligent person must strategically neglect.'[1]
(Jon Bloom)

---

[1] Bloom, J. (2016). *Lord Keep Me From Wasting My Life.* See https://www.desiringgod.org/articles/lord-keep-me-from-wasting-my-life.

RESOLVED.

Resolved 38

Resolved to never use the Lord's Day for my own entertainment, for
foolish words or for foolish behaviour.

The land enjoyed its Sabbath rests; all the time of its
desolation it rested.
(2 Chronicles 36:21)

There remains, then, a Sabbath-rest for the people of God.
(Hebrews 4:9)

Dear Friends,

Sundays 1950: rest, reflection, worship, contemplation, family, serve
others, a good book, a walk, the Lord, recovery.

Sundays February 2020: the Mall, restaurants, golf, work, serve self,
the gym, the job, sports, wash the car.

Sundays March 2020: rest, reflection, worship, contemplation, family,
serve others, a good book, a walk, the Lord, recovery.

While I doubt that anyone will ever name a son 'Covid', there is one
great redeeming quality this virus has for us, if we will take it; it is
forcing us as individuals and as a culture to *rest*.

What a gracious God we have! He, our Maker, Our Redeemer, has
given us the *gift* of 52 days off a year and we, as a culture, have said,
'Thanks but no thanks!' Frazzled and frayed we have landed with a
thump.

199

RESOLVED.

In our Scripture at the top from 2 Chronicles, a disobedient and godless Israel has been hauled off into exile. And *finally,* the land is getting the 'Sabbath rest' it is due and desperately needs. (You can almost hear the sigh of relief.)

I want us to rediscover the goodness of God in the gift of the Sabbath.

Do I hear a chuckle at Jonathan's earnestness? We tend to think keeping Sabbath - resting and worshipping on Sunday - as a quaint old thing our grandmothers did. Let's be careful! Whenever we smirk at the past, we need to remember that some of us are not doing particularly well at world-changing, culture-shaping discipleship these days. Perhaps we had best be quiet and learn from those who have done better then we.

Sabbath. God's appointed Rest. A time to *abide.* A rhythm in our lives. A Day to pause, pray, and ponder on the forgotten realities of another world.

We receive it to our blessing; we reject it to our peril.

For Christians, the Sabbath - the Lord's Day, Sunday - is a powerful statement to God, to ourselves and to the watching world. When we stop to rest, re-create, revive, and revere, we say to God, 'We *treasure* You, Lord, above work and play. We *trust* your goodness as we come away from other things to draw near to You. We *trust* in Your finished work for us in Christ and, as we rest, we enjoy the Rest of the Gospel'. We say something to ourselves. We say, 'We believe that time spent *apart* will keep us *together.* We are resting from our labours as a statement that we have entered the Rest of the Gospel. Jesus has delivered us from the labour of earning our salvation!' We say something to the watching world: 'We are citizens of another Kingdom, where we honour Jesus, who has given us Rest from our enemies and brought us into the peace and safety of salvation'.

RESOLVED.

Let's quickly dispense with the obvious extremes in regard to Sundays:
1) Legalism. A day to dread. One dare not laugh, or play. One dear old English saint was so against any form of ball game on a Sunday, he used to say, 'If it's round, its *wrong!*' Perhaps (and who am I to say?) Jonathan errs on this side.

2) License: Sunday is just an extension of Saturday. Get church over with (or, better yet, worship God on the golf course) and then work, indulge, watch sports, and shop-till-you-drop. Perhaps (and I say this from my own experience) you and I err on this side.

Can we agree that both are extremes?

Now, what can we learn from our Covid-19 forced rest? How can we repent to God for casting aside His gift of Sabbath Rest? How can we best keep our Rest?

Firstly, we can learn of - or remember - the goodness of God and our own foolishness. I do not think it is possible to live a meaningful, joyful, and impactful Christian life without a meaningful, joyful, and impactful Sabbath. John the Revelator tells us, 'On the Lord's Day I was in the Spirit' (Revelation 1:10), not, 'On the Lord's Day I was in the shopping mall'. It is safe to conclude that there was a direct relation to where he was on that day, and what he received on that day. He had set apart time to meet with Jesus...and, boy, did he! I seriously doubt that he would have had his encounter with Jesus at the local Stuff Mart.

Then, we need to earnestly apologize to God for mocking His design and gift. We have made a day that our grandparents reverently called 'The Lord's Day' into 'Our Day'. We *do* waste it in entertainment, worldly pursuit, and foolishness. Even if we squeeze church in, many of us exhaust ourselves with our agendas. Our bodies, our families, our

RESOLVED.

friendships, and mostly *our souls* are suffering greatly for our foolish, arrogant disobedience. For Jonathan, his consecration of this day reflected his consecration to the Lord. Likewise, for us, our disregard of this day may reflect our disregard of the Lord. Our current crisis affords us a perfect time to rethink our own consecration to God and God's appointed Rest.

So, how can we best keep our Sabbath Rest? Bearing in mind that our generation – a generation which proudly rejects God and His appointed Rest - really no longer has a clue about the basics of life, I suggest we take our instruction from God and His Book.

While I cannot go into a thorough theology of the Sabbath here, you will recall that it was instituted right at creation:

> *By the seventh day God had finished the work he had been doing;*
> *so, on the seventh day he rested from all his work. Then God*
> *blessed the seventh day and made it holy, because on it he rested*
> *from all the work of creating that he had done.*
> (Genesis 2:2,3)

You will remember that after God redeemed Israel from Egypt, God enshrined it in the Ten Commandments, saying,

> *Remember the Sabbath day by keeping it holy. Six days you shall*
> *labour and do all your work, but the seventh day is*
> *a Sabbath to the Lord your God.*
> (Exodus 20:8)

Then, many times God promised blessings for Israel for keeping the Sabbath, (and warned of consequences for playing fast and loose with it):

RESOLVED.

If you keep your feet from breaking the Sabbath
and from doing as you please on my holy day,
If you call the Sabbath a delight and the Lord's holy day honourable,
and if you honour it by not going your own way
and not doing as you please or speaking idle words,
then you will find your joy in the Lord...
(Isaiah 58:14)

Eventually, the religious rulers of Israel ruined the Sabbath by making certain observances of it a demarcation of true spirituality. They forgot that it was a gift from God (52 days off a year!) and turned it into a burden. This made Jesus really mad:

Then Jesus asked them, 'Which is lawful on the Sabbath: to do
good or to do evil, to save life or to kill?' But they remained
silent. He looked around at them in anger and, deeply distressed
at their stubborn hearts, said to the man, 'Stretch out your hand.'
He stretched it out, and his hand was completely restored.
(Mark 3:4-6)

Jesus, God the Son, taught the Sabbath as a gift from God to people, not as a religious ritual that crushes people. He delivered the Sabbath from religious abuse but did not abolish the Sabbath. He re-booted it:

Then he said to them, 'The Sabbath was made for man,
not man for the Sabbath.'
(Mark 2:27)

Now get this: for Christians, the Sabbath is ...

Jesus and His Gospel!

RESOLVED.

Jesus is our Sabbath. He is our Rest. Jesus, the One who saves us from the yoke of religion and sin, is the Sabbath Rest for the believer:

> *There remains, then, a Sabbath-rest for the people of God.*
> (Hebrews 4:9)

So, if we have Jesus, do we still need the day?

The *day* is still important because it points to the *Person* we treasure. We *do not* keep Sunday to justify ourselves before God, but we *should* keep Sunday as a testimony - to God, to ourselves, and to others - that we have found Rest in Jesus Christ. To keep Sunday without knowing Jesus is just old-fashioned legalistic religion. But to keep the day as a celebration that we have found the Reality to which it points is precious, powerful, rejuvenating, and joyful.

The big message of the Sabbath is of a 'finished work': creation in the Old Testament, redemption in the New. And you know from experience that whenever work is finished, rest is welcomed.

There then! A very brief theology of Sabbath.

We are not smarter than God. Most of us are not better Christians than most of our forefathers. God has ordained that we need a corporate day of rest and worship to declare and celebrate our Rest in Christ. For Edwards, Sunday was not a day to wash the car, but to celebrate the Gospel by ceasing from regular activities.

Let's not waste this. Let's rethink things. It is time to re-set priorities. Our relationship with Jesus Christ, our enjoyment of His Gospel, our prosperity and health, and our usefulness for His cause, cannot prosper without a true Sabbath. My fear is that we won't learn our lesson the first time around. But, while we cannot control what our culture will do, we can determine what we will do, and in so doing, be salt and light to our world.

You and I have freedom here. No one is policing you. This is a *gift*. Don't let Jonathan - or me - legislate the details of the Lord's Day for you. But don't let culture either. Be earnest in receiving this gift from the Lord as a tonic for your soul and a testimony to your world. Don't let Sunday just be another Saturday. Discover how God wants you to spend it. Let it be a day in which you deliberately draw away from the things which weary your soul and towards the One who refreshes.

If we learn only this from the virus, then we will have learned much.

I will leave you with two wonderful old 'Sunday Hymns' to reflect on.

Sweet is the work, my God, my King,
To praise Thy Name, give thanks and sing,
To show Thy love by morning light
And talk of all Thy truth at night.

Sweet is the day of sacred rest,
No mortal cares disturb my breast.
O may my heart in tune be found,
Like David's harp of solemn sound!

My heart shall triumph in my Lord,
And bless His works and bless His Word.
Thy works of grace, how bright they shine!
How deep Thy counsels, how divine!
(Isaac Watts, 1674-1748)

RESOLVED.

Dear Lord and Father of mankind,
forgive our foolish ways;
reclothe us in our rightful mind,
in purer lives thy service find,
in deeper reverence, praise.

O Sabbath rest by Galilee,
O calm of hills above,
where Jesus knelt to share with thee
the silence of eternity,
interpreted by love!

Drop thy still dews of quietness,
till all our strivings cease;
take from our souls the strain and stress,
and let our ordered lives confess
the beauty of thy peace.

Breathe through the heats of our desire
thy coolness and thy balm;
let sense be dumb, let flesh retire;
speak through the earthquake, wind, and fire,
O still, small voice of calm.
  (John Greenleaf Whittier, 1807-1892)

RESOLVED.

Resolved 39

Resolved to never do anything that I question the lawfulness of, unless the prospect of not doing it appears to be equally unlawful.

So, whatever you believe about these things keep between yourself and God. Blessed is the one who does not condemn himself by what he approves. But whoever has doubts is condemned if they eat, because their eating is not from faith; and everything that does not come from faith is sin.
(Romans 14:22,23)

...holding on to faith and a good conscience, which some have rejected and so have suffered shipwreck with regard to the faith.
(1 Timothy 1:19)

Dear Brothers and Sisters,

I want to follow Jesus with all my heart! But sometimes, in some situations, I do not know what to do!

Before we dive into this *Resolution*, I think we need to confirm ourselves in the profound freedom of life in Christ. There is the danger lurking in this *Resolution* for the unwary. If we are not keeping our eyes on Jesus and His finished work for our redemption, it can lead to over-introspection and an unhealthy fear of 'getting it wrong' which freezes rather than frees us.

Every believer lives under the banner of God's super-abundant grace. We need not hug the shore, forever afraid to venture out to the deep lest we somehow displease God and He washes His hands of us. I have known dear children of God who are so afraid of 'getting it wrong' that they never try anything at all! We need to ever remember that Christians live in a state of grace and walk in the mercy and forgiveness of God. It is from that place of security that we leave the shallows and dare go to the depths.

We can be sure that Jonathan does not want himself, or us, frozen in inaction through fear of making a mistake. He understands the grace of God too fully for that! His life of daring faith and full-on following is evidence of a free, not a frozen, spirit.

So, with a firm and joyful understanding of our security and freedom in Jesus, let's explore this *Resolution* – one which urges us toward caution, toward careful listening to the Holy Spirit's voice to our consciences. Just like every car needs *both* an accelerator *and* a brake, our conscience needs to act like a brake in our lives. Schooled by the Word of God, we need to be able to hear the Holy Spirit when He prompts us to tap the brakes or come to a screeching halt and change direction.

In the Christian life there are matters of black and white … no need for discussion, no need even to pray about them! But there are grey areas. We might not want to admit that, but there are. There is wriggle (USA 'wiggle'!) room. There are points upon which Christians differ. There are things we need to wrestle over and seek God about. There are times when we move forward in faith, only to find that we are on thin ice and need to turn back.

In the Scripture at the top of this letter, the Apostle Paul is giving some guidance for just such times. The issue Paul was addressing was eating of certain foods. That may seem trivial and silly to us today, but in the Roman church, where Jewish Christians - endless food laws - and Gentile Christians - '…pass the ribs!' - were learning to follow Jesus together, the issue was hot and serious. Paul's principle applies far beyond food. It is very simple: if I cannot move forward in faith, that is, engage in a particular activity with confidence that it is right to do so before the Lord, then if I proceed, I am sinning against my conscience. 'I really should not eat this pork chop, I do not feel right about it before God, but … pass the BBQ sauce!' Take 'pork chop' out and put in 'go to war' or 'marry this person' or 'vote for this politician', and the principle still applies.

Jonathan's *Resolution* affirms that unless the weight upon one's conscience of *not* proceeding with an action is equal to - or greater than - that of proceeding, then it is wrong to proceed when one's Bible-instructed conscience is saying 'hit the brakes'. There have been many times in Christian history when believers have had to make hard decisions and they were guided by this principle. A clear example was when Dietrich Bonhoeffer was faced with the evil of Adolph Hitler and his regime. The young pastor was a pacifist by conviction. He could not see room for violence in the life of a Christian, particularly in defence of the state. However, he finally saw that love demanded that Hitler be stopped. To *not* do something was a clearer sin than to *do* something. So, his Bible-guided conscience led this pacifist to engage in a plot to kill Hitler, for which he was arrested in 1943 and hanged in 1945.

I once pastored a woman who was told by her husband to tell lies on his behalf to his boss. The Bible instructs a wife to submit to her husband. But it teaches us to honour God above all. Her conscience told her it was wrong to lie. Unfortunately, in this case, she sinned against her conscience and lied for her husband. The results allowed her husband to continue on a sinful course with tragic results, even her husband's death.

Perhaps another follower of Jesus identifies with Daniel in Babylon. The king – who should normally be obeyed – issued an edict that none should pray to any god for a month. So, here is a godly and prayerful Daniel: 'Should I obey the king and not pray? Will this honour God? Or should I defy the king and pray?' Daniel's godly conscience responded to the Holy Spirit's promptings.

> *Now when Daniel learned that the decree had been published, he went home to his upstairs room where the windows opened towards Jerusalem. Three times a day he got down on his knees and prayed, giving thanks to his God, just as he had done before.*
> (Daniel 6:10)

Daniel knew that God was above the king and, therefore, to cease to pray weighed more heavily upon his conscience than the thought of committing the 'crime' of praying.

Many Christians have had to make such decisions, and we may find ourselves making them someday too.

I asked some friends for help with this, and they provided some of the following examples where we may have to learn to hear the Holy Spirit's promptings and obey ... and some Christians may draw different conclusions than others:

- Enter a closed country for mission work on a tourist visa because that is the only way in.

- Once inside, if questioned, do I say 'Yes, I have Bibles', or keep quiet? A 'lawful lie' (Joshua 2:4), like Rahab, in a way?

- Allow your child and their same sex 'spouse' to share a room when they visit you.

- Give a homeless person money. Maybe they will only use it for alcohol, but what if they starve because I don't give?

RESOLVED.

- Bail a child out of another financial mess with a bookie. Lawful? But if I don't, they get injured or killed.

- Attend a friend or family same sex wedding. Yes? No? They may get no godly input if I don't relate to them.

- Attend a family event I don't approve of. If I go, I must consider the family effect. If I don't attend it may cause bad family results for a long time. Which is worse?

Such situations are real and increasingly pressing in upon us as our culture spins away from God, and the Church cannot and must not legislate every nuance of life. May the *Resolution* of a young disciple who lived in a saner age give us wisdom and courage to honour God and live for Jesus in our world today.

In the end, we are cast upon the grace of God, knowing that His mercy is greater than our discernment. Trust the Gospel, seek to be obedient in all situations, and go live for Jesus!

*Trust in the Lord with all your heart and lean not on your own
understanding; in all your ways submit to him and he
will make your paths straight.*
(Proverbs 3:5-6)

'Every day my conscience makes confession relying on the hope of
Your mercy as more to be trusted than its own innocence.'[1]
(Augustine of Hippo)

---

[1] *The Confessions of Saint Augustine: Books I – X*, (1886), p. 183. London: Griffith, Farran, Browne and Co. Limited.

211

RESOLVED.

Resolved 40

Resolved to consider, at the close of each day, the habits of that day, especially in regard to my eating and drinking.

I have the right to do anything,' you say – but not everything is beneficial. 'I have the right to do anything'– but I will not be mastered by anything.
(1 Corinthians 6:12)

For, as I have often told you before and now tell you again even with tears, many live as enemies of the cross of Christ. Their destiny is destruction, their god is their stomach, and their glory is in their shame. Their mind is set on earthly things. But our citizenship is in heaven. And we eagerly await a Saviour from there, the Lord Jesus Christ.
(Philippians 3:18-20)

Dear Friends,

Jonathan! You have gone too far this time! We are happy for you to speak of the sins of others, of sin in the abstract, we are happy for you to talk about holiness in vague, undefined terms. Carry on! But,

> now you have begun to meddle in our private world …
> now you are sticking your nose too far into our business …
> now you have touched a nerve …
> now you have …
> … offended one of our sacred *idols!*

There is a new 'super-spirituality' doing the rounds today that divides your spirit from your body. It wants to tell you that what you believe in your private heart about Jesus need not affect what you do with your

212

body. Actually, this super-spirituality is not new. It invaded the first century church in a heresy called Gnosticism. Gnosticism taught – and teaches – that salvation is a secret inner thing, a private knowledge, that need not in any way affect your outward living. The Apostle John was speaking against Gnosticism when he wrote:

> *We know that we have come to know him if we keep his commands. Whoever says, 'I know him,' but does not do what he commands is a liar, and the truth is not in that person. But if anyone obeys his word, love for God is truly made complete in them. This is how we know we are in him: whoever claims to live in him must live as Jesus did.*
> (1 John 2:3-6)

The modern Gnostic, super-spiritual Christian will recoil at this *Resolution*:

What does what I do with my body have to do with what I feel in my soul?
Moderation in food and drinking - taking stock of it every day?
What does that have to do with discipleship?
Isn't following Jesus an 'inner', 'private' thing?
What does faith have to do with how I live?

In fact, bringing eating and drinking under the Lordship of Jesus Christ *is not advanced discipleship*! It is basic discipleship. Refusing to be mastered by anything, including – especially – food and drink is vital to learning to bring every aspect of our lives under the wonderful Lordship of Jesus.

OK. Let's make sure we have some balance here. Is this *Resolution* not moving us too far toward austerity and asceticism? Are we next going to be wearing burlap and sleeping on a bed of nails? Theologically speaking, Jonathan Edwards was essentially a Puritan who was born a century too late. But the Puritans have been grossly misrepresented by history. They were *not* dour, pouting, black-wearing, witch-burning, killjoys! Yes, they were earnest about Jesus and His Gospel; yes, they were disciplined in all aspects of their lives, but they could party and rejoice and feast with the best of them. Jonathan's resolve to be diligent with what he put into his body must not be mistaken for crusty, grim, tasteless Christianity!

God gave us taste buds. He invented flavours and textures and smells. Throughout the Bible, God invited Israel to stop all other distractions and *feast*. God is no killjoy; He is the source of all joy.

But.... Satan's whole career is based around taking the good things God has given and enticing us to pervert them. He has done just that with sex, work, creativity, and just about any and every good thing; food and drink are no different. We end up becoming enslaved to food. We harm our God-given bodies through food and drink abuse. We dull our senses, shorten our lives, and reduce our usefulness.

Tom Brady, the football player (for my UK friends, by 'football' I mean the American kind that you play with your hands), winner of *five* Super Bowls, widely called 'The Greatest of All Time' (the GOAT), is famous for his careful use of food. He has his own diet regime known as the TB12 Diet. His whole goal is to reach peak performance for the sake of throwing a ball.

No one thinks he is strange or excessive! The world applauds him for his diligence and determination, right down to what he puts in his body.

But! How dare Jonathan Edwards suggest to a follower of Jesus that they do *the very same thing*! But hang on a minute before we wave the 'legalism' flag. Like Tom Brady, Jonathan's goal is also 'peak performance', but for Jonny this is all about Jesus and Eternal Kingdom and a crown that will last!

This *Resolution* is about stewardship of one of our most valuable resources, our bodies. Christians cannot, dare not, divide the physical life from the spiritual. Reading my Bible while I polish off a few donuts might be a contradiction. It is *not* that we cannot feast and relish and enjoy food, but it *is* that we will not – to quote the Apostle Paul – 'be mastered by anything' (1 Corinthians 6:12). This *Resolution* recognizes that we are no longer our own, we belong to Jesus, and have been bought at a great price.

> *Do you not know that your bodies are temples of the Holy Spirit, who is in you, whom you have received from God? You are not your own; you were bought at a price. Therefore, honour God with your bodies.*
> (1 Corinthians 6:19-20)

Friends, '[t]here is a time for everything, and a season for every activity under the heavens' (Ecclesiastes 3:1). How wonderful is our God that He has given us wine to make us glad and food to feast upon! But we want to be at our best for Him, for His call, for His service. May we in joy, not in sorrow and servitude, bring every aspect of our lives under the Lordship of Jesus ... especially our food and drink habits. If Tom Brady can do it for trophies that will tarnish, God will give us all grace to do so for trophies that will last forever!

> *Do you not know that in a race all the runners run, but only one gets the prize? Run in such a way as to get the prize. Everyone who competes in the games goes into strict training. They do it to get a crown that will not last; but we do it to get a crown that will last forever. Therefore, I do not run like someone running aimlessly; I do not fight like a boxer beating the air.*

RESOLVED.

No, I strike a blow to my body and make it my slave
so that after I have preached to others, I myself
will not be disqualified for the prize.
(1 Corinthians 9:24-27)

'It is altogether fitting and proper that we should enjoy things made for us to enjoy. What is not at all fitting or proper is that we should set our hearts on them. Temporal things must be treated as temporal things – received, given thanks for, offered back, but enjoyed. They must not be treated like eternal things.'[1]
(Elizabeth Elliot)

---

[1] Elliot, E. (2006), *Discipline, the Glad Surrender*, p.111. Grand Rapids, Michigan: Fleming H. Revell Company.

Resolved 41

Resolved to ask myself at the end of every day, week, month and year, how I could possibly in any respect have done better.

Examine yourselves to see whether you are in the faith;
test yourselves. Do you not realise that Christ Jesus is in
you - unless, of course, you fail the test?
(2 Corinthians 13:5)

And this is his name by which he will be
called, The Lord Our Righteousness.
(Jeremiah 23:6 NKJV)

Dear Friends,

There is a big difference between self-examination and introspection. One is a good thing. One is a bad thing. One is healthy. One is not.

Should Christians examine their hearts, motives, actions, and intentions? Yes. Should followers of Jesus battle against indwelling sin, search their hearts, and repent often? Of course. Self-examination is vital to our growth in grace and to following Jesus well.

But ... there is a tendency among many of us to be forever looking inwards, ever scraping our insides, hunting for evidence of righteousness, ever looking for the vestiges of sin, in intense, navel-gazing introspection. This is not what God would have us do. True faith looks up and away from self. As A.W. Tozer taught us, true faith is the gaze of the eyes of the soul away from itself and onto the God who saves. This means we need to avoid over-introspection. It is unhealthy and detrimental to our well-being in Jesus, and as such it gives the enemy opportunity for condemnation. The answer for a

RESOLVED.

Christian is not found *within* but *without*. It is not *inside* but *outside*. I look to *Jesus* not to *myself*.

Introspection leads either to pride or to morose, joyless, Christless, sub-Christian living. You cannot look to Jesus, beholding His saving beauty, and look to yourself at the same time. Our righteousness is found in Christ, not in ourselves. Don't look inside for it because you will never find it. Look always to Jesus.

But if introspection is a bad thing, self-examination is a good and necessary thing. In the Scripture at the top of this letter, the Apostle Paul urges us to examine ourselves with one aim in view: to see whether we are 'in the faith', so that we might discover and ensure that 'Jesus Christ is in [us]': in other words, that within us is a living faith in Christ and not in ourselves, which yields to the Word of God and the promptings of the Holy Spirit in our hearts.

Jonathan determines to 'ask myself at the end of every day, week, month and year, wherein I could possibly in any respect have done better'.

Let's explore this *Resolution* through the lens of the Gospel. If we remove the lens of the Gospel and merely focus on the words 'wherein I could possibly have done better', we will inevitably default to introspection and end up either proud of ourselves or in despair. Everything must always be viewed through the Gospel!

So ... how does a Gospel-believing man or woman examine him or herself? Below I offer key questions to ask oneself daily, weekly, monthly, yearly. These questions are not just 'how am I doing?' questions, but - and the difference is vital – 'How am I doing *in Jesus*?' questions. Asking them of yourself will help a proper self-examination that will help you to grow in grace. Neglecting self-examination will inhibit your growth in grace and allow sin to take root and lies of the enemy to enter and take hold, proving detrimental to both your joy and usefulness in Jesus' Kingdom.

Questions to ask myself at the close of a day and at other seasons of self-examination:

1) Have I looked away from myself today and to the God who saves, or have I been consumed by looking to myself for righteousness?

It is because of him that you are in Christ Jesus, who has become for us ... our righteousness, holiness and redemption.
(1 Corinthians 1:30)

2) Have I looked at others, especially those nearest to me, through the Gospel, receiving them in Christ, giving and receiving forgiveness and grace or have I merely looked with a critical, selfish eye?

So, from now on, we regard no one from a worldly point of view. ... Therefore, if anyone is in Christ, the new creation has come; the old has gone, the new is here!
(1 Corinthians 5:16,17)

3) In what ways have I chosen Christ today as my source of life and joy, and in what ways have I turned from Him and sought joy in things that cannot satisfy?

My people have committed two sins: They have forsaken me, the spring of living water, and have dug their own cisterns, broken cisterns that cannot hold water.
(Jeremiah 2:13)

RESOLVED.

*Jesus stood and said in a loud voice, 'Let anyone who is thirsty
come to me and drink. Whoever believes in me, as Scripture has
said, rivers of living water will flow from within them.'*
(John 7:37,38)

4) Have I sought grace to love my neighbour, including those who do
not love me back? Have I reached out to serve others or have I merely
pursued my own wants?

*Sitting down, Jesus called the Twelve and said, 'Anyone
who wants to be first must be the very last, and
the servant of all.'*
(Mark 9:35)

5) Have I promoted the fame of Jesus and loved others by speaking the
Gospel as God has granted openings or have I been silent and unloving,
hiding my light under a basket?

*You are the light of the world. A town built on a hill cannot be
hidden. Neither do people light a lamp and put it under a bowl.
Instead, they put it on its stand, and it gives light
to everyone in the house.*
(Matthew 5:14,15)

6) Have I been open to the leading of God's Spirit, wanting to walk in
His purposes for me, saying 'no' to self and 'yes' to Jesus, or have I
selfishly pursued my own agenda?

*For we are God's handiwork, created in Christ Jesus to do good
works, which God prepared in advance for us to do.*
(Ephesians 2:10)

RESOLVED.

7) Have I honoured Jesus in my inner thought life and in the secret place, or have I allowed sin to have its way in my unseen life, allowing lies of the enemy to overwhelm me?

Let the words of my mouth, and the meditation of my heart, be acceptable in thy sight, O Lord, my strength, and my redeemer.
(Psalm 19:14)

8. Have I repented of any sin of commission or omission, received the cleansing blood and let go of regret?

If we confess our sins, he is faithful and just and will forgive us our sins and purify us from all unrighteousness.
(1 John 1:9)

God wants us to do well! He is for us! By all means, examine yourself daily, weekly, often. Be deliberate about it. You will do well if you do. Perhaps the questions above will help you. If you have some other method, that is fine. But always do so through the Gospel, seeing Christ as your source and your sufficient supply. Avoid self-imploding introspection, thinking that somehow in your own sufficiency you can and will become the person God wants you to be. Look up and away to the God who saves, and then, in the light of His love and constant supply of grace, examine your heart and life.

It is a good practice to spend a few moments at the end of the day, perhaps as you lie down to sleep, and just go over your day in this way. Thank God for the blessings and obediences and repent and receive cleansing for the failings. Ask God for His perspective on your day and then receive God's peace.

RESOLVED.

Search me, God, and know my heart;
test me and know my anxious thoughts.
See if there is any offensive way in me,
and lead me in the way everlasting.
(Psalm 139:23,24)

'Do all the good you can, by all the means you can, in all the ways you can, in all the places you can, at all the times you can, to all the people you can, as long as ever you can.'[1]
(John Wesley)

---

[1] Attributed to John Wesley and a partial match to quotes from the 1799 work 'Sermons on Several Occasions': Sermon 36, p. 486, and Sermon 50, p. 675.

RESOLVED.

Resolved 42

Resolved to frequently renew my dedication to the Lord, even as I was dedicated to Him at my baptism and was renewed when I was received into the fellowship of the church, and as I have renewed it today.

Then he said to them all: 'Whoever wants to be my disciple must deny themselves and take up their cross daily and follow me.
(Luke 9:23)

The fire on the altar must be kept burning; it must not go out.
(Leviticus 6:12)

These are my appointed festivals, the appointed festivals of the Lord, which you are to proclaim as sacred assemblies.
(Leviticus 23:2)

Dear Friends,

The Lord knows what we need better than we do. He knows that our hearts quickly grow cold, that zeal abates, that desire dies down, that distractions overtake us. He knows that our memories fail us, that our resolve is often paper thin, and that the call of the world can deafen us to His voice.

Before all else, we are called to Jesus. We are saved from sin to Him. But we are a fickle and fragile lot. We wander and wobble. The flame on the altar of our hearts sometimes burns dangerously low. We hear Jesus' call to *daily* take up the cross and follow Him, but we do not always heed. How wonderfully patient God is with us!

RESOLVED.

Jonathan is wise beyond his years. Recognizing the woefulness of his ways, he resolves to 'frequently renew his dedication to the Lord'. This does not mean he has to 'get saved' all over again. No, justification, that is, the act whereby God declares us forgiven and right with Him through faith in Jesus, is a one-time, permanent pronouncement of God (phew!). But the walking out of our salvation requires the frequent renewal of our consecration to Jesus. This is a *relationship* not simply a legal contract. And relationships require attention.

In ancient days, God called Israel to Himself. They - of all peoples - were uniquely *His.*

> *For the Lord's portion is his people, Jacob his allotted inheritance.*
> (Deuteronomy 32:9)

> *He has revealed his word to Jacob,*
> *his laws and decrees to Israel.*
> *He has done this for no other nation;*
> *they do not know his laws.*
> (Psalm 147:19,20)

Knowing that they, like us, were fickle and failing, He gave them help in regularly renewing their dedication to Himself. Israel had a rhythm of feasts throughout the year. God instituted seven of them. Each one had a different emphasis in regard to their salvation history, each one provided opportunity for God's people - from individuals, to families, to Israel as a nation - to stop and think, to reflect and repent, and to rededicate themselves to their saving God.

Now, we are not obliged to keep these feasts today. Each one, in some way, looked not only back to Israel's saving history but forward to Jesus Christ. As such, they are fulfilled in Jesus. But do we not still need today 'helps' in keeping us aflame for Jesus? Does not the fire in our hearts sometimes burn dangerously low? Do we not need to pray with Charles Wesley,

> 'O thou who camest from above
> the fire celestial to impart,
> kindle a flame of sacred love
> on the mean altar of my heart'?

Many wonderful followers of Jesus throughout history have built into the rhythm of their lives, seasons of reflection, repentance, and rededication. We think of Advent, Lent, Christmas, Easter, and other days and seasons that many have used well to keep the flame for Jesus burning for themselves, their families, and their churches.

Of course, these can become mere formalities that hold no value and in fear of this many of us have dispensed with most of them. But is there a whiff of arrogance in our readiness to throw off things that helped our fathers follow Jesus? For generations people have followed Jesus better than I have. Can I not learn from them? I have to confess to you that in my early Christian days, in my youthful zeal, I brazenly threw overboard almost anything that was more than five years old. I was arrogant in my assertion that I did not need the faith of my fathers. Had I to do it over again, I would root myself much more firmly in the wonders and ways of those who had already followed well before me.

We have, of course, kept Communion as a constant reminder of the Atonement and – hopefully – as a regular help in reflection, repentance, and rededication - once a month in many churches, weekly in others. Clearly, we keep this in obedience to the plain command of Jesus to remember Him (He knows we forget!) until He returns.

RESOLVED.

But … can I venture out with you for a moment? Hang in there with me for just a little longer and try to hear me out. … I want to make a case here for history.

Most of us who pride ourselves in being 'Bible-believing Evangelicals' (I am one) have impoverished ourselves by ignoring the richness of our fathers and mothers in the faith. For two thousand years, men and women have followed after Jesus, living and dying for Him. I want to make a case for using the devotional wealth of our forebears to regularly rededicate ourselves to Jesus. The book of Hebrews exhorts us to do just this:

> *Remember your leaders, who spoke the word of God to you.*
> *Consider the outcome of their way of life and imitate their*
> *faith. Jesus Christ is the same yesterday and today and forever.*
> (Hebrews 13:7,8)

We can (and I think should) stand on the shoulders of giants when we embrace the best of Christian history. We can affirm our faith and refresh our walk with Christ when we recite a creed *and mean it.* We can rededicate ourselves to Jesus when we *earnestly* pray the Lord's Prayer. We can do business with God – serious business – when we sing a great hymn. Why not use a great, proven devotional to help you in your daily prayer life? Why not prayerfully read one of the great catechisms of our Faith? Just take a moment and re-read the 'First Question' of the 1563 Heidelberg Catechism which we already looked at in *Resolution* 11, but which merits another moment. It has been called by some 'an ageless summary of everlasting comfort'.

Question: What is your only comfort in life and death?

Answer: That I am not my own, but belong with body and soul, both in life and in death, to my faithful Saviour Jesus Christ. He

226

has fully paid for all my sins with His precious blood and has set me free from all the power of the devil. He also preserves me in such a way that without the will of my heavenly Father not a hair can fall from my head; indeed, all things must work together for my salvation. Therefore, by His Holy Spirit He also assures me of eternal life and makes me heartily willing and ready from now on to live for Him.

Can I come up with anything more profound than that? (The answer is 'no'). Cannot such great truth be used by us today to replenish our hearts for Christ? Can we not learn from those great souls who went before us? Can you and I think better than they could? Really?

In our quest to stay authentic and fresh with Jesus, can I urge you to walk the paths that others have walked. We do not have to reinvent what it means to live well for Jesus! The trails are forged, the way is well marked!

Here are a few great 'helps' that you might find to be a rich source to aid you in your devotion to Jesus:

My Utmost for His Highest by Oswald Chambers,

Morning and Evening by Charles Spurgeon,

The Valley of Vision: A Collection of Puritan Prayers and Devotions,

If by Amy Carmichael.

None of these are a substitute for your Bible, and there are many others that could be added to this brief list, but this is my plea - that we do not fall into the post-modern trap of believing that *we* are somehow the

RESOLVED.

pinnacle of wisdom and that those who went before us have little to offer us. Let us humble ourselves and learn from those who have run well how to live lives truly dedicated to Jesus.

This is what the Lord says: 'Stand at the crossroads and look; ask for the ancient paths, ask where the good way is, and walk in it, and you will find rest for your souls.'
(Jeremiah 6:16)

'Jesus, confirm my heart's desire
to work, and speak, and think for thee;
still let me guard the holy fire,
and still stir up the gift in me.'
(Charles Wesley)

RESOLVED.

Resolved 43

Resolved, remembering my last *Resolution*, to aim to live all my days knowing that I am not my own, but that I wholly belong to God.

Do you not know that your bodies are temples of the Holy Spirit,
who is in you, whom you have received from God? You are not
your own; you were bought at a price. Therefore,
honour God with your bodies.
(1 Corinthians 6:19,20)

For you know that it was not with perishable things such as silver
or gold that you were redeemed from the empty way of life
handed down to you from your ancestors, but with the precious
blood of Christ, a lamb without blemish or defect.
(1 Peter 1:18,19)

Dear Friends,

Purchased!

No longer my own!

The priceless and prized possession of Jesus Christ!

Settle the matter today, and remind yourself every day, that you are no longer your own. Jesus Christ, the Eternal Son of God, has purchased you for Himself with His own blood.

You are worthy ... because you were slain, and with your blood
you purchased for God persons from every tribe
and language and people and nation.
(Revelation 5:9)

RESOLVED.

The sobering truth is we are not, nor have we ever been, sovereign lords over ourselves. We *want* to be, we *think* we are, but we are not. Once we were slaves to sin (see Romans 6:17; John 8:34). Our will was bound and subject to our natures, which were sinful and themselves enslaved to Satan. But! Having been set free from sin through the blood of Christ, we are now slaves to Jesus:

> *But thanks be to God that, though you used to be slaves to sin,*
> *you have come to obey from your heart the pattern of teaching*
> *that has now claimed your allegiance. You have been set free*
> *from sin and have become slaves to righteousness.*
> (Romans 6:17,18)

> *Paul, a servant of Jesus Christ ...*
> (Romans 1:1)

What a wonderful Master to whom we are now bound! We find ourselves now owned by, and enslaved to, the One who made Himself nothing and took upon Himself the very nature of a slave (see Philippians 2:7). I am the servant of the One who did not come to be served, but to serve and to give His life as a ransom for me and for many (see Mark 10:45). Here is wonderful Jesus, and *He* owns *me*! Give me slavery to Jesus over sovereign rule over myself any day. As believers we are subjects in a Kingdom ruled over by a Servant-King.

So, whenever we speak of being under the Lordship of Jesus, of belonging to Him, of being bought and owned by Him, of giving up all rights to Him, of being ready – without complaint or protest – to do His bidding at all times, we need to remember:

1) The only thing we are free to decide is whose servant we will be, not whether or not we will be a servant.

RESOLVED.

2) That if we do not serve Jesus, we will serve sin, Satan, and self.
3) That Jesus is altogether wonderful and service to Him is sweet because He is sweet.
4) Slavery to sin leads to death. Slavery to Jesus leads to life.

It is when we forget these foundational truths and begin to think of ourselves as sovereign lords over ourselves that we fall right into the trap the evil one set for our ancient mother, Eve:

> *For God knows that when you eat from it your eyes will be*
> *opened, and you will be like God, knowing good and evil.*
> (Genesis 3:5)

The essence of sin is the desire to 'be like God,' that is, be sovereign. But Jonathan makes the only *sane* choice! His reasoning is simple:

I am not *autonomous.*
I will be servant to *something.*
I can serve sin which leads to death or Jesus who brings life!

I choose Jesus!

It is when I want to try to 'make a deal' with God that following Jesus becomes a joyless ball-and-chain. When I offer God part of myself, even most of myself, but hold back that sweet spot for my own direction and delight, discipleship becomes an impossible chore. When, failing to see myself as totally His and with no rights of my own, I see God as somehow obliged to *my* agenda and wants, then I am surely headed to crash upon the rocky reefs of disillusionment and disappointment. But…there is the twist in the story!

RESOLVED.

Surrender to Jesus brings ... *(drum roll)* ... Freedom!

Seeing yourself as 'not your own', reckoning yourself as 'wholly belonging to God', enslaving yourself to Jesus, *sets you free* from the tyranny of slavery to sin, Satan, and self. The Christian – being enslaved to Jesus, being the servant of all people – is in fact the freest man or woman you will ever meet. Sin is a terrible master. Satan is a tyrannical lord. Self is impossible to satisfy. But Jesus is wonderful. He commands, but then empowers. He directs, but first goes before. He is easy to please and delights in our efforts.

I have read so many biographies of men and women who have given up everything to be happily enslaved to Jesus. I have read of their sufferings and marvelled at the challenges they faced. But I have rarely, in fact never, read of them complaining that service to Jesus has been a wrong choice. *He* has been a delightful and tender Master, and *He* has always given to *them* more than they give to *Him*.

Hear with me from John G. Paton (1824-1907), the Scottish missionary to the New Hebrides in the South Pacific. Linger over his words. Know that they are not unique, but typical of those who have bound themselves in servitude to Jesus:

> Let me record my immovable conviction that this is the noblest service in which any human being can spend or be spent; and that, if God gave me back my life to be lived over again, I would without one quiver of hesitation lay it on the altar to Christ, that He might use it as before, in similar ministries of love, especially amongst those who have never yet heard the Name of Jesus. Nothing that has been endured, and nothing that can now befall me, makes me tremble — on the contrary, I deeply rejoice — when I breathe the prayer that it may please the blessed Lord to turn the hearts of all my children to the Mission Field and that He

RESOLVED.

may open up their way and make it their pride and joy to live and die in carrying Jesus and His Gospel into the heart of the Heathen World.[1]

Friends! When you find your peace abating and your joy deflating, check your heart. Chances are you are staging a – sure to fail – *coup d'état* against the Lordship of Jesus. Stop everything and repent of your holding back from your wonderful Saviour! We are not our own, we were bought with the blood of Jesus. We have been freed from slavery to death to become slaves to the Giver of Life. He has total rights over us, and whatever He chooses for us can and will only be for His Glory and our good. Total surrender leads to total peace and to true freedom.

Perhaps you will take a few minutes and earnestly pray John Wesley's Covenant Prayer. It exalts the Lordship of Jesus and binds the humble believer to His wonderful service:

I am no longer my own, but thine.
Put me to what thou wilt, rank me with whom thou wilt.
Put me to doing, put me to suffering.
Let me be employed for thee or laid aside for thee,
exalted for thee or brought low for thee.
Let me be full, let me be empty.
Let me have all things, let me have nothing.
I freely and heartily yield all things to thy pleasure and disposal.
And now, O glorious and blessed God, Father, Son and Holy Spirit,
thou art mine, and I am thine.
So be it.
And the covenant which I have made on earth,
let it be ratified in heaven. Amen.

---

[1] https://bethanygu.edu/blog/stories/john-g-paton-working-among-the-cannibals/

RESOLVED.

To him who is able to keep you from stumbling and to present you
before his glorious presence without fault and with great joy – to
the only God our Saviour be glory, majesty, power and authority,
through Jesus Christ our Lord, before all ages,
now and for evermore! Amen.
(Jude 24,25)

'God always gives His best to those who leave the
choice with him.'[2]
(Jim Elliot)

---

[2] Widely attributed to Jim Elliot.

RESOLVED.

Resolved 44

Resolved that I shall live for no other purpose than to know and glorify God, and that all that I do - even the small things - shall be motivated by nothing else besides living for Jesus.

I want to know Christ – yes, to know the power of his resurrection and participation in his sufferings, becoming like him in his death, and so, somehow, attaining to the resurrection from the dead. ... [O]ne thing I do: forgetting what is behind and straining towards what is ahead, I press on towards the goal to win the prize for which God has called me heavenwards in Christ Jesus.
(Philippians 3:11-14)

One thing I ask from the Lord, this only do I seek: that I may dwell in the house of the Lord all the days of my life, to gaze on the beauty of the Lord and to seek him in his temple.
(Psalm 27:4)

For to me, to live is Christ ...
(Philippians 1:21)

Dear Friends,

Is Jonathan Edwards a fanatic? Should we be worried about him? Has he become unbalanced? For an eighteen-year-old young man to say that he wants to 'live for no other purpose than to know and glorify God', and that he 'shall be motivated by nothing else besides living for Jesus', is this not a concern?

Jonathan!
What about finding a wife?

RESOLVED.

Don't you like sports?
How about your career goals?
Have any healthy hobbies?

Forgive me if I feel a need to defend my young hero. Perhaps he is sprinting out of the starting blocks, but, like a wise long-distance runner, our zealous follower will mature and settle into his stride as the years pass. But should his zeal abate? Should mine? Should yours? Should we begin well only to finish poorly, if at all? Should there not be a 'kick' to our stride as we 'round the last bend and see the finish ahead? Should we, like a dying fire, 'cool off' with the passing of time? Or rather, should we not find our hearts warming as we get closer to seeing Jesus, even as our excitement grows as we reach a journey's end and the long-desired destination is in view?

I would caution us against judging Jonathan's zeal by modern standards. We modern Western Christians are not the 'Gold Standard' for discipleship. Better to learn from one who ran well and finished his race - even if he sprinted too hard at the start - than from our sofas to criticize him too harshly.

Jonathan's *Resolution* for all-out consecration of every aspect of his life to Jesus makes total sense and takes on beauty if we do one thing: dispense with the false and dangerous 'sacred/secular' divide in our lives. We have already talked about how insidious this can be and I will take the time to reiterate that we need to see *all* of life as a consecration of ourselves to Jesus, not just aspects of our lives. If we only see parts of our lives as 'religious' and the rest of our lives as 'regular' then we will forever be struggling with the impossible question, 'Am I *doing* enough spiritual stuff to satisfy God?'

The divide is a false divide because '[t]he earth is the Lord's, and everything in it ...' (Psalm 24:1). That means there is nothing outside of

236

the Lordship of Jesus for a Christian. Reading my Bible is sacred, but so is cutting the grass. Praying is spiritual, but so is eating a meal with friends. A well-seasoned Jesus-follower sees everything she does as done before the Lord, unto the Lord, and as a worshipful expression of devotion to Jesus. If I cannot offer a thought or a word or a deed up to Jesus with a thankful, worshipping heart, then I should not do it. If I can, then I can proceed with freedom.

As a matter of fact, if one is reading their Bible when they should be helping with the dishes (as super-spiritual house guests have often done), then at that point reading the Bible might be offensive to God. Rolling up your sleeves is a holy thing. Embracing your wife, swinging a bat, taking a nap, hiking a trail, going to work, are all expressions of worship for the understanding Christian. The resolve to 'live for no other purpose than to know and glorify God' need not drive one to a monastery. In fact, it is almost certainly better if it does not. The monk in his habit is not holier than the mother in her household. The priest in his parish is not necessarily closer to God than the boy with his ball.

The secularist sees the material, physical world as all that there is. The Christian sees the material world as an expression of the Eternal God, who made the seen world and called it 'good', but who also made an unseen world that transcends time. For the believer, all of life, both the 'hallelujah' and the 'ho-hum' are holy. Well-taught Christians have always understood this and have thus been enabled to offer up every part of their lives in worship, devotion, and freedom to God.

When salted with a bit of maturity, that is what Jonathan is saying in this *Resolution*. This is exactly what the Apostle Paul is presenting to the Philippians when he says, 'For me to live is Christ ...' (1:21). A desire for total consecration to Jesus is not weird. It is wonderful. I want it.

RESOLVED.

Are you free from the tyranny of trying to make sure that your 'religious' part is counterbalancing your 'regular' part? Are you delivered from striving to ensure that the 'spiritual' section of your life is big enough to keep God happy? Have you entered into the freedom of *enjoying* all of life as received from the good hand of a generous God and offered back to Him in thankful worship? We are redeemed from sin so that all of our lives, and our deaths – whether they be gentle and timely or shocking and sudden; whether they come through sorrow and suffering or through the hands of a persecutor – may be a sweet offering to God.

In 1646 and 1647, a group of English Christians got together and forged a document that could be used to teach believers the heart of the Gospel. Their finished work, The *Westminster Shorter Catechism,* begins with a question that is one of the most important questions that can ever be asked. And then it gives an alarming answer which is glorious in its freedom:

Question: What is the chief end of Man?

Answer: Man's chief end is to glorify God and to enjoy Him forever.[1]

When it is time to read your Bible and pray, by all means do so. When it is time to wrestle with the kids, go ahead, but do it all for the Glory of God!

The crack of a ball on a cricket bat can be as sacred a sound as a church choir if offered to Jesus from worshipping hands.

---

[1] See also **Resolved 1**.

RESOLVED.

*And whatever you do, whether in word or deed, do it all in the name of
the Lord Jesus, giving thanks to God the Father through him.*
(Colossians 3:17)

'Till you can sing and rejoice and delight in God, as misers do
in gold, and kings in sceptres, you will
never enjoy the world.'[2]
(Thomas Trahern)

---

[2] Trahern, Thomas. (1908). *Centuries of Meditations,* p.31. London: Dobell, P.J. &
A.E.

RESOLVED.

Resolved 45

Resolved to surrender not only my actions, but my inner life – my emotions and the affections of my heart – to the Lord Jesus, to the end that joy and grief, pleasure and sorrow and all the circumstances that bring them about, will together serve His greater purpose.

May these words of my mouth and this meditation of my heart be pleasing in your sight, Lord, my Rock and my Redeemer.
(Psalm 19:14)

We demolish arguments and every pretension that sets itself up against the knowledge of God, and we take captive every thought to make it obedient to Christ.
(2 Corinthians 10:5)

Friends in Jesus,

Ah, the inner life, the secret place - so often ignored, yet seen and cherished by God and as important as the visible outer life! Like an iceberg, or the deep foundation of a building, most of your life is not seen, except by God. What goes on in the secret place is as vital to who we are as what we do in public before people.

God is concerned with our hearts. He is not a slave driver who is only interested in our outward productivity. We are not workers on an assembly line. To Him, we are children in a family, friends in a friendship, lovers in a marriage. Your boss may only care that you get your job done. He might not be the least bit concerned about your attitude your motives or your heart. Jesus is not like that. He loves us to the very depth of who we are. He wants to save us not just from sin's penalty but from sin's deep damages. He wants not merely to lop off the weed's flower but dig out the roots.

RESOLVED.

Our emotions need redemption as surely as do our actions. Our thoughts are as significant to God as are our deeds. We need to be as careful with our inner life as with our outer life. Jesus is to be enthroned in the secret places of our hearts as surely as He is to be evident in our public appearances. And most of us find that the secret place is a tougher battlefield than the public place. Some of us are *pretty weird* deep down. Many of us have given up even trying to honour Jesus 'on the inside'.

So, here is some *wonderful* news for you: the blood of Jesus, shed once on Calvary's cross, does *deep* work. Never be afraid to recognize pain and confess sin – including sins of thought and feeling – because Jesus is always ready to cleanse. Our souls can be very sick and sinful. Greed, lust, envy, bitterness, irritability and wrath are all deep heart-sins that will erupt as surely as will a volcano. They offend God as surely as do outward acts. Left to themselves, they fester and seek a fissure through which they can vent themselves. They can lead to grave illness of the mind and inner life. Carelessness with the inner life will surely result in public pain and fractured friendships.

But we have a Saviour! Look what His blood can do!

Let us draw near to God with a sincere heart and with the full
assurance that faith brings, having our hearts sprinkled to
cleanse us from a guilty conscience and having our bodies
washed with pure water.
(Hebrews 10:22)

Do you see those words *'cleanse us from a guilty conscience'*? That is *deep cleaning.* That is what Jesus can and wants to do. So, why would any of us hold back from bringing not just our obvious outward sins, but the hidden things of our hearts to Him? What joy and peace we can have when we learn to watch over our thoughts and emotions and bring wayward ideas and impulses to our ready and willing Saviour!

And it is not just our inner *sins* that we can bring to Jesus, but our inner *sadness* and grief that we can bring to Him. Why let pain simmer away in your soul until it cripples you when you can tell Jesus about it and ask Him to heal your heart? Even as the inner affects the outer, the outer affects the inner. Circumstances outside of us deeply shape us on the inside.

The old children's rhyme, 'Sticks and stones may break my bones, but words will never hurt me', simply is not true! Things from the outside *do* hurt on the inside and, if left undealt with, re-appear in some poisonous form on the outside again.

But look at what Jesus has done:

> *Surely, he has borne our griefs, and carried our sorrows ...*
> (Isaiah 53:4 NKJV)

And look at what Jesus still does:

> *Cast all your anxiety on him because he cares for you.*
> (1 Peter 5:7)

With Jesus being so wonderful and so ready to have us bring all of our *crud* to Him, why do we fail to do so? Sometimes we get a strange, even perverse comfort from old hurts, wayward thoughts, and tangled emotions. We hang on to our inner sins and brokenness like a toddler does a filthy and frayed old comfort blanket. But this dishonours God, does damage to us and to those around us.

Don't look upon Jonathan's resolve to look after his inner life with all diligence as a burden. Don't respond with an 'ug' but rather with a 'hooray'. Hooray! I have a place to go with my sadness, my lust, my envy, my wayward thoughts, my obsessions, my compulsions, my crud. If we did not have a wonderful Saviour whose blood cleanses and heals to our very depths, caring for our inner selves would just be another impossible task. But we *do* have a wonderful Saviour and, therefore, it is possible to be *free*. So, to be lax with our thoughts and emotions is to give in to living beneath God's purposes for us. The key here is *not* to 'try harder' but to bring your sin and brokenness to Jesus, over and over, for He will forever receive you and you will never weary Him with your coming:

> *Come to me, all you who are weary and burdened, and I will give*
> *you rest. Take my yoke upon you and learn from me, for I am*
> *gentle and humble in heart, and you will find rest for your*
> *souls. For my yoke is easy and my burden is light.*
> (Matthew 11:28-30)

Many times, I have failed to fight the battle for my inner life. I have thought that as long as my outward conduct was passable, then all was 'OK'. But Jesus did not come so that I would be 'OK'. He came because He loves me and wants to redeem all of me. Yet I have allowed thoughts to run wild over me and unhelpful emotions to rule me. I am coming to learn (why am I such a slow learner?) that Jesus *cares* about what goes on inside of me, that my inner world is every bit as real as my outer world, and what plays in the theatre of my mind determines what I will play out in the public theatre. *Jesus* has battled for *my* joy and purity on the cross. Therefore, so should I. But remember! Every Christian battle takes place before the cross on one's knees where sin is cleansed, hearts are healed, and grace is received. We do not battle in our own energies, but we battle by continually coming to Jesus. Let's learn to pray with the Psalmist:

RESOLVED.

Search me, God, and know my heart;
test me and know my anxious thoughts.
See if there is any offensive way in me,
and lead me in the way everlasting.
(Psalm 139:23,24)

Friend, you and I have a wonderful, wonderful Saviour. With your Bible open, go to Him continually. Bring your thoughts, your emotions, your *weirdness* to Him! He *will* receive you. He will never tire of you. He will cleanse you and strengthen you. You go to the gym or to the doctor to care for physical body. Do not wait another day to go to Jesus and ask Him to deal with your inner life. Jesus is for you!

May God himself, the God of peace, sanctify you through and
through. May your whole spirit, soul and body be kept blameless
at the coming of our Lord Jesus Christ. The one who calls you is
faithful, and he will do it.
(1 Thessalonians 5:23,24)

'Sow a thought, reap an act. Sow an act, reap a habit.
Sow a habit, reap a character.
Sow a character, reap a destiny.'[3]
(Ralph Waldo Emerson)

---

[3] Widely attributed to Emerson. Brought to my attention by a helpful friend, Steve Johnston, in 1986.

RESOLVED.

Resolved 46

Resolved to carefully guard my attitude toward my parents, and
toward all of my family. Resolved that my speech, my eyes, and
my expressions will portray a good attitude
of heart toward them.

*Then He [Jesus] went down to Nazareth with them [His
parents]and was obedient to them.*
(Luke 2:51)

*My son, give me your heart
and let your eyes delight in my ways.*
(Proverbs 23:26)

*If someone curses their father or mother, their lamp will
be snuffed out in pitch darkness.*
(Proverbs 20:20)

Dear Friends,

Our young Jonathan is not leaving a stone unturned. He sees clearly
that following Jesus impacts every aspect of life. We cannot have
'compartments' that do not belong to Jesus!

I find it heartening to see an eighteenth-century young man concerned
about his attitude toward his mom and dad. Apparently, this is not a
modern problem! In fact, the Bible has so much to say about attitude
toward parents that we must conclude that the problem is as old as
human history. But the battle is raging hot today, perhaps hotter than
ever. There is a disdain for authority in our day that is nowhere more
evident than in the realm of children toward their parents (which then
spills over into a wider disdain for God and all that is good). The

RESOLVED.

Apostle Paul saw this day coming and warned of it when he said, 'People will be lovers of themselves, lovers of money, boastful, proud, abusive, **disobedient to their parents**, ungrateful, unholy (2 Timothy 3:2 emphasis mine).

Jonathan's *Resolution* goes deeper than the outward action, to the inward attitude. Actions are birthed in attitudes and God therefore sees our attitudes as clearly as we see our actions. How destructive it is to self, and to society to dishonour parents! Yet here is a *command* that comes with a promise, first to Israel as a nation, then expanded in the New Testament to Christians in every time and culture:

> *Honour your father and your mother, so that you may live long*
> *in the land the Lord your God is giving you.*
> (Exodus 20:12)

> *'Honour your father and mother' – which is the first commandment*
> *with a promise – so that it may go well with you and that you may*
> *enjoy long life on the earth.*
> (Ephesians 6:2,3)

But Jonathan's *Resolution* embraces not just his parents, but his family.

Honouring our parents and loving our families is not optional if we are setting out to follow Jesus. Now, I must be careful here: we are *not* to idolize them. We are *not* to forsake Christ for them. Parents and families are *not* more important than others and following Jesus demands that we be willing to leave them for the mission field (Mark 10:29). But - our discipleship has to start with loving our neighbours; our parents, our spouses and our children are, in fact, our nearest neighbours.

RESOLVED.

For me to be Christ-like and sweet everywhere but home is offensive to God. To be charitable to those far away while I entertain a critical spirit toward those with whom I live is hypocrisy.

I have to humble myself before Jesus over this. How easy it is to entertain a critical attitude, to roll the eye, to cut with the word. How deadly it is! How I need to pray about my attitudes and bring them under the lordship of Jesus! And here is a thought: my parents have long since gone home to be with Jesus, but I still need to honour them. Their values, what they would want to see me do and, their teachings, need to move and motivate me today as surely as when I was a boy in their home. I need to feel my father's guiding hand upon my shoulder today. For me to steal or commit adultery or lie at this point in my life would dishonour them as surely as did climbing out the window at midnight to go cavorting with my friends when I was fifteen. The clear command in Proverbs 1:8, 'Listen, my son, to your father's instruction and do not forsake your mother's teaching', does not have an expiration date!

More often than not, our parents and our families get the worst of us, not the best of us. Yet can there be a more important place for the wonderful, sweet, goodness that Jesus wants to produce in us to be manifested? Why should my wife be the recipient of my bad attitude, or my rolling eyes and cutting words? Should one's parents – or one's children – be on the sharp end of sarcasm, cynicism, and critical words? Should my family not be the first port of call for my love and Christian expression? Again…are not my parents, my wife, and my children *my nearest neighbours*?

In Mark's Gospel, Jesus delivers a demonized man from Satan's power. He then gives him the toughest mission assignment of all:

Go home to your own people and tell them how much the Lord has done for you, and how he has had mercy on you.

247

RESOLVED.

(Mark 5:19)

The man wanted to leave town and follow Christ wherever he went. Jesus' commission to start with his family is telling. For that man – or for me – or for you – to be off changing our world without first loving our families with the love of Jesus is never what Jesus wants from us. Yes, again, we do not idolize our parents, our kids, our families, and yes, again, many of us will be called to leave them and go elsewhere for Jesus, but, again, grace *must* begin in the attitude of our hearts toward our nearest neighbours – our families.

This is tough but telling. It is almost always easier to have a good attitude toward 'farther' neighbours. The problem must be with my parents (or wife, or kids). I can get along with everyone except them! Ah, but you do not have to *live* with anyone except them! They jolt your pride and expose your selfishness like no-one else does, not because there is something wrong with them, but simply because you are around them so much. Believe me, your office mate, your gym buddy, your friends in the book club chew just as loudly and sneeze just as weirdly as your parents do … you just do not have to put up with it. We are all bothersome, not just your parents or your husband. The ladies in the bridge club 'pass vapours' (a polite British term) just as surely as do the guys on the ball team. We all have gross habits, you just don't see (or hear, or smell) them in others like we do in our own family.

I need help!

Lord Jesus! Forgive my sour attitude toward those closest to
me! Give me sweetness in my heart that spills over in my actions,
glances and words!

RESOLVED.

Will you join with me, and can we join with Jonathan, in pursuing, with all conviction, Christ-like attitudes toward our nearest neighbours. It is the toughest assignment and the most telling school of discipleship. If you can follow Jesus at home - beginning with your parents, your spouse, your siblings, and your children - you can follow Jesus anywhere.

The father of a righteous child has great joy;
a man who fathers a wise son rejoices in him.
May your father and mother rejoice;
may she who gave you birth be joyful!
(Proverbs 23:24,25)

'The light that shines farthest shines brightest nearest home.'[1]
(C.T Studd)

---

[1] Widely attributed to C.T. Studd and Oswald J. Smith. I first heard it from my old Cornish farmer mentor Stuart V. Pearce in 1987.

RESOLVED.

Resolved 47

Resolved to seek to cultivate a sweet, benevolent, contented, serving spirit, and to say 'no' to whatever might threaten the growth of such a spirit. Resolved to examine myself weekly in this regard.

I am the vine; you are the branches. If you remain in me and I in you, you will bear much fruit; apart from me you can do nothing.
(John 15:5)

... the unfading beauty of a gentle and quiet spirit, which is of great worth in God's sight.
(1 Peter 3:4)

Beloved in Christ,

The cultivation of a sweet and godly spirit is a deliberate work. God will produce it in us, but we must cooperate. We need to understand the distinction between *Justification* and *Sanctification*. Here is a brief theology lesson for us all. (Humour me if you already know this!)

Justification is the glorious work whereby God pardons our sin and graces us with His righteousness *solely by the merits of Jesus and his death and resurrection*. We contribute nothing to our justification except our need and we receive our justification by faith alone. It is instantaneous and complete the moment we believe in the Gospel.

Sanctification is the glorious work within us whereby we grow in Christlikeness. Whereas in justification we contribute nothing but simply receive, in sanctification we cooperate with God. It is a process which is not complete until we die and are glorified in Jesus' presence. Some Christians grow to be more like Jesus than others because they are more diligent than others.

RESOLVED.

Jonathan's *Resolutions* deal largely with sanctification, that is, with growing in Christ likeness. The *Resolution* above is all about sanctification. Jonathan is earnest in his desire to cultivate a spirit, a disposition, that reflects the very nature of Jesus.

Stop and think about this desire with me for a minute. This is *not* harsh legalism! Why wouldn't he want to be more like Jesus? Why wouldn't you? Why wouldn't I? The only plausible reason (not a very good one) is that we do not see the beauty of holiness and the ugliness of sin. The best thing I can do for myself, for my family, and for my generation, is to become more like Jesus. If His nature can be increasingly formed within me, what a blessing that will be to myself and to all who come into the orbit of my life!

I promise you that your wife will be blessed if you grow to be more like Jesus.

So will your kids …

So will your neighbours …

So will you!

So, please do not look upon this *Resolution* as a burden, but rather as a blessing. Do yourself (and others) a favour and be diligent with your soul. Cultivating 'a sweet, benevolent, contented, serving spirit' will not happen by accident. Even as cultivating a verdant and fruitful garden requires attention, so does cultivating a Christlike spirit. Oh, but what a blessing to many is a well-loved garden! What a blessing to many is a well-loved spirit!

251

RESOLVED.

The key to growing in Christlikeness is given to us by Jesus Himself in John's Gospel. I'll use the King James Version because it employs the wonderful word 'abide', which means 'to stay with' or 'to live with'.

Abide in me, and I in you. As the branch cannot bear fruit of itself, unless it abides in the vine; no more can you, unless you abide in me. I am the vine, you are the branches: He that abides in me, and I in him, bears much fruit: for without me you can do nothing. ...

If you abide in me, and my words abide in you, you shall ask what you desire, and it shall be done for you. By this my Father is glorified, that you bear much fruit; so you will be my disciples.
(John 15:4,5;7,8 NKJV)

The picture Jesus gives is of a vine, a branch, and fruit. It is a beautiful and obvious image. The vine has life in it. The branch 'remains' or 'abides' in the vine, and fruit is the natural consequence. The vine does not 'try' to bear the fruit. It does not fret over fruit-bearing. It is inevitable. The *life* of the vine produces fruit in the attached branch. Our 'job' in all of this is to 'abide'. Our job is to remain, to stay with, to stick to Jesus. This means that we must treasure Him above all other pretenders. If I choose sin, I will not remain in Jesus. I will then be like a branch that withers. You see in Jonathan's *Resolution* that he will be careful to say 'no' to whatever might threaten the growth of a Jesus-like spirit within him. Please do not see this as a chore! It is a wonderful wonder that we can be transformed into the image of Jesus by abiding with Him. Indeed, we have been saved from sin for nothing less:

For those God foreknew he also predestined to be conformed to the image of his Son, that he might be the firstborn among many brothers and sisters.

252

RESOLVED.

(Romans 8:29)

I am *not* 'Exhibit A' of what it means to be a Jesus-like Christian. But I am married to 'Exhibit A' (Perhaps I might be 'Exhibit L', or 'P'! I really do want to be like Jesus and have a 'sweet, benevolent, contented, serving spirit'.) I have had the privilege for four decades of watching a person be continually transformed into Christ's likeness, and it has been a beautiful thing to behold. I have seen *four* things (she does not know I am writing this!):

> - My wife has made it her priority to abide with Jesus. She has day by day prioritized some time to be alone with Jesus. She has worn Bibles out and read good books that have nourished her inner life: all this with seven children. She taught our children to value *her* time with Jesus. She has done this because she sees something of the beauty of Jesus and she wants to be like Him.
> - My wife has been careful to not allow what will threaten her life with Jesus to gain a foothold in her spirit. It has been remarkable to watch this. She simply will not put up with a bad attitude, Satan's lies, bitterness, unforgiveness, and other poisons of the heart. She consistently takes every thought and attitude captive and makes them obedient to Christ (2 Corinthians 10:5).
> - My wife has consistently valued substance over shadow. In a world where appearance is valued above character, I have watched my wife cultivate character as a first priority because the Bible tells her that her 'beauty... should be that of [her] inner self, the unfading beauty of a gentle and quiet spirit, which is of great worth in God's sight' (1 Peter 3:3,4).
> - My wife has been deliberate in cultivating a spirit of contentment. In a world which constantly clamours for more, she has made unseen things her treasure and deafened her ears to

253

the siren-song of 'more is better', believing that the Bible tells the truth when it says that '...godliness with contentment is great gain' (1 Timothy 6:6).

In these ways (and others) my wife has been diligent to cultivate a sweet and godly spirit. She has grown increasingly into the likeness of Jesus and bears much fruit. How many have been blessed to be in her presence!

Perhaps we can all learn from 'Exhibit A'!

If you make abiding with Jesus the non-negotiable priority of your life, He will pour His Life into you, transforming you to be more like Him, and His wonderful fruit will be the inevitable result. *He* guarantees it.

> *For this reason ... we have not stopped praying for you. We*
> *continually ask God to fill you with the knowledge of his will*
> *through all the wisdom and understanding that the Spirit gives, so*
> *that you may live a life worthy of the Lord and please him in*
> *every way: bearing fruit in every good work, [and] growing in the*
> *knowledge of God.*
> (Colossians 1:9,10)

> 'The branch of the vine does not worry, and toil, and rush here to
> seek for sunshine, and there to find rain. No; it rests in union and
> communion with the vine; and at the right time, and in the right
> way, is the right fruit found on it. Let us
> so abide in the Lord Jesus.' [2]
> (Hudson Taylor)

---

[2] Taylor, H. cited in George, D. (2014), *The Daily Thought Shaker, p.191.* Bloomington: West Bow Press.

RESOLVED.

Resolved 48

Resolved to never assume that all is well with my soul, but to
diligently and earnestly keep vigilance over myself, being sure, at
any and all times, that all my trust is in Jesus, and that I am not
allowing sin to take root. In this way I shall be ready both to live
for Christ and to die in Christ.

*Examine yourselves to see whether you are in the faith; test
yourselves. Do you not realize that Christ Jesus is in you—unless,
of course, you fail the test?*
(2 Corinthians 13:5)

Dear Friends in Christ,

John Bunyan (the humble tinker - maker of pots and pans) wrote over
sixty books. Perhaps his theology can be summed up in one great
sentence: 'God justifies us by bestowing on us, not by expecting from
us'.[1] Those are his wonderful words.   Put into my comparatively
cumbersome words, I would phrase it in this way:

We are declared right with God by *receiving* from God,
not by *striving* for God.

It is of utmost importance that we understand this and do not take a
breath without remembering it. We are not made right before our Holy
God through anything we do or offer. Neither effort nor energy, neither
emotion nor exuberance, neither education nor exactness, make us right
before God.   As is so often the case, the poet says it better than the
theologian:
Not the labours of my hands
can fulfil thy law's demands;

---

[1] Quoted in Dane Ortlund's wonderful book *Gentle and Lowly,* p.81.

255

RESOLVED.

could my zeal no respite know,
could my tears forever flow,
all for sin could not atone;
thou must save, and thou alone.
(Augustus Toplady)

But this is not to say we should be passive. This is not to say that we become complacent. A true work of God awakens us and makes us alive to God. We become concerned for things that we used to ignore. Things that were once of no importance to us become matters of great importance.

One such matter is the health and well-being of our souls. Where we once ignored and abused them, we now realize the eternal value of our unseen selves and begin to exercise diligent care over them. A child of grace knows that Jesus has placed His caring hands upon him. He knows that he is saved and safe forever. But he is *alive* and *aware* where he once was *dead* and *dulled* and as such, he is careful over his life in a new way.

Assurance and *assuming* are not to be confused! A Jesus-follower has a wonderful *assurance* that He belongs totally and forever to Jesus. But that does not cause him to *assume* that all is as it should be with his heart and that he need not exercise care over it. Trusting in Jesus wholly and totally for my safety and salvation does not mean that I have nothing to do.

Hence, Jonathan's resolve to diligently and earnestly keep vigilance over himself at all times does not in any way mean that he is striving in his own strength to be saved. It does not mean that he is ignoring the Gospel and thinking that he can and must establish his own righteousness before God. It does not mean that he thinks he will lose his salvation if, in a given moment, his zeal abates or sin grabs him.

RESOLVED.

Self-examination is not introspection.[2] Introspection, as we have observed earlier[3], is the dangerous imploding practice of looking within for goodness, righteousness, holiness, and justification. It inevitably leads to pride or despair.

Self-examination is not about looking inward so much as looking outward. It only looks inward to make sure that the soul is looking outward. It constantly re-orients the soul to Christ.

For Jonathan this means that he will be careful moment by moment to look to Christ and not to himself for his justification and his security. It means that he will preach the Gospel daily … hourly … constantly… to himself, applying the wonders of Jesus as mediator, sin-bearer, intercessor, and advocate to his own sin-plagued life. It means that he will watch that Christ be Lord of his attitudes and relationships. It means that he will live daily ready to die, knowing that at any moment his Saviour may summon him home.

Keeping careful watch over one's soul is not optional if one expects to live well and die well – and not all Christians do either well!

Here are five simple but searching questions a careful Christian should ask himself often if he is to cultivate a healthy, sweet, Jesus-like, ready-to-live and ready-to-die inner life:

1) Am I looking *away from myself* and to my Saviour Jesus for my hope, salvation, joy, and righteousness, or am I somehow

---

[2] For a helpful exploration of the necessary difference between the two, see Dr Martyn Lloyd-Jones remarkable book *Spiritual Depression: Its Causes and Cure,* or read the relevant passage at https://twilson901.wordpress.com/2014/03/18/introspection-vs-self-examination/

[3] See **Resolved 41.**

believing that I can establish my own righteousness apart from Christ?

Jesus, ... has become for us wisdom from God – that is, our righteousness, holiness and redemption.
(1 Corinthians 1:30)

2) As I invite God the Holy Spirit to search my heart, is He putting His finger on any sin that is lurking? If so, am I quickly taking it to Jesus in confession and repentance, knowing that He is ever willing to receive me and cleanse me?

Search me, God, and know my heart;
test me and know my anxious thoughts.
See if there is any offensive way in me,
and lead me in the way everlasting.
(Psalm 139:23,24)

3) Am I walking in sweetness and forgiveness towards my brothers and sisters or am I allowing roots of bitterness to worm their ways into my heart?

But if we walk in the light, as he is in the light, we have fellowship with one another, and the blood of Jesus, his Son, purifies us from all sin.
(1 John 1:7)

4) Am I asking and trusting Jesus to empower me every day, every moment, to deny self and love Him and others, to say 'yes' to God and 'no' to Satan, or am I believing that I can live a Christ-honouring life in my own strength?

I can do all this through him who gives me strength...

RESOLVED.

... apart from me you can do nothing.
(Philippians 4:13; John 15:5)

5) Am I living every day realizing that very soon, indeed, at any moment, my life on earth will end and I will be summoned to give my account to God, or am I foolishly forgetting the fragility of my mortal frame?

Why, you do not even know what will happen tomorrow.
What is your life? You are a mist that appears for a
little while and then vanishes.
(James 4:14)

May we learn to be diligent over our souls, to the honour of Jesus who purchased them, to the blessing of ourselves who must spend eternity with them, and to the good of others who must bear the burden or blessing of them.

I delight greatly in the Lord; my soul rejoices in my God. For he
has clothed me with garments of salvation and arrayed me in a
robe of his righteousness, as a bridegroom adorns his head like a
priest, and as a bride adorns herself with her jewels.
(Isaiah 61:10)

As I began with John Bunyan, let me finish with words from the thinking tinker:

'It is sad to see how the most of men neglect their precious souls
... when, in the meanwhile,
their bodies are well provided for,
their estates much regarded,
and the things of this present life are highly prized,

259

RESOLVED.

as if the darling was of less value than a clod of earth;
an immortal soul, than a perishing body;
a precious Saviour, than unsatisfying creatures.'[4]

[4] Bunyan, J. (1658), *A Few Sighs from Hell...* p.1.Printed by Ralph Wood for M. Wright at the Kings Head in the Old Bailey, London.

Resolved 49

Resolved that, with reference to my previous *Resolution*, it shall never be that when I come to die, I will realize that I have been careless with my life.

If anyone builds on this foundation using gold, silver, costly stones, wood, hay or straw, their work will be shown for what it is, because the Day will bring it to light. It will be revealed with fire, and the fire will test the quality of each person's work. If what has been built survives, the builder will receive a reward. If it is burned up, the builder will suffer loss, but yet will be saved – even though only as one escaping through the flames.
(1 Corinthians 3:12-15)

Friends,

There are numerous ways to be careless with one's life.

One is to ignore eternity and your soul altogether, forgetting that there is more to 'you' than meets the eye, and more to life than these brief years. In so doing, you see yourself as nothing other than a 'higher animal'. Christ and the Gospel are foolishness to you. This is the tragic position of many in today's world. Many are materialists who view themselves as nothing more than an accidental gathering of matter that somehow sparked to conscious life.

Another deadly way to be careless is to ostensibly believe in Jesus and His Gospel but not take faith beyond mere outward appearance and conformity to a group. Here faith becomes a matter of simple and shallow intellectual assent to a few facts, but as for a personal pursuit of God, there is no desire. Salvation is seen as nothing more than an insurance policy against hell (if there happens to be one).

RESOLVED.

Then, Jesus warns us, one can be seemingly very spiritual and even be deep into ministry, but in fact have no saving knowledge of God. Yikes! It is all too easy to attempt to substitute a full religious calendar for a humble walk with God, but God is not interested in our busyness and is unimpressed by our boasts of demons driven out and miracles performed. He has heard every sermon ever preached and neither yours nor mine are going to impress Him when what He wants is that we simply walk with Him.

In these and other ways we can ruin our lives and souls and miss Heaven by an inch or by a mile.

But I do not think that our Jonathan is concerned with missing Heaven when he resolves to not be careless with his life. There is clear evidence in the Bible that it is possible - easy - to be a genuine believer, one who truly knows Jesus as Saviour and friend, and yet to be careless and thereby effectively waste your life. I think this is a greater danger to many of us than we might think.

Can we explore this together?

First, can you agree with me that *this life* ... our earthly journey ... is valuable and should not be wasted? For a Christian to waste the grace given for each earthly day is a tragedy not only for himself, but for the cause of Christ in this world. For a Christian to yawn or fuss his way through the gift of each and every day in this present realm is surely to offend the loving heart of his good and wonderful God. Jonathan does not want to get to the end of his earthly journey and realize that he blew his chance to relish his precious days on earth. (How many days have *we* wasted with sin, fear, irritability, laziness or selfishness?)

RESOLVED.

The sad little book of Ecclesiastes tells the story of a man's (probably Solomon's) regret for wasting his earthly days in vanity. His summary is one you do not want to repeat:

> *So, I hated life ... All of it is meaningless,*
> *a chasing after the wind.*
> (Ecclesiastes 2:17)

You do not want to do that! Neither do I!

But then, agree with me that *time* affects *eternity*. *This life* affects *the next life*. It seems that it is possible for a blood-bought child of grace to squander much of his inheritance and leave himself, though saved and safe, comparatively impoverished.

Oh dear! I want to avoid this at all costs!

Take a few minutes and carefully read the Scripture at the top of this letter again. The Apostle Paul is using a word picture to depict two kinds of people, the lives they live, and the eternal results of the lives they live. Paul presents vastly different outcomes. Clearly *both* are saved from a deserved Hell, but they are not equal in their undeserved Heaven.

One life is a picture of the well-nourished soul and the resultant fruitful life. This life and life's work is built upon precious and costly things: gold, silver, rare and valuable gems. Note with me that these things are usually *unseen* and *slow to produce*. They occur away from the obvious eye - often in secret - and take a lot of digging to discover and bring to light. But they are solid and substantial and will withstand fire.

The other's life and work are built upon wood, hay and straw. Such are *seen* and *fast to produce*. They are on display and obvious to all, but ... they cannot endure for long, especially when the fire tries them. Their lack of substance is indicative of an inner life that is feeble and frail. All that is left is a heap of ashes. There is nothing substantial and enduring.

Clearly in Paul's word picture the fire is a picture of a judgment that all believers will go through ... not a judgment to decide our eternal destiny. That has already been determined as we have been graciously delivered from wrath. But it is a judgment upon our works, our ways, our lives, our efforts. Some take the grace of God and apply themselves to growth and usefulness, some are comparatively careless and therefore stunted in their growth and usefulness.

Jesus spoke many times of *rewards* for believers. Clearly, salvation is free and by grace through faith alone. So, what can He mean? I think we have to deduce that we are not all the same in Heaven. This life affects Eternity! Hear the words of Jesus:

> *Rejoice in that day and leap for joy, because*
> *great your reward in heaven.*
> (Luke 6:23)

> *But love your enemies, do good to them, and lend to them without*
> *expecting to get anything back. Then your reward will*
> *be great, and you will be children of the Most High,*
> *because he is kind to the ungrateful and wicked.*
> (Luke 6:35)

Jesus also spoke of the ability *now* to invest in *then* when He said:

> *Sell your possessions and give to the poor. Provide purses for*
> *yourselves that will not wear out, a treasure in heaven*
> *that will never fail, where no thief comes near*
> *and no moth destroys.*
> (Luke 12:33)

RESOLVED.

Clearly Jesus tells us that some will invest more into their eternity than others through the choices and moves they make today. How is your 'Eternity Portfolio' looking?

I might be wrong, but I think the difference will be our eternal capacity for joy. Jonathan, as we have already seen,[1] proposed that the differing states of believers in Heaven might be likened to vessels (jars) with different capacities for joy – each one plunged into the sea of God's eternal happiness, and therefore each one full to the brim, but each one not having the same capacity – some being bigger, some smaller, than others, and, that capacity having been determined in *this* life, by one's response to grace and desire to know and honour Christ.

I do not want to waste *this life* and I do not want to have poor choices in the present spill over into my eternity. We will live well if we live with an eye constantly on Heaven! We will be most useful, joyful, and full *here and now* if we seek to be ready to be all that we can be in Jesus *there and then*. God is pouring grace out in super-abundance for you and for me. May we open our hearts wide to receive it.

> *Teach us to number our days, that we may*
> *gain a heart of wisdom.*
> (Psalm 90:12)

'The Christian ideal has not been tried and found wanting; it has
been found difficult and left untried.'[2]
(G.K. Chesterton)

---

[1] **Resolved 17.**

[2] Chesterton, G. K. (1912). *What's Wrong with the World*, p.22. London; Toronto: Cassell.

RESOLVED.

Resolved 50

Resolved to live and act in such a way that, upon my coming to Heaven, I will see that I lived my earthly life well and wisely.

He regarded disgrace for the sake of Christ as of greater value than the treasures of Egypt because he was looking ahead to his reward.
(Hebrews 11:26)

He will wipe every tear from their eyes.
(Revelation 21:4)

Dear Friends in Jesus,

Jonathan's *Resolutions* are coming at us fast and hard. So.... take a momentary breather with me and remember that God is all grace and goodness. He is *for us*. His heart for us is *huge*. He *wants* us to do well and will meet our meagre efforts will pleasure and power. In fact,

His divine power has given us everything we need for a godly life through our knowledge of him who called us by his own glory and goodness.
(2 Peter 1:3)

So, take a few deep gulps of grace before we pick up our stride again.

OK. Ready? Here goes ...

I want you to do some thinking with me. What I am about to propose I cannot be 'dogmatic' about. I might be wrong, but I might be right (and I think I am).

RESOLVED.

I trust that every follower of Jesus is looking for that day when Jesus will open wide His grace-filled arms and greet us with a joyous, 'Well done, my good and faithful servant! Come and enter into my joy!' I know that is God's heart for us. What a reward that will be for every battle-weary believer!

But ... I think it is possible for a Christian to have some regrets - at least for a while - in Heaven.

Hear me out before you slam the book shut!

Jesus uses the motive of future reward (a warm 'Well done' will be plenty of reward for me!) to motivate us in discipleship today. There are about a dozen times in the Gospels when Jesus speaks of rewards for believers.

> *For the Son of Man is going to come in his Father's glory with his angels, and then he will reward each person according to what they have done.*
> (Matthew 16:27)

Clearly Jesus wants us to learn to make decisions with more than just the weekend in view. He wants us to think and act in the light of eternity and of being with Him forever.

We have already seen in previous *Resolutions* that this brief earthly life affects our eternity. There is no disconnect between our days here on earth and our life in God's Heaven. We have been created to inhabit eternity and forever begins *now* for every believer (as it, in fact, does in a sad way for every unbeliever). We need to see the impact that temporal today has upon our eternal tomorrow.

RESOLVED.

There is a *continuity* between now and then. This is made clear in Paul's letter to the troubled, worldly, eternity-forgetting church in Corinth:

> *So will it be with the resurrection of the dead. The body that is*
> *sown is perishable, it is raised imperishable; it is sown in*
> *dishonour, it is raised in glory; it is sown in weakness, it is raised*
> *in power; it is sown a natural body, it is raised a spiritual body.*
> (1 Corinthians 15:43,44)

It is reasonable and right to infer that if there is continuity of our physical selves, from perishable to imperishable, from weakness to power, from mortal to immortal, that there will likewise be continuity of our mental selves, of our spiritual selves, and of our relational selves, our emotional selves. Everything will be enhanced, not diminished. Who we are here will have a continuance, but in a glorified manner, into eternity. (Likewise, it is reasonable to infer that the wicked will know a continuity as well but expressed in enhanced regret and agony.)

So, will we be able to look back upon our lives here? Is there any biblical evidence for such a thought? And if so, might a saved and safe person in any way look back with any regrets? Might there be any room, even for a short season, for tears in Heaven?

There is some evidence in the Bible that after we die and at least while we await the final renewal of all things (as promised in Revelation 21), that there will be a remembrance and awareness of our brief earthly sojourn. For instance, clearly the redeemed multitude gathered before the throne of God in Revelation 6 are fully aware of what happened and is happening on earth as they await God to avenge their blood:

> *They called out in a loud voice, 'How long, Sovereign Lord, holy*
> *and true, until you judge the inhabitants of the earth and*
> *avenge our blood?'*

268

RESOLVED.

(Revelation 6:10)

Also, in Jesus' story of the wicked rich man and Lazarus the beggar (Luke 16:19-31), there is a clear and conscious connection, at least for a while, between paradise, earth, and the place of torment. This connection, continuation, between this life and the next life teaches us that in reality we live *one* life, with death being a bridge between two aspects of it.

It is interesting to me that it is not until the final consummation of all things and the glorious appearing of 'a new Heaven and a new earth' in Revelation 21, that God finally wipes away every tear (v.4). Could it be that only *then* is any residue of pain, sorrow, and regret from this life finally and totally expunged from our consciousness and we enter into *total* and *consummate* joy? Could it be that, for a season, before the final presentation of the Kingdom in all its fulness, the redeemed who are living in the wonderful presence of their wonderful Lord still experience some degree of sorrow relating to this present life? Why else would Jesus have to wipe away tears in Heaven?

For a season, and to a degree, even in the Paradise of God, there might be room for regret amongst the redeemed.

Jonathan does not want to get to Heaven and then wish he had lived differently while on earth. Neither do you. He is not doubting his salvation. He is not striving to gain Heaven by his own merits. But he is realizing that he has *one* life, and that this earthly sojourn continues beyond death and into eternity. We saw in his previous *Resolution*, particularly in the passage likening some Christians' lives and labours to 'wood, hay and straw' (1 Cor 3:12), that it is possible to be a Christian, but waste much of your life in futility. Can we not see regret in that picture of one's efforts being proven to be nothing but a pile of ashes? How could there not be?

RESOLVED.

Jonathan's resolve to enter Heaven with no regrets *will only make him live better now*. How can it not? Do we not all regularly experience the power of anticipation to transform the present? If I know that what I do today will enhance or diminish my joy tomorrow, then my today is transformed. My choices are changed, my direction is determined, my attitude is adjusted, my stride is strengthened by anticipations of future happiness or sadness resulting from today's decisions.

I think that it is only in eternity that we will get a proper perspective upon this life. So, should we not live this life in the light of Eternity? Will we not live better *now* if we are living with an eye on *then*? Without question, those Christians who have lived best while on earth have been those who have lived each day with an eye on Heaven. C.S Lewis put it well:

> If you read history, you will find that the Christians who did most for the present world were precisely those who thought most of the next. It is since Christians have largely ceased to think of the other world that they have become so ineffective in this [world]...[1]

(Certainly, the biggest reason to rejoice in Heaven and the biggest reason for regret must have to do with loving others (or not) enough to share Jesus with them. If there is joy in Heaven over one sinner who repents (Luke 15:7), then there must be joy in Heaven when one looks back and sees the episodes where he or she was faithful to help a sinner repent. But could there be sorrow at the times where we allowed the fear of man or the love of comfort to silence us? I fear so!)

Thank you, Lord Jesus for forgiving me for all the times I was silent and failed to love enough to speak of you!

---

[1] Lewis, C. S. (2001). *Mere Christianity*, p.143. Grand Rapids, Michigan: Zondervan.

RESOLVED.

Wow!

Lord teach me to live with a wonderful anticipation of future glory - falling into your grace-filled arms and so much more - always in view!

Look, I am coming soon! My reward is with me.
(Revelation 22:12)

'Aim at Heaven and you will get earth 'thrown in': aim at earth and you will get neither.'[2]
(C.S. Lewis)

---

[2] Lewis, C. S. (1996). *Joyful Christian*, p.138. New York: Simon and Schuster.

Resolved 51

Resolved, by God's grace and not wanting at the last to discover that I was a false follower, to prove my faith genuine in how I live and act in every way and at all times.

But someone will say, 'You have faith; I have deeds.' Show me your faith without deeds, and I will show you my faith by my deeds. You believe that there is one God. Good! Even the demons believe that – and shudder. You foolish person, do you want evidence that faith without deeds is useless?
(James 2:18-20)

Then he will say to those on his left, 'Depart from me, you who are cursed, into the eternal fire prepared for the devil and his angels. For I was hungry and you gave me nothing to eat, I was thirsty and you gave me nothing to drink, I was a stranger and you did not invite me in, I needed clothes and you did not clothe me, I was ill and in prison and you did not look after me.'
(Matthew 25:41-43)

Dear Friends,

That glorious pillar of our Faith, that bedrock of scriptural Christianity, that wondrous truth that has kept millions of believers sane and secure - that is,

justification by grace through faith alone -

does not any way teach or imply that how I *live*, how I *act*, what I *do* is now of no importance since I have faith in Jesus.

It is a caricature of something great, a perversion of something wonderful, to suggest that receiving the Gospel by faith alone absolves me from any responsibility as to how I then live ... as to what I *do* and what I *do not do*. The best followers of Jesus over the vast years of Christian history have been those whose faith has been proven by their works. Let's be clear on this – for them, works were never a substitute for faith in the finished work of Jesus on the cross. But equally, faith was never allowed to exist in a vacuum, free of works. Faith produced works and thereby, proved itself as genuine. Faith in Jesus followed from and existed through a deep inner work of God's Holy Spirit that moved and motivated them to labour and love in new and often supernatural ways.

Yes, the poet said well:

> Not the labours of my hands
> Can fulfil Thy law's demands.[1]

But, likewise, the poet said this well:

> I cannot work my soul to save,
> For that my God alone has done.
> But I will work like any slave
> For the love of God's dear Son.[2]

Faith is a living thing that produces acts of faithfulness. It keeps us *from* doing certain things and moves us *to* do certain things. Young Jonathan understood this from the earliest days of his journey with Jesus. I actually softened up the tone of this *Resolution* as it originally said:

> Resolved, that I will act so, in every respect, as I think I shall
> wish I had done, if I should at last be damned.

---

[1] Augustus Montague Toplady, (1740-1778).
[2] Author unknown.

RESOLVED.

No! He is not getting morbid and negative in this *Resolution*. But he is being healthy and realistic. There needs to be a bit of a tremble, a touch of reserve, a hint of caution in the heart of every true believer. You might want to call it *reverence*. Assurance – that wonderful inner witness, based upon the promises of God in the Bible – that one is saved and safe forever with Jesus, is the birthright of every believer. But alongside it should exist a moment-by-moment realization: 'I dare not take this salvation for granted. I dare not play fast and loose with God's grace'. The psalmist said it well:

Serve the Lord with fear [reverence]and rejoice with trembling.
(Psalm 2:11 NKJV)

Jonathan imagines a horrific future scene in order move him to faithfulness in all he does today. Imagining this scene does not mean he thinks he can lose his salvation, or that somehow Jesus cannot keep him. But it does mean he sees the clear and present danger that he can be a false follower, and that only his deeds can prove his faith genuine. He imagines what John Bunyan's Pilgrim had dreamily (nightmarishly) imagined a hundred years before him:

> Then I saw that there was a way to Hell, even from
> the gates of Heaven.[3]

He imagines getting to the end of his life only to find his assumptions were false and his assurance was misplaced. Such thinking moved Jonathan Edwards (and John Bunyan) to avoid assumption, arrogance, and carelessness in his profession of faith in Jesus.

---

[3] Bunyan, J. (1857) T. *Pilgrim's Progress*, p.191. Edinburg, Scotland: Nelson and Sons. But take courage! For indeed, there is also *a way to Heaven even from the gates of Hell!*

RESOLVED.

John Wesley called false following 'antinomianism', that is, lawlessness.

Bonhoeffer called it, 'cheap grace'.

The Apostle James called it 'dead' faith.

So ... take a moment and dare to imagine getting to the end of your life, all along having been confident of your eternal safety, only to find that there is indeed a gate to Hell adjacent to the gate of Heaven ... and it has swung wide for you. Imagine discovering that your repentances were shallow, that your motives were self-serving, that your life was, in fact, in orbit around yourself, and that your profession of Christ was little more than an opinion and a feeling or two. Can this not cause you to tremble? Can this not cause you to check yourself? Can this be anything but good for you? Do not many perish for simple lack of such examination? Will you ever be harmed by taking serious stock of things? Can there ever be harm in being diligent to prove your faith genuine by what you do and do not do?

Read some of Jesus' parables and you will find a recurring theme that we tend to view ourselves as better, more 'spiritual' than we really are:

Once the owner of the house gets up and closes the door, you will stand outside knocking and pleading, 'Sir, open the door for us.'
But he will answer, 'I don't know you or where you come from.'
Then you will say, 'We ate and drank with you, and you taught in our streets.'

But he will reply, 'I don't know you or where you come from.
Away from me, all you evildoers!'
(Luke 13:25-27)

RESOLVED.

It seems the day will come when everyone will want to be known as Jesus' friend. It seems that Jesus is warning that such friendship needs to begin today. It seems that it is dangerously easy to assume oneself to be 'OK with God' because, 'We ate and drank with you, and you taught in our streets'.

No one will ever get to the end of their earthly pilgrimage and say,

> 'Dang! I was too diligent with my soul!'
> 'I took salvation too earnestly!'
> 'I followed too closely!'
> 'I watched too carefully!'

But many will say 'Open the door for us!'

May it not be so with you, or with me.

> *In the same way, faith by itself, if it is not accompanied*
> *by action, is dead.*
> (James 2:17)

> 'Cheap grace is the grace we bestow on ourselves. Cheap grace is
> the preaching of forgiveness without requiring repentance,
> baptism without church discipline, communion without
> confession...Cheap grace is grace without discipleship, grace
> without the cross, grace without Jesus Christ,
> living and incarnate.'
> (Dietrich Bonhoeffer) [4]

---

[4] Bonhoeffer, D. (1959) *The Cost of Discipleship,* p.47. New York: Macmillan.

Resolved 52

Resolved, as I often hear old people say that they would live their lives differently if given the chance, that I, by God's grace, may live as I can imagine I will wish I had done, should I live
to one day be an old man.

But whatever were gains to me I now consider loss for the sake of Christ. What is more, I consider everything a loss because of the surpassing worth of knowing Christ Jesus my Lord, for whose sake I have lost all things. I consider them garbage, that I may gain Christ and be found in him, not having a righteousness of my own that comes from the law, but that which is through faith in Christ – the righteousness that comes from God on the basis of faith. I want to know Christ – yes, to know the power of his resurrection and participation in his sufferings, becoming like him in his death, and so, somehow, attaining to the resurrection from the dead.
(Philippians 3:7-11)

Dear Friends,

Perhaps the most popular tourist attraction in Cairo is the gilded burial treasure of the young King Tutankhamun. While his embalmed body lies entombed in the Valley of the Kings, the gold that was buried with him has been removed to the Museum of Egyptian Antiquities for all to see. Fabulously wealthy, his life still speaks as a testimony of the 'best' this present, visible life has to offer...and of its final emptiness.

While a flood of the intrigued and envious make their way to the Cairo Museum, a mere trickle finds their way to the inconspicuous grave of another young man buried in Cairo. A son of the Kingdom-yet-to-come, William Borden (1887-1913) had no earthly treasure with which to be buried, for he had long given his fabulous wealth away. Captivated by Christ, he, like many other subjects of this coming Kingdom, 'regarded disgrace for the sake of Christ as of greater value than the treasures of Egypt, because he was looking ahead to his reward' (Hebrews 11:26).

Borden, a millionaire by age eighteen, gave his wealth away and, upon graduating from Yale, headed for the mission field, treasuring the eternal well-being of a certain Chinese Muslim tribe above his own earthly comfort. While studying Arabic in Cairo he contracted meningitis and died at 25. His death sent a shockwave throughout the Christian world of his day, but his brief life motivated many to likewise 'consider everything a loss because of the surpassing worth of knowing Christ Jesus'.

His gravestone bears a single sentence epitaph:

Apart from Christ, there is no explanation for such a life.

In his Bible, six simple words were written which summed up his values:

No Reserves
No Retreats
No Regrets.

William Borden was a soul mate to our Jonathan - just born 150 years later. He, too, lived his brief days in light of Eternity and made decisions every day in light of his last day.

Compare William's life to the young Tutankhamun's, who very well might have breathed his last in the same spirit of regret as another king, Solomon, who, 'having it all', could only survey his vanity and confess:

RESOLVED.

I hated life...
(Ecclesiastes 2:17)

 Getting to the end of one's earthly journey regret-free will not happen by accident. It requires one great goal: the Glory of God over self. Then come many crisis moments of redirection, and thousands of little daily choices and adjustments to keep one on course.

But until we understand the heart God has for us, we will never get far in the Christian life. God is not a cosmic killjoy. Actually, He is the universal source of all true joy. He alone possesses infinite joy, and He is ready and willing to give it liberally away. The problem is that we seek fullness apart from the One who alone can give it. We seek joy in the back-alleys (meaning in the dark recesses), pleasure in the tenement slums, hidden away from Him whose heart longs to meet ours with His very own Life.

We are too easily satisfied, which keeps us from ever being truly satisfied, which causes us to end our days in a sigh instead of a shout. Let's remind ourselves of C.S. Lewis' lesson, that we looked at right at the beginning, in the first *Resolution*:

> It would seem that Our Lord finds our desires not too strong, but too weak. We are half-hearted creatures, fooling about with drink and sex and ambition when infinite joy is offered us, like an ignorant child who wants to go on making mud pies in a slum because he cannot imagine what is meant by the offer of a holiday at the sea. We are far too easily pleased.[1]

---

[1] Lewis, C. S. (2001). *Weight of Glory*, p.1. Grand Rapids, Michigan: Zondervan.

RESOLVED.

Jesus makes plain to us the heart and mind of the Eternal God in regard to our good, profit, and pleasure:

> *I have told you this so that my joy may be in you and that*
> *your joy may be complete.*
> (John 15:11)

> *The thief comes only to steal and kill and destroy; I have come*
> *that they may have life and have it to the full.*
> (John 10:10)

But there is a cost! Jesus tells us that His Kingdom is like a valuable pearl for which a merchant will *gladly give up everything else*! His life-long search is over, for he has found the ultimate treasure (Matthew 13:45). Jesus warns that loving anything or anyone above Him makes joy-giving, God-glorifying discipleship impossible (Matthew 10:37).

Jonathan Edwards is aiming for the stars. He is not an austere ascetic. He is not a mystic trying to extinguish all desire. No! He is refusing all lesser desires because he is choosing the highest desire. He is not content with anything less than living for the highest purpose of all: the Glory of God - a life lived to know, love, and enjoy his Creator. Jonny, like William, knows why he has been made. He has been made for nothing less than to give pleasure to God and to receive pleasure from God.

Do we see this? The pursuit of a life which gives Glory to God and the pursuit of one's own *highest* good, profit, and pleasure, are not mutually exclusive goals. But, as Lewis rightly says, the problem is that we are 'far too easily pleased'.

Call it Life vs. life.

RESOLVED.

Call it True Living vs. merely existing.

Call it Soaring Like an Eagle vs. scratching around like a turkey.

Jesus makes it plain: When we 'lose our lives for His sake' we actually 'find Life'.

Far from simply having a 'passing religious phase' in their lives, these two, William and Jonathan, were bent on living for Jesus and Joy for all their days and into forever, no matter the cost. Edwards and Borden both knew that God Almighty had apprehended them for nothing less than fullness in Himself. Therefore ... to settle for mere existence would be practical unbelief and virtual blasphemy.

Call it a Magnificent Obsession.

　　Call it a Steely Resolve.

　　　Call it a Consuming Passion.

Let these purposeful young men wrestle you to the mat and pin you, as they have me.

Now to him who is able to do immeasurably more than all we ask or imagine, according to his power that is at work within us, to him be glory in the church and in Christ Jesus throughout all generations, for ever and ever! Amen.
(Ephesians 3:14-21)

Let me leave you with a power-packed quote, not form a youngster, but from a proven war-horse, British journalist Malcomb Muggeridge:

RESOLVED.

'I can say that I never knew what joy was like until I gave up
pursuing happiness, or cared to live until I chose to die.
For these two discoveries I am beholden to Jesus.' [2]

---

[2] Muggeridge, M. in conversation with William Buckley cited by Mathwin D. *A Stick
in the Mud* blog (Feb 18, 2021)

RESOLVED.

Resolved 53

Resolved, on my good days, when I am in the best frame of mind, to never miss an opportunity to draw closer to Jesus, to trust Him in new ways, to embark on new adventures in following Him, and to make fresh consecration of myself to Him. In so doing I will confirm my assurance in Christ Jesus as my Redeemer and that I am eternally safe in Him.

*Go to the ant ... consider its ways and be wise ...
it stores its provisions in summer and gathers
its food at harvest.*
(Proverbs 6:6-8)

*If you stumble in safe country, how will you manage in the
thickets by the Jordan?*
(Jeremiah 12:5)

Dear Friend in Jesus,

The wisest followers of Jesus have learned, like the ant, to capitalize on the good times, knowing that lean times are never far away and sure to come.

Let's be realistic:

There will be stormy times,
Dry seasons,
Many questions,
Few Answers,
Overwhelming challenges,
Days when Heaven seems far off,
Times when God seems silent,

RESOLVED.

There will be days when obedience is hard - and disobedience is easy. There are sure to be storm clouds brewing. We still live in the battle-zone. We still inhabit the sin-stricken planet. Some days will be sunny. Many will be stormy.

Charles Wesley said it well:

> Hide me, O my Saviour, hide,
> till the storm of life is past;
> safe into the haven guide,
> O receive my soul at last!

We had better brace ourselves.

Here is Jonathan's counsel: we had better take advantage of every good day, every sweet season, every day of health and strength to store up, to build up, to prepare to venture out in faith.

We will do well to press into Jesus on the good days. Habits of consecration learned when the wind is at our back will serve us when the gale is blowing straight in our face. Spiritual disciplines need to be learned *before* the tough phone call comes. Friendship with Jesus needs to be cultivated *before* the world comes knocking on our door. While it is true that tough times are unique seasons of grace in which God can do deep work in our lives, we dare not waste the sunny times when we have the strength and sanity to 'grow in the grace and knowledge' (1 Peter 3:18) of our wonderful Saviour. It will not always be easy to get up early and pray, so do it now. You will not always have time to read your Bible, so read it today. You might not have the capacity one day to read great books of faith, or to spend days seeking God, so take the chance while you have it.

RESOLVED.

When the young Hudson Taylor - preparing for a life of service in China - was still living in the comparative ease of London, he took that time to learn the spiritual and life disciplines that he figured he would need if he was to survive in the harsh frontier of inland China. The faith lessons he learned 'in the safe county' served him well 'in the thickets' of the mission field. Indeed, years into his life's work, having suffered trials beyond his strength, it was from the deep well of Christ, dug in his stronger days that he was able to say: 'I am so weak that I cannot read my Bible...even pray, I can only lie still in God's arms like a little child, and trust'.

Somewhere on our shelves at home is my wife's 'pre-marriage and children' Bible. Every page is worn. Every margin is written in. Line after line is highlighted. Its yellowed pages speak of a young woman taking advantage of the (comparatively) easy years to prepare herself for the rigours of what would turn out to be a large family, a busy ministry, and a (nearly) impossible husband. It has not been by accident that she has continued steadfast in Jesus and useful in her Master's hands through countless trials and challenges.

It is hard to strike out on some new adventure of faith and service when tribulation is unending and the waves are overwhelming. Better to lift your sails and hoist your anchor when the wind is favourable than to spend the fair-weather days loitering about the harbour only to find yourself unprepared for the adventure God has for you somewhere over the horizon.

We find ourselves living in such emotionally fragile days. We are a culture of quitters. Our feelings are easily hurt and our feathers quickly ruffled. Many of us have had so much leisure and pleasure that we cannot endure even brief periods of trial, let alone long seasons of hardship. We have failed to make good of the sunshine in anticipation of the storm-clouds. We would do well to go to the ant and learn a lesson or two. We would learn to 'store provisions in summer' before the sure onset of winter.

As a pastor, I have been privileged to walk through sacred seasons of life with many dear people. Please take it from me, some true believers in Jesus enter such painful trials, particularly when death approaches, that had they not 'stored provisions in summer', they would not have endured. I have seen believers too sick to pray, too distraught to read their Bibles, to battered to battle. At such times, the deep wells already dug have supplied them with grace unseen. It is foolish to think that you will get serious with your relationship with Jesus when the onslaught is upon you. It is wise to take every sunny day, and your years of strength to get to know Jesus as deeply and fully as you possibly can! Wise was 'The Preacher' when he counselled:

> *Remember your Creator*
> *in the days of your youth,*
> *before the days of trouble come*
> *and the years approach when you will say,*
> *'I find no pleasure in them'.*
> (Ecclesiastes 12:1)

God does not give us sweet seasons and times of clarity and strength so that we can forget Him, but so that we can learn of Him. His kindness is meant to lead us to repentance and to tenderness and to intimacy with Him. If I waste the good seasons, I will be unprepared for the tough times. (By the way, have we not done this as a culture? Have we not forgotten the Lord in these great years of blessing and peace He has given us as a nation? Have we not failed to press on to know Him and instead become Godless and lazy? Have not our Bibles grown dusty and our hearts grown worldly?) Those who have gone far and deep with Jesus through the storms of life have been those who have made good use of the balmy times, the early mornings, the pain-free days, the quiet

286

evenings, the times of unique Divine favour, to multiply grace in their lives.

 Friend, the Lord Jesus will give you all grace to know Him deeply and truthfully. He will give you all strength for the storms which are sure to come. Take advantage of every good year, day, moment. Receive every sweet season, every calm moment as a chance to pray, read, repent, venture out, and learn of Jesus. Learn of Him on the smooth plain before you are called to ascend the rugged peaks or traverse the deep valley. Teach your children to know the Lord in the days of their youth, knowing that trials await them when the Lord will be all they have.

There will never be an easier time for you to get real with God and earnest with His Son than today.

The Lord is good to those who wait for Him, To the soul who seeks Him. It is good that one should hope and wait quietly for the salvation of the Lord. It is good for a man to bear the yoke in his youth.
(Lamentations 3:25-27 NKJV)

Whatever is your best time in the day, give that to Communion with God.[1]
(Hudson Taylor)

---

[1] Widely attributed to Hudson Taylor.

RESOLVED.

Resolved 54

Resolved, whenever I hear of or see something praiseworthy in another person to seek to imitate it in my life.

Walk with the wise and become wise,
for a companion of fools suffers harm.
(Proverbs 13:20)

Remember your leaders, who spoke the word of God to you.
Consider the outcome of their way of life and imitate their faith.
(Hebrews 13:7)

Dear Friends in Jesus,

Envy: a bad thing.

Admiration: a good thing.

Envy is to want what someone else has. The dictionary defines envy as:

Desire to have a quality, possession, or other desirable attribute belonging to (someone else).

Admiration might also involve wanting what someone else has, but there is no bitterness attached to it. The dictionary defines admiration as:

Respect and warm approval; something regarded as impressive or worthy of respect.

Everyone is better than me at *something* and I can learn from them if I am ready and willing. You know when you see something praiseworthy in another person and respond with envy in your heart. It feels terrible. I remember reading a godly author - I think it was Roy Hession - who astutely pointed out that jealousy (envy) is the only sin that *never* feels good. All other sins have seasons of pleasure, but envy is never any fun.

> *Envy rots the bones.*
> (Proverbs 14:30)

But it can be a wonderful thing to admire a godly trait in another and desire it in yourself. The Bible actually counsels us to observe others, to see noble things in their lives, to hear of praiseworthy things in their character, and desire them:

> *We did this [worked night and day], not because we do not have*
> *the right to such help, but in order to offer ourselves*
> *as a model for you to imitate.*
> (2 Thessalonians 3:9)

> *We do not want you to become lazy, but to imitate those who*
> *through faith and patience inherit what has been promised.*
> (Hebrews 6:12)

> *Follow my example, as I follow the example of Christ.*
> (1 Corinthians 11:1)

The wise, old apostle Paul counselled the young, green Timothy to run alongside those who were running well when he said, 'Flee the evil desires of youth and pursue righteousness, faith, love and peace, *along with those who call on the Lord out of a pure heart*' (2 Timothy 2:22 , italics mine).

RESOLVED.

It is a beautiful thing to see young Jonathan wanting to find in himself the godliness that is evident in others. Rather than envying them he admires them. In a life-giving way he desires in himself what he sees as life-giving and God-glorifying in another. Indeed, if envy 'rots the bones', admiration inspires the heart. It *feels good.*

Now the *caveat.* It is good to admire and desire what is good in others … but we dare not fool ourselves. The Lord may no doubt be doing a good work in another's life, and admirable traits may be evident and desired, but even the finest saints have 'feet of clay'. We finally look to Jesus for what is good and beautiful. We want to be like *Him.* All people, even the most admirable, are flawed and if we move from admiration to idolatry, we are sure to be disappointed and hurt.

We should desire what we see in another only to the extent that what we see in them is a Jesus-like trait. That being said, it is spiritually healthy to seek out the wise and those who have walked well and long with Jesus and want to be like them. The Bible tells many stories of men and women who grabbed onto the coat tails of someone 'godlier' than they and hung on.

    - I think of Elisha all but demanding of Elijah, 'Let me inherit a double portion of your spirit' (2 Kings 2:9). Envy? No. He saw something of God in his mentor that he admired and desired.

    - Joshua attached himself to Moses. I wonder what he learned? He no doubt imitated him in many ways.

    - Ruth saw something admirable in broken Naomi: faith in a God that a wreck could return to. That is why Ruth boldly declared, 'Don't urge me to leave you or to turn back from you. Where you go, I will go, and where you stay, I will stay. Your people will be my people and your God my God' (Ruth 1:16).

- Timothy pursued Paul who was pursuing Jesus. Paul came right out and unashamedly said, 'You ... know all about my teaching, my way of life, my purpose, faith, patience, love, endurance ... the things you have heard me say in the presence of many witnesses entrust to reliable people who will also be qualified to teach others' (2 Timothy 3:10; 2:2).

- Mary, when told of the child within her, went to stay with the godly Elizabeth for three months. I wish I could have been a fly on the wall as the older mentored the younger.

It is a noble and good spirit that is teachable, receptive, and ready to see the good work of God in another and, rather than reacting in jealousy ('Why does *he* get picked to be a (fill in the blank) and not *me*?'), runs up alongside and says, 'I want what you have! I like what I see! I am ready to learn!'

I want to venture farther with this. *Every Christian,* no, wait, *every person* has something admirable about them that I can discover if I am humble enough to see it, and that I can seek to imitate, if I am hungry enough to want it. Every person is better at something than I am and, therefore, should be an inspiration to me ... if I am willing to be humble, rather than critical or envious, and learn from them.

Every Christian ... even ones that bug me ... in some wonderful way has a knowledge and experience of Jesus and the Gospel that I know nothing of in my experience and life. There is some gem of grace in them that I should desire to have in me. There is some wonder they have seen in Christ which has produced something good in them which I have yet to see and have in my life. Rather than envy them or write them off, I need to ask, 'Lord Jesus, show me what they know about You that I have yet to discover, and begin to form that within me'.

But admirable traits are not the sole reserve of Christians! God's common grace and goodness is at work in every person's life (Matthew 5:45) and, if I will look, I will see admirable things in not-yet-believers that I should want to find in me. As I write this, a new book, *Talking to GOATS*, has just landed on my doorstep (*GOATS = Greatest of All Time*). It is far from a 'Christian' book. But I can learn much from it. In it, author and sports-caster Jim Gray tells the stories of greats in their respective fields, from Michael Phelps to Michael Jackson, from to Jack Nicklaus to Tom Brady, and many more. I cannot wait to read it.

I want to *learn* from them. I want to be *inspired*. I want to *imitate the good*. What do these 'people of this world' know that this 'person of the light' (*cf.* Luke 16:8) needs to learn?

Do you want to become a well-rounded, mature, fully useful follower of Jesus? Do you want to function in your gifting and grow into areas yet uncharted in your life? Then learn to run with those who are running well. *Everybody* is really good at *something*. Every person has in them something you can desire and endeavour to imitate in your life.

Refuse envy and embrace admiration and see what God might birth and grow in your life.

> *Finally, brothers and sisters, whatever is true, whatever is noble, whatever is right, whatever is pure, whatever is lovely, whatever is admirable – if anything is excellent or praiseworthy – think about such things.* (Philippians 4:8)

RESOLVED.

'People should remain two things throughout their lifetimes:
Curious and teachable.'[1]
(Roger Ebert)

---

[1] Ebert, R, (2009) *I'm a Proud Brainiac,* https://www.rogerebert.com/roger-ebert/im-a-proud-brainiac.

RESOLVED.

Resolved 55

Resolved, to aim to live and to act as I would if I had seen the wonders of Heaven and the torments of Hell.

The time came when the beggar died and the angels carried him to Abraham's side. The rich man also died and was buried. In Hades, where he was in torment, he looked up and saw Abraham far away, with Lazarus by his side. So, he called to him, 'Father Abraham, have pity on me and send Lazarus to dip the tip of his finger in water and cool my tongue, because I am in agony in this fire.'
(Luke 16:22-24)

He will wipe every tear from their eyes. There will be no more death or mourning or crying or pain, for the old order of things has passed away.
(Revelation 21:4)

Friends,

It will do us well to live every day with an eye on eternity. Saints of old did this as a matter of habit, as a spiritual discipline. They lived well in *time* because they were conscious of *eternity*.

Hear John Wesley:

I am a creature of a day, passing through life as an arrow through the air. I am a spirit come from God and returning to God: just hovering over the great gulf; till, a few moments hence, I am no more seen; I drop into an unchangeable eternity! I want to know one thing - the way to heaven; how to land safe on that happy shore.[2]

RESOLVED.

John Bunyan wrote an entire book on eternity entitled *Visions of Heaven and Hell.*

Richard Baxter wrote 800,000 words on eternity in his book *The Saints' Everlasting Rest.*

Charles Spurgeon preached endless sermons on the theme of eternity. It seems that he never preached without an eye on forever. In 1855 he preached a sermon entitled *Heaven and Hell.* Hear him:

> Tonight, I shall, I hope, encourage you to seek the road to heaven. I shall also have to utter some very sharp things concerning the end of the lost in the pit of hell. Upon both these subjects I will try and speak, as God helps me. But I beseech you, as you love your souls, weigh right and wrong this night; see whether what I say be the truth of God. If it be not, reject it utterly, and cast it away; but if it is, at your peril disregard it; for, as you shall answer before God, the great Judge of heaven and earth, it will go ill with you if the words of his servant and of his Scripture be despised.[3]

Such words seem almost quaint today. But perhaps their 'eternal' perspective caused the believers of old to be healthier, more robust, than does our 'time-bound' perspective. The strange fact is that in ignoring eternity, we end up making a mess of time, too. In thinking too little of Heaven and Hell we think too much of this brief life and in so doing we ruin it.

---

[2] Wesley, J. (1747) *Sermons on Several Occasions: Volume One, Preface.*

[3] Spurgeon, C. (1855) *Heaven and Hell,* Sermon 39, delivered on September 4th.

RESOLVED.

As C.S. Lewis observed, and as we have already noted just a little while ago in the 50th *Resolution*:

> Aim for Heaven and you will get Earth 'thrown in'.
> Aim for Earth and you will get neither.[4]

We have much to learn from those who have travelled before us and who lived valiant lives for Jesus. These Christians of old did not simply muse about Heaven and Hell and come up with their own ideas and notions. They drew from their Bibles truths to live and die by. The Bible gives data on eternity. Not exhaustive data, not enough to answer every question and satisfy every curiosity, but enough data to give us cause to set our course, straighten our gait, and to fix our gaze.

Jonathan is resolved to live today as if he has already seen both the wonders of Heaven and the torments of Hell. Let me ask you, how might such a resolve affect you? Do you live with an eye on eternity? Or are your thoughts and sights earth-bound? Do you live as though you have a soul? Are you remembering that you are built to last? When did you last contemplate your eternal destiny? How often do you allow the joys of Heaven and the sorrows of Hell to persuade you away from sin and self and toward Jesus and godliness?

When we read our Bibles, particularly the Gospels, we are confronted with eternity. I think I will capitalize it: Eternity. Jesus spoke often on Heaven and Hell. He often spoke in very graphic terms. When speaking about Eternity perhaps He was speaking literally, perhaps He was using metaphor (word pictures to explain the unexplainable). We cannot be sure, and we do not need to argue the point. Either way, Jesus was loving us enough to speak persuasively to us about realities unseen.

---

[4] Lewis, C. S. (1996). *Joyful Christian*, p.138. New York: Simon and Schuster.

RESOLVED.

Jesus doesn't only reference hell, he describes it in great detail. He says it is a place of eternal torment (Luke 16:23), of unquenchable fire (Mark 9:43), where the worm does not die (Mark 9:48), where people will gnash their teeth in anguish and regret (Mattew13:24), and from which there is no return, even to warn loved ones (Luke 16:19-31). He calls hell a place of 'outer darkness' (Matthew 25:30), comparing it to 'Gehenna' (Matthew 10:28), which was a trash dump outside the walls of Jerusalem where rubbish was burned and maggots abounded. Jesus talks about hell more than he talks about heaven and describes it more vividly. There's no denying that Jesus knew, believed, and warned about the absolute reality of hell. [5]

Why did Jesus do this? Could it be that He wanted us to live today as though we had already seen the torments of Eternity - separated from God and all that is good? Could it be that He wanted us to see the end result of a life of selfish choices and forgetfulness of God?

But Jesus spoke much about Heaven! Take courage! If Hell has no exit, there is a way to avoid it and a sure door to Heaven! Jesus spoke of Heaven as His 'Father's house' (John 14:2), with a place prepared especially for us. He called it 'paradise' (Luke 23:43). He taught that it is a tangible place where we can make secure eternal investments (Luke 18:22). It is a place of comfort (Luke 16:22), joy (Luke 16:7), reward (Luke 6:23). It is 'home'. It is worthy of the costliest repentance (Matthew 18:8). According to Jesus, Heaven, wonderful Heaven, is worth more than the entire world. In fact, to gain the world but to lose one's soul and God's Heaven is an immeasurable loss (Matthew 16:26). Most wonderfully, Heaven is where Jesus is in His eternal Glory with His Father and the Holy Spirit, *and He wants us there*!

---

[5] Schmucker, L. (2017) *The Uncomfortable Subject Jesus Addressed More Than Anyone Else,* The Gospel Coalition, https://www.thegospelcoalition.org/

RESOLVED.

Father, I want those you have given me to be with me where I am,
and to see my glory, the glory you have given me because you
loved me before the creation of the world.
(John 17:24)

Why does Jesus speak to us so earnestly about Heaven? Without question Jesus presses the reality of Eternity upon us because He wants us to run hard after Him. As the old timers used to say, 'There is a Heaven to hope for and a Hell to shun'.

We have a Saviour who has purchased us not just from Hell to Heaven, but, more wonderfully, from sin to Him.

Living today in anticipation of the unspeakable glories to come is transformational. Nothing severs the cord of sin and temptation, nothing is a balm for the wounded heart, nothing adds strength to the stride and zeal to the labour like a glimpse of the wonders of Heaven.

Richard Baxter taught himself to contemplate Eternity for thirty minutes every day. We would do well if we could muster a minute. The benefits would be out of this world.

Eye has not seen, nor ear heard, nor have entered into the heart of
man, the things which God has prepared for those who love him.
(1 Corinthians 2:9 NKJV)

'Once more consider, there is nothing, but heaven,
worth setting our hearts upon.'[6]
(Richard Baxter)

---

[6] Baxter, R. (1814), *The Saints Everlasting Rest*, p.222. Leeds, England: Davies and Booth.

RESOLVED.

Resolved 56

Resolved never to give up the fight against my own heart sins, nor to go easy on them, no matter how long the battle rages or how many times I fail and have to start again.

Finally, be strong in the Lord and in his mighty power.
(Ephesians 6:10)

Brothers and sisters, I do not consider myself yet to have taken hold of it. But one thing I do: forgetting what is behind and straining towards what is ahead, I press on towards the goal to win the prize for which God has called me heavenwards in Christ Jesus.
(Philippians 3:13,14)

If God is for us, who can be against us?... No, in all these things we are more than conquerors through him who loved us.
(Romans 8:31,37)

Friends,

In 1983, upon the advice of the godly, aged evangelist Leonard Ravenhill, I purchased a copy of *The Christian in Complete Armour* by the English pastor William Gurnall (1616-1679). The book is a 1,200 page commentary on just eleven verses of the Bible, Ephesians 6:10-20. Have a look at its subtitle!

A treatise of the saint's war against the Devil, wherein a discovery is made of that grand enemy of God and his people, in his policies, power, seat of his empire, wickedness, and chief design he hath against the saints; a magazine opened, from whence the Christian is furnished with spiritual arms for the battle, helped on with his armour, and taught the use of his weapon; together with the happy issue of the whole war.[1]

I think we can be sure that the book is not destined for the *New York Times* Best-Sellers List.

But I think it might be on *God's* Best-Sellers List.[2]

In those pages Gurnall describes the holy war that believers are engaged in and sets out the do-or-die strategy for victory. The very first directive he offers, is this:

The Christian is to proclaim and prosecute an irreconcilable war against his bosom sins.

Ah! How good we are at 'proclaiming and prosecuting irreconcilable war' against other people's sins! We can go against our wife's sins with a vengeance! We can pray against them and rail on about them to God and to her. We can be relentless against the sins of our political opponents and bothersome neighbours…

But!
                    The only heart I have jurisdiction over is my own!

I wonder if Edwards had well-worn a copy of Gurnall on his shelf (mine is held together with duct-tape), for it seems that Jonathan and William were cut from the same bolt of cloth, both being resolute in going after their own heart-sins (Jon called his heart-sins *corruptions*, Bill called them *bosom-sins*.) I want to have some useful fun here: in

---

[1] Thankfully, James Bell has recently provided us with a far more 'useable', *Daily Readings from The Christian in Complete Armour,* (2015) Moody Press, USA.

[2] John Newton said, 'If I might read only one book beside the Bible, I would choose *The Christian in Complete Armour.'*

commenting on Jon, I want to paraphrase Bill. That way we will get the best of two great men, and just to top it off, I might throw in some Augustine of Hippo, too.

From Gurnall:

> It is our nearest and dearest sins – the ones that lay in our hearts – which we now must war against. What courage it requires to go after your own sin! Especially the deep, darling ones! Think of when God came to Abraham and said, 'Take your son, your only son, whom you love – Isaac – and sacrifice him as a burnt offering on a mountain that I will show you' (Genesis 22:2). So, God comes to you and to me and says, 'Take your lust, your dearest lust, which has at times given such pleasure and laughter, lay your hands upon it and offer it, and delay not!' And! Our lust will not lie so still on the altar as did Isaac! No! It will wriggle and writhe and roar, doing all it can to break you with its passionate cries.
>
> Or it will reason with you: 'I am just a little sin. Spare me. I will not kill your soul! You can have me *and* your Jesus. I will not mind. You can keep me and your ministry. I promise to stay in secret, to be polite, to stay away from the sight and hearing of others. Put me in the deepest, most secret room and I promise to stay there. If only now and then you will embrace me in secret, that will be enough for me. Or … if not that, then at least stay my execution for a short season that we might yet embrace and frolic, if just for a little while!'
>
> All the while that sin pleads: it knows – and we need to know – that secret sins *do not stay in their place and reprieved lusts will one day get their full pardon.*

RESOLVED.

The most valiant warriors of the world have proven to be cowards when dealing with their own hearts! The greatest emperors of ancient Rome, riding in triumph over others, have themselves been conquered by their own lusts and desires. [3]

Indeed,

> *'Better a patient person than a warrior, one with self-control*
> *than one who takes a city'*
> *(Proverbs 16:32).*

But friend! If you will not hear Jonathan or William, will you hear Augustine? He himself confessed that his will, being enslaved, had made a chain for him, and bound him. And from his enslaved will was a lust made; and then when that lust was served it became a habit, and, not resisted, became necessity, 'by which links, as it were, joined together (whence I called it a chain) a hard bondage held me enthralled'.

So, he prayed, 'Lord, make me pure, but not yet!' For he feared God would too soon answer his prayer. Sin was ever whispering, 'Can you part with me?' He was in the habit of hearing sin plead, 'You cannot live without me!'
But then! Grace awakened in him a vision of the beauty of holiness, and he set himself against his own sins. Let me paraphrase his immortal words:

Where I had trembled to go, there appeared unto me the beautiful dignity of Purity. She was serene – where sin was like a tossing sea. She was gay and honest, alluring me to come and not doubt. She stretched forth to receive and embrace me, her holy hands full of

---

[3] My paraphrase from Gurnall, W. (1964) *Christian in Complete Armour,* p. 13. Edinburg: Banner of Truth Trust.

multitudes of good examples of those who had said 'no' to sin and 'yes' to holiness. Here were so many young men and maidens, a multitude of youth and every age, widows and aged virgins. And Purity herself not barren (as Sin had said Purity would be), but a fruitful mother of joyous children, by You, Lord, her Husband. And she smiled on me and with persuasive words said: 'Can you not have what these have? The Lord their God gave me unto them. Why stand in your own strength and in so doing not stand against sin? Cast yourself upon Him. Fear not! He will not withdraw Himself that you should fail and fall. Cast yourself fearlessly upon Him and He will receive you and will heal you'. And I blushed exceedingly, for I was still hearing the muttering of those sins and toys I had loved so long and hung there in suspense. And she again seemed to say, 'Stop your ears against those thy unclean habits and wicked earthly sins. Kill them! They tell you of delights, but they lie. Delight is found only in the way of God'.[4]

There will never be a better day than today to declare war upon your heart sins. All Heaven will come to your aid. You will find an ever-gracious God enabling you by His Spirit and providing His very own Son as your Advocate. Take courage! You may fail a thousand times, but Jesus will never give up on you. Your weakness is no obstacle, but rather a bridge to His grace and power.

"Lord Jesus! *Make* me hate my heart-sins!"

Fight the good fight of the faith. Take hold of the eternal life to which
you were called when you made your good confession…
(1 Timothy 6:12)

---

[4] My paraphrase from Book VIII Augustine, S. (1876). *The Confessions*, pp. 201, 202. Ed: Clark, G. University of Liverpool, England.

303

RESOLVED.

We cannot do better than to hear again from our thinking tinker, John Bunyan. Oh! To recover today a great sense of the greatness and holiness of God, the marred majesty of mankind, and the ruin and tragedy of sin!

'Sin is the dare of God's justice, the rape of His mercy, the jeer of His patience, the slight of His power, and the contempt of His love.' [5]

---

[5] From *John Bunyan's Dying Sayings* in Miscellaneous Pieces, (2021) Google-generated PDF.

RESOLVED.

Resolved 57

Resolved, rather than give way to fear of bad things that might happen or adversities that may come my way, that I will seek instead to make certain that I am doing my duty to God and others and battling for holiness of heart and life. Then I know that I can simply trust God's providence and accept His ordering of my life as good and best.

Now I want you to know, brothers and sisters, that what has happened to me has actually served to advance the gospel.
(Philippians 1:12)

I eagerly expect and hope that I will in no way be ashamed, but will have sufficient courage so that now, as always, Christ will be exalted in my body, whether by life or by death. For to me, to live is Christ and to die is gain. If I am to go on living in the body, this will mean fruitful labour for me. Yet what shall I choose? I do not know! I am torn between the two: I desire to depart and be with Christ, which is better by far.
(Philippians 1:20-23)

Friends,

What a timely *Resolution*! There is a spirit of fear roaming about these days that seems to have taken many captive. Our culture is seeking iron-clad guarantees that we will be safe at all times. Indeed, we are in danger of making safety an idol. And idols *never* deliver what they promise and *always* demand more and more from their devotees.

Jonathan lived in an age of ever-present danger and death. Few made it to old age (Jonathan would die at 54, Sarah, his wife, at 48). A cut could kill you with tetanus. A growling appendix could be lethal.

RESOLVED.

Small-pox, measles, tuberculosis were found in every family. There was no health service to rely upon. There were no paramedics to show up, no 911 (UK, 999), no hospitals, no anaesthetic. Vaccines were few and as dangerous as the illnesses they were designed to prevent (Jonathan actually died of a small-pox vaccine gone wrong). Indeed, there were endless threats to life that today have all but been eliminated by advances in science, medicine, and safety protocols.

But the death rate is still 100% and there are *no* guarantees of safety. In fact, Jesus Himself *guarantees* danger and adversity for everyone who follows Him:

> *I have told you these things, so that in me you may have peace. In*
> *this world you will have trouble. But take heart!*
> *I have overcome the world!*
> (John 16:33)

And Paul's words sound strange - other worldly - to our modern ears:

> *However, I consider my life worth nothing to me; my only aim is*
> *to finish the race and complete the task the Lord Jesus has given*
> *me – the task of testifying to the good news of God's grace.*
> (Acts 20:24)

I wonder what Jonathan would make of we moderns. We are insured to the hilt, vaccinated to the brim, and medicated to the max. We have a pill or a procedure for almost everything. We are buckled and belted, helmeted and pillowed in almost every way possible … Yet we are perhaps the most fearful generation ever. Having moved away from God and toward anything and everything else, we have become prey to a spirit of fear that threatens to totally redefine 'normal' life.

But … do we *love this life* too much?

RESOLVED.

And … do we *trust God* too little?

Jonathan - living in a world fraught with dangers and imminent death - has a simple and powerful strategy for living above fear and walking in divine purpose. Here it is: He is going to pursue Jesus, serve others, and run after holiness of heart and life … then he is going to leave his well-being up to the providential care of his loving and good Heavenly Father. This strategy is not fool-hearty or brash. It is freeing and empowering. This is how Christians are supposed to live. It is *not* how Satan wants us to live. The enemy of our souls wants to isolate us and inject us with fear. He wants us to be more concerned with our own well-being and survival than with God's purposes for our lives. He wants us to miss Life while we are trying to preserve our lives.

A.W. Tozer was right when he said that, in the end, every issue of life is theological – it all boils down to how we view God. God is *good.* The Christian is to make it his consuming passion to know Him, love others, and hate sin. If we are doing that, we can then rest in God's overseeing care for us. We can then say with the Apostle Paul, 'If we live, we live for the Lord; and if we die, we die for the Lord. So, whether we live or die, we belong to the Lord' (Romans 14:8).

COVID. Ah, COVID! It has taught us so much! It certainly has brought the idol of safety out into the open. Of course, we need to be prudent and use all reasonable precautions. God expects us to. Likewise, He expects us to be mindful of one another, caring for the concerns of those around us who are particularly vulnerable. But as a follower of Jesus, I am not called to pursue 'safety first', but 'faithfulness first'. The two are not always mutually exclusive, but they sometimes are. This world does not offer me, or any of us, guaranteed safety. We are living through a storm. We are pilgrims in a desert. We are part of a fallen and broken race living on a fallen and broken planet. Things will go wrong. We will all get sick. We will all die. We cannot

307

RESOLVED.

pursue safety and well-being with more determination than we pursue Jesus. To do so is idolatrous and, again, idols *always* fail to deliver what they promise and are forever asking for more allegiance. They are unfaithful and insatiable.

The Psalmist has wisdom for us here. In Psalm 112 he observes that the 'man who fears the Lord' (that is, the man who regards God above all things) *'has no fear of bad news'* (v.7).

Notice the Psalmist does not say that the man who fears the Lord *will never get* bad news. He says he will not be held captive to the *fear* of bad news. And why? Or better, how? How can he live free from fear? He tells us: *'(His) heart is steadfast, trusting in the Lord'* (v.8).

He knows God and God's character, and that is enough for him. His heart is held fast by a clear view of God.

If you want to see Jonathan's strategy lived out before your eyes, go watch the film *Hacksaw Ridge*. It is a true story. Desmond Doss, a committed Christian and conscientious objector, serves a as medic in the battle of Okinawa. Refusing fear, and defying safety, he relentlessly commits his way to his good God and Saviour as he perseveres under hours of hostile fire, rescuing 75 wounded marines off the field of battle. It was his knowledge of God that allowed him to not love his life more than he loved others and to live bravely in the midst of incredible danger. In doing so Desmond Doss became the only conscientious objector to ever win the Medal of Honour.

Warning! Once we give way to fear and bow at the false altar of safety, discipleship and purposeful living will be all but impossible. Jesus warns us against loving our lives in this world too dearly. If it is fear of COVID that captures us today, it will be something else tomorrow. By all means, take reasonable measures. Buckle your seat belt. Take the medicine. God is not calling us to be foolish and cavalier.

But guard yourself …

The spirit of the age is begging you to preserve yourself in this world at all costs, and Jesus is calling you to lose yourself for His Kingdom and for others. We cannot do both. Which voice are we going to listen to and obey?

Anyone who loves their life will lose it, while anyone who hates their life in this world will keep it for eternal life.
(John 12:25)

'The real purpose of this training,' Mr. Dinnen told me, 'is to teach our students that they can trust God to do what He has said He would do…They cannot be effective if they are afraid or if they doubt that God really means what He says in His Word. So here we teach not so much ideas as trusting.'[1]
(Brother Andrew)

---

[1] Sherill, E., Andrew, B., & Sherrill, J. (2015). *God's Smuggler*, p.70. London: Hachette.

RESOLVED.

Resolved 58

Resolved, when engaging with others in conversation, to refuse a
proud, argumentative, easily angered spirit and to exhibit
instead a loving, cheerful and gracious spirit.

*Let your conversation be always full of grace, seasoned with salt,
so that you may know how to answer everyone.*
(Colossians 4:6)

Let your gentleness be evident to all. The Lord is near.
(Philippians 4:5)

*A gentle answer turns away wrath, but a harsh word stirs up anger.
The tongue of the wise adorns knowledge, but the mouth
of the fool gushes folly.*
(Proverbs 15:1,2)

Dear Friends,

The desire to 'be right' is a wicked desire. It is fuelled by pride and
selfish ambition. It causes conflicts, produces pain, and fractures
friendships. The quarrel in the kitchen is no different in essence from
the fight on the frontlines. For sure the battlefields of the World Wars
broke God's heart, but so do the battlefields of the breakfast table, the
Waffle Wars.

Whether it is an army on the march to war or a strutting brother ready to
risk a friendship for the sake of 'giving a piece of his mind', the same
scripture holds true:

For where you have envy and selfish ambition, there you find

310

RESOLVED.

disorder and every evil practice.
(James 3:16)

Our world is living in a time of barbarism. The desire to shout another down, the willingness to walk away from an argument having 'wiped the floor' with our opponent, the readiness to 'give as good as we get', is all straight from the pit. The common courtesy of listening, understanding, and replying kindly has given way to making sure we get our point across even at the risk of a relationship.

In the midst of this, the Christian is called to a higher standard. He follows the One who, when 'they hurled their insults at him … did not retaliate; when he suffered, … made no threats. Instead, he entrusted himself to him who judges justly' (1 Peter 2:23). Our Lord and Master is the One of whom it was foretold:

He will not shout or cry out, or raise his voice in the streets.
A bruised reed he will not break, and a smouldering
wick he will not snuff out.
(Isaiah 42:2,3)

While we live in a world that loves to shout out and raise the voice and break the bruised reed, we are subjects of another world. Jesus was misunderstood, misrepresented, and misjudged. He did not retaliate. He did not have to win every argument or prove anything to anyone. He entrusted all things to His Father, and that was enough for Him.

We are called to be like *Him,* not like our culture.

What a freedom it is to not have to be right all the time! Hooray! What a relief it is to not have to always have the final word! Phew! What a peace and joy it is to be misunderstood and just give it to Jesus and walk in peace with our brothers! Indeed, the Bible speaks of a 'peace

311

that passes all understanding' (Philippians 4:7), but we also have a 'peace that passes all *mis*understanding'!

We have been taught to 'win at all costs' but the Bible actually teaches that it 'is to one's honour to avoid strife' because only a 'fool is quick to quarrel' (Proverbs 20:3). Many times, I have walked away from a hot conversation, bloodied sword in hand, congratulating myself for my deadly duelling skills, when in fact I have either:

1) made a total fool of myself or
2) wounded my brother for whom Christ died.

Paul had to admonish the worldly, carnal, babyish Corinthians with the simple but penetrating question:

> *Why not rather be wronged?*
> (1 Corinthians 6:7)

There is a great peace in cultivating an *unoffendable spirit.* An old Cornish farmer once said these wise words to me, ''Tis as much a sin to *take* offense as it is to *give* offense!' In order to grow such a spirit, I need to know that I am safe in Jesus and, therefore, I do not have to walk around hurt and wounded all the time, ready to strike out with venomous words. I can *leave it.* I also need to view every single person through the lens of the Gospel (2 Corinthians 5:15) and seek to see them as Jesus does – redeemed or redeemable, eternal beings of inestimable value to God. Those people I rehearse arguments with in my head (interesting how I never lose my imaginary arguments) are not just the bothersome nuisances I see them as, but people worth the blood of Jesus Christ.

There is great spiritual value in praying for a sweet spirit. To ask Jesus regularly to fill me with sweetness and tenderness toward others, especially those with whom I disagree, is actually vital spiritual warfare. In addition to my old Cornish farmer named above, I also used to pray regularly with an old-time Arkansas Pentecostal Preacher (you bet I did!) whose words I related earlier but will reprise because they are so good! This dear man used to pray every week 'Oooo Lord! When someone kicks me, let them get honey all over their foot!' (followed by some words I could not understand...). I learned a lot from that old preacher!

Oh, for a sweet, unoffendable, Jesus-protected spirit that does not strive and argue and wrangle with others! If I am going to be *useful* to Jesus, I simply do not have the time to embroil myself in trying to prove my point, be the expert (again), or be right – unless it is truly a *Gospel issue*. Indeed, for any lesser issue, I must not. So, Paul commanded Timothy:

> *Don't have anything to do with foolish and stupid arguments,*
> *because you know they produce quarrels. And the Lord's servant*
> *must not be quarrelsome but must be kind to everyone,*
> *able to teach, not resentful.*
> (2 Timothy 2:24)

And Peter commands us all:

> *Always be prepared to give an answer to everyone who asks you*
> *to give the reason for the hope that you have. But do this with*
> *gentleness and respect, keeping a clear conscience, so that those*
> *who speak maliciously against your good behaviour in Christ*
> *may be ashamed of their slander.*
> (1 Peter 3:15,16)

Believers in Jesus! We need to rise above the spirit of the age. The world has sneezed and the Church has caught the cold! But it was not for nothing that the Lord gave us *two* ears and *one* mouth (old Cornish farmer again). Indeed:

> *My dear brothers and sisters, take note of this: Everyone should*
> *be quick to listen, slow to speak and slow to become angry,*
> (James 1:19)

Jonathan resolves not merely *not* to fall into the cesspit of argument, he actually wants his words to be life-giving. He desires that his speech 'exhibit instead a loving, cheerful and gracious spirit'. He wants people to leave his presence edified, built up, blessed, refreshed. (Lord Jesus! I want that too!) This is right on! We are needed as channels of love and blessing in an angry, blaming culture. We are to be tender where the world is tough and sweet where the world is bitter. Our words are to be 'always full of grace, seasoned with salt'. Salt brings flavour, pleasure, purity wherever it goes. In a recipe, its presence is unmistakable, its absence inexcusable.

Jesus will help us. We do not have to do anything in the Christian life in our own strength, including this. We dare not even try. As we increasingly surrender ourselves unto Him, He will work His sanctifying grace in us. I would be surprised if Jonathan read much of St. Francis of Assisi. But I would not be surprised if he read, and prayed, this timeless prayer of the humble 12th century Italian:

> Lord, make me an instrument of your peace.
> Where there is hatred, let me bring love.
> Where there is offence, let me bring pardon.
> Where there is discord, let me bring union.
> Where there is error, let me bring truth.
> Where there is doubt, let me bring faith.
> Where there is despair, let me bring hope.
> Where there is darkness, let me bring your light.

RESOLVED.

Where there is sadness, let me bring joy.
O Master, let me not seek as much
to be consoled as to console,
to be understood as to understand,
to be loved as to love,
for it is in giving that one receives,
it is in self-forgetting that one finds,
it is in pardoning that one is pardoned,
it is in dying that one is raised to eternal life.

(Giovanni di Pietro di Bernardone, *aka*, Francis of Assisi,
1181-1226)

Resolved 59

Resolved, when I am feeling irked, when my attitude is bad, when I am aware of emotions of anger or feelings of ill nature, to act in exactly the opposite manner to my feelings. Even if it seems that it will be to my disadvantage to not act according to my negative feelings, it is always best to obey God and act in a gracious manner, not only when I feel like doing so.

For the grace of God has appeared that ... teaches us to say 'No' to ungodliness and worldly passions, and to live self-controlled, upright and godly lives in this present age ...
(Titus 2:11,12)

Friends,

If I waited until I 'felt like it', I would:

>   rarely get up early to read my Bible and pray,
>   often ignore my wife's needs and just think of myself,
>   *never* go to the gym.

The popular thought these days is that the *will* must follow the *feelings*. People think that *emotions* should determine *actions*. If I do not feel like doing something, then I need not do it. ('Unless my heart tells me to do something, I should not do it' can sometimes be the 'Christian' way of saying the same thing.) In a culture that is collapsing inwards, being 'true to myself' (often code for 'doing what I feel like doing') has become the supreme virtue.

Older Christians knew nothing of this way of thinking. To them, almost across the board, the *will* was to lead the way and the emotions were told to fall in step. The will was subject to the Word, and the 'affections' (feelings) were expected to comply … without arguing. Feelings were told to follow, never allowed to lead. This does not mean that our feelings, our affections, our emotions are not important! But it does mean that they cannot rule us.

We do not wait on our feelings before we go forward. We obey God's Word and tell our feelings to get in line or be quiet. Actions precede attitudes. Feelings and attitudes are to be *subject* to, never *sovereign* over, the will which is itself subject to Jesus and His Word. A godly person who taught me this was Henry Scougal (1650-1678) in his remarkable book *The Life of God in the Soul of Man.* I had the privilege of re-writing that wonderful book a couple years ago, and here is my rendition of Henry's vital teaching:

> If we are having trouble getting our inner life changed, then we can begin with our outer life. I know that many say that without the heart, the actions are hypocritical, but that is not always the case. The heart can actually follow the actions. It can engage once the actions are engaged. In other words, there may be times when we do our duty, regardless of our hearts, and we find the heart follows the will. If we are not on fire with love towards God, then let's not just be passive and wait. Let's do what we are commanded to do! We can give God our best whether we feel like it or not. … External actions can have value in moving you toward a warm heart. … It is always good and right to do what we can, knowing that God will have mercy on us and help us with even our weak efforts. [1]

Like Henry's advice, Jonathan's *Resolution* is strange to our modern way of thinking. But it is actually refreshing and brings hope with it. He is telling us that we need not be held captive to miserable

---

[1] Gillespie, J. (2017). *The New Life of God in the Soul of Man,* p.102, Myrrh Books.

attitudes, bitter feelings, sour emotions, and cold hearts. Even if we think that returning blessing for someone's bad actions toward us will not serve our immediate advantage, Jonathan instructs us that it is *always* the best path to act in a gracious manner. This is exactly what Jesus teaches us to do!

> *If you love those who love you, what reward will you get? Are not*
> *even the tax collectors doing that? And if you greet only your own*
> *people, what are you doing more than others?*
> *Do not even pagans do that?*
> (Matthew 5:46-48)

Clearly Jesus is teaching us here to rise above our feelings and emotions and act according to the grace that we have received from our Heavenly Father. Remember this: Jesus will help us to say 'no' to our miserable, selfish, moping, morose selves and say a hearty 'yes' to moving in the opposite direction. We are *never* asked to move in our own strength. But we need to get over the notion – because it is erroneous – that our feelings and moods need to set the direction for our wills to follow. No! Listen to Paul on this:

> *We demolish arguments and every pretension that sets itself up*
> *against the knowledge of God, and we take captive every*
> *thought to make it obedient to Christ.*
> (2 Corinthians 10:5)

A few years ago, I became very deeply convicted that my irritability was a sin. Giving in to morose moods and sour attitudes was dishonouring to the God who saved me and promised to pour His Joy into me (John 15:11). I had allowed Satan to build a stronghold in my life by failing to battle for joy and by caving into the mood of the moment. Failing to 'demolish arguments' in my own head and not bothering to take my every though captive to Christ had allowed the enemy to gain ground in my inner life. All the while Christ Jesus had been giving me all grace to deny self (which includes self-pity, self-hatred, self-seeking, self-introspection, etc.). 'Going into my cave', brooding, thinking the worst of others, responding irritably, sarcasm, fault-finding, holding grudges, being irked, and peevishness are all grace-denying ways of worshipping at the throne of myself. What a painful - then blessed - revelation it was to see all this! Dismantling this stronghold is proving to be a long, but vital, work. But I have no choice if I am to be a faithful follower of the One whose 'divine power has given [me] everything [I] need for a godly life through [my] knowledge of him who called [me] by his own glory and goodness' (2 Peter 1:3).

Jonathan's advice is revolutionary in today's world: Forget yourself and *go do the opposite to how you feel.*

This is *not* hypocritical.
> It is spiritual warfare.
>> It is taking a stand against yourself.
>>> It is agreeing with God …
>>>> … It is *willing* instead of *wallowing.*

And, again, it is the consistent testimony of endless Jesus-followers, who have already run well and finished the course, that feelings will follow when they are told - in no uncertain terms - that they are not in charge. It was Elizabeth Elliot who astutely observed that so much of what we call 'struggling' is simple delayed obedience.[2] If you lie in bed waiting until you feel ready to get up and get going, you might end up spending the day lusting and loafing. If you nurse your hurts rather than forgive the offender, they are going to grow until they cripple you. If you stroke your irks rather than repent of them and go serve that irksome person, they will grow until the relationship is ruined. It

---

[2] Elliot, E. (2013) *Leaving Self Behind*, Radio Broadcast.

RESOLVED.

is *always* right to respond in grace and obedience and let Jesus work out the results. It is *never* right to respond according to your sinful nature and try to engineer the result *you* want. You are on far safer ground when you respond to a bothersome person, or a destructive feeling, with humility and grace, trusting Jesus to fix it, than you are to give in to your lower self by trying to 'fix it' in a sinful way.

I think I can honestly say that whenever I have acted out of anger, moved by irked, judgmental, irritated or lazy feelings, *I have never been glad that I have done so the next day.* Obeying my sinful, selfish feelings has never produced a good, peaceful, and godly result. Why? 'Because human anger [or irritability, or laziness, or moodiness, or bad attitude] does not produce the righteousness that God desires' (James 1:20).

Lord Jesus! Help me to deny myself, get off the throne, stop feeling entitled, quit following my moods, and man up! Thanks, Jonathan for loving me enough to 'put me in my place' (UK) / 'whip my butt' (USA).

> *Better a patient person than a warrior, one with*
> *self-control than one who takes a city.*
> (Proverbs 16:32)

> 'Refuse self-pity. Refuse it absolutely. It is a deadly thing
> with power to destroy you.'[3]
> (Elizabeth Elliot)

> 'If I can in any way slight another in conversation, or even in
> thought, then I know nothing of Calvary's love.'[4]
> (Amy Carmichael)

---

[3] Elliot, E. (2002), *Passion and Purity*, Revell.
[4] Carmichael, A. (2011) *If,* p. 15. CLC Publications.

Resolved 60

Resolved, whenever I begin to lose my peace within, when my heart is the least bit uneasy, or whenever my outward behaviour begins to be inconsistent with being a follower of Jesus, that I will waste no time in subjecting myself to a strict examination.

Why, my soul, are you downcast? Why so disturbed within me? Put your hope in God, for I will yet praise him,
my Saviour and my God.
(Psalm 42:11)

Dear Friends,

Roy Hession alarmed me with these words: 'Everything that disturbs the peace of God in our hearts is sin, no matter how small it is, and no matter how little like sin it may at first appear to be.'[1]

Remember what Jonathan is teaching us: diligence is not anti-grace. Being careful with your heart is not legalism.

It is a proper response to being delivered from the ruin of sin.

Jonathan Edwards did not believe that he was saved by works. He knew he could not perform his way into Heaven. He fully understood that salvation was totally a free gift of God's grace that could never be earned or deserved.

But he did not cheapen the Gospel. He knew he was saved from sin to holiness. He knew that grace was not license for laziness but power for purpose. He knew that it was easier to head sin off at the pass than it

---

[1] Hession, R. (2016). *The Calvary Road*, p.8. CLC Publications.

was to watch it whizz by and then try to chase after it, lasso it, and wrestle it to the ground. He knew sin unchecked could run wild.

Look at this *Resolution* carefully. Jonathan does not want to give a head start to destructive thoughts or behaviour. Come with me to Joshua chapter 7, to the secret (or so he thought) sin of a careless man named Achan:

> *Achan replied, 'It is true! I have sinned against the Lord, the God of Israel. This is what I have done: when I saw in the plunder a beautiful robe from Babylonia, two hundred shekels of silver and a bar of gold weighing fifty shekels, I coveted them and took them. They are hidden in the ground inside my tent, with the silver underneath.*
> (vss. 20,21)

Do you see a progression here? If you remember the story, Israel went up against Jericho and won a resounding victory by the grace and goodness of God. But! They were clearly commanded to touch *none* of the pagan artifacts of that city. Achan acted secretly, stealing some of their articles of devotion. But, ah! Sin never stays secret! You can trace its origin, but rarely predict its destination. How foolish was Achan! How wise he would have been if he had examined his own heart and wasted no time in redirecting his course!

Hear Achan's own words:

This is what I have done:

1) *I saw.* No crime yet! Achan! Check your heart! Look away now! Listen to your inner unease! Your behaviour is soon to be inconsistent with your beliefs. Get out of there!

322

RESOLVED.

2) *I coveted.* Crime is now being committed at heart level! God sees the heart. God sees the crime. But! There is still time to flee. Sin is starting to gallop. Get out of the way! Repent *now*.

3) *I took.* Now we have gone from eyes to heart to hands. Achan! You have suppressed your conscience! Sin *never* stays put. You must slay it, or it will slay you. At this point…. he still could have put those trinkets back, or thrown them in a well, or something, and run away!

4) *I hid.* Secrecy. Dishonesty. Cover up. Lying. Can't sleep. Can't eat. Can't look you in the eye. 'What's up with Achan?' the friends say. Sin has a grip on Achan's soul.

If you know the story you will know that Achan's sin affected not only Achan, not only his family, but all Israel.

Again, you may know sin's origin, but rarely can you imagine its final impact. But be sure of this: Whether the rill turns to a raging river or a meandering mudflow, it will be a broader and deeper destruction than you ever dreamed of.

Better stop sin in its infancy. Better not give it any ground.

The psalmist, in Psalm 42 enquires within, 'Why are you downcast, soul?' He knows there must be a reason for his loss of joy. He knows he needs to find out why his peace has left. Did he take a wrong turn? Has he fallen out with a friend? Has he ignored God? Is there a little idol running around working mischief in his inner life? 'Why is my inner life so disturbed?' Whatever the discovery, the remedy is *Godward.* 'Put your hope in God!' Get back on track with Jehovah. Whether it is attitude or action, the answer is *always* to move toward God, never to step away and into the shadows. Here, in the Bible, we find a God who, when offended, invites us to approach. Imagine that! The Bible tells us of a *welcoming* God: in it we learn of a *willing* God.

323

RESOLVED.

Roy Hession, in his amazing book, *The Calvary Road*, cited above, helped me understand that the peace of God in my heart is meant to act as an umpire for my life.

Look at the verse below:

And the peace of God, which transcends all understanding, will
guard your hearts and your minds in Christ Jesus.
(Philippians 4:7)

Roy teaches that when the peace of God is nowhere to be found, it is as though an umpire has blown a whistle and called foul! When my peace is gone, it is time to stop and take stock. 'Why has the Holy Spirit blown the whistle? What is the offence?' It is *not* time to be pig-headed and just keep going in the same direction. It is a sign of spiritual growth and maturity to learn to listen to your heart and to the Holy Spirit within. It is a sign of spiritual health to learn to be sensitive to your loss of peace, your inward unease, recognizing that it is God addressing you in His love and seeking to halt your way before you bring yourself to trouble, or even disaster.

We do not have to stumble from crisis to crisis. We do not have to leave a trail of tears behind us. We do not have to have a life that forever seems to resemble a demolition project more than a building site. The life of a Jesus-follower is a life of many little corrections, numerous repentances, countless trips to the cross, not a few tears, all followed by renewed joy and vigour as sin is cleansed, attitudes are changed, relationships are restored, and peace is refreshed. We must never be hesitant to allow God to lead us in a strict examination if it helps us to discover sin, repent of it before a gracious Jesus, and know the cleansing that His atoning blood continually gives.

Search me, God, and know my heart; test me and know my

RESOLVED.

anxious thoughts. See if there is any offensive way in me,
and lead me in the way everlasting.
(Psalm 139:23,24)

But if we walk in the light, as he is in the light, we have fellowship
with one another, and the blood of Jesus, his Son,
purifies us from all sin.
(1 John 1:7)

'This peace is to 'rule' our hearts, or (a more literal translation)
'be the referee' in our hearts. When the referee blows his whistle
at a football match, the game has to stop, a foul has been
committed. When we lose our peace, God's referee in our hearts
has blown his whistle! Let us stop immediately, ask God to show
us what is wrong, put by faith the sin He shows us under the
Blood of Jesus, and then peace will be restored, and we shall go
on our way with our cups running over.'[2]
(Roy Hession)

---

[2] Hession, R. (2016). *The Calvary Road*, p.8. CLC Publications. See also
Resolved 35.

RESOLVED.

Resolved 61

Resolved to rise above laziness. Whether laziness is tempting me
to let my mind wander away from being fixed upon God and His
grace or inciting me toward apathetic neglect of my duties, I
realize it is always best to keep my mind on the Lord
and my hands to my calling.

Lazy hands make for poverty, but diligent hands bring wealth.
(Proverbs 10:4)

Set your minds on things above, not on earthly things.
(Colossians 3:2)

*We want each of you to show this same diligence to the very end,
so that what you hope for may be fully realized. We do not want
you to become lazy, but to imitate those who through faith and
patience inherit what has been promised.*
(Hebrews 6:11,12)

Dear Friends,

Goodness, it is hard to imagine Jonathan Edwards struggling to
overcome apathy! My first thought upon wrestling with this *Resolution*
is simply: If Jonathan has an issue with laziness, where on earth does
that leave the rest of us?

The fact of the matter is, none of us are machines. Jonathan Edwards
was not a machine. The Lord Jesus knows this. The fact is that we can
all lapse into apathy and the temptation is there to yawn our way
through an hour or a day, or an entire season of life. But before we
explore the problem and excise the root cause, I think we need to draw a
sharp demarcation between laziness and legitimate rest and re-creation,

for we have an enemy who will always lead us to extremes. Anything to ruin us. As the old (Cornish farmer again!) saying goes: If Satan cannot rock us to sleep, he will ride us like a horse. Either will do. Both will render us useless, and that is his sinister goal.

So first, a look at rest and re-creation. We need look no farther than Jesus Himself for the model and the balance. Here is the One who was able to say of Himself:

> *Very truly I tell you, the Son can do nothing by himself; he can do*
> *only what he sees his Father doing, because whatever*
> *the Father does the Son also does.*
> (John 15:19)

He lived and breathed His Father's will. I think we are on safe ground to say that Jesus did not succumb to laziness on the one hand or drivenness on the other. He worked hard (go read Mark chapter 1!) and He took time off. Look at Jesus in the midst of a very busy stretch:

> *And he said unto them, 'Come ... apart into a desert place, and*
> *rest a while', for there were many coming and going,*
> *and they had no leisure so much as to eat.*
> (Mark 6:31KJV)

My old Cornish farmer friend put it to me this way: 'Jesus will have you "come apart", lest you come apart!'

Also, Jesus kept the Sabbath as a day of rest. (Remember that quaint old gift from our loving Heavenly Father?)[1] Rest, including Sabbath, would have been part of the rhythm of His God-guided life. And He invites us into His rest:

---

[1] **Resolved 38**.

327

RESOLVED.

Come to me, all you who are weary and burdened, and I will give you rest. Take my yoke upon you and learn from me, for I am gentle and humble in heart, and you will find rest for your souls. For my yoke is easy and my burden is light.
(Matthew 11:28-30)

So, we explore laziness against the background of a wonderful Saviour who invites us to His rest and to a life rhythmed by work and rest. Laziness can be fuelled by exhaustion. I am sure that if we allowed our lives to be shaped by a work-rest rhythm, which would include a regular Sabbath, we would go a long way toward conquering laziness and apathy.

Now on to laziness. We need to see laziness as sin. It is wasting a treasure. Jesus addressed laziness directly in His story of the servant who buried his master's treasure in the ground rather than investing it. He called that servant 'wicked and lazy' (Matthew 25:26). Ouch! Sloth is seen in Catholicism as one of the Seven Deadly Sins. Our word comes from a Latin lexeme which means 'to not care'. It is interesting that we have named a ponderously slow-moving creature, that spends most of its life hanging upside down in trees, after this sin. The tree sloth might be cute and cuddly but the sofa sloth is a tragedy. For Jesus has created us for purpose and redeemed us from sin (including sloth) for adventure and meaning.

For we are God's handiwork, created in Christ Jesus to do good works, which God prepared in advance for us to do.
(Ephesians 2:10)

Notice with me that Jonathan combats sloth not just in his deeds, but in his thinking as well. He does not want his mind to be upside-down, where his thoughts can just dribble downward. He wants it right-side up, remaining on God and His grace and goodness. He wants to

328

discipline himself to 'take every thought captive', making each one 'obedient to Christ' (2 Corinthians 10:5). He aims to direct his thinking upward, to keep it focused, not allowing it to leak out like an unconscious drip:

Since, then, you have been raised with Christ, set your hearts on things above, where Christ is seated at the right hand of God. Set your minds on things above, not on earthly things.
(Colossians 3:1,2)

While I cannot present myself as 'Exhibit A' of diligence, I want to venture to tell you what I have learned / am learning to do. I do find this to be a never-ending battle, and the enticement of inertia is constant, but I offer the following, knowing that there are many examples who will be better than I!

First, I need to recognize that I am not a machine, and that some days will be better than others. On some days, it will be easier to 'get after it' than others. Jesus understands this, because He made me, and He has saved me by His grace, not by my diligence. No guilt and condemnation are attached to the normal reality of human frailty.

Then, I need to know that while He has indeed saved me by His grace, it is for purpose and meaning. Satan does not want me to walk in purpose. Jesus' purpose is in fact 'good, pleasing and perfect' (Romans 12:2), and for me to submit myself to my Heavenly Father and refuse apathy will bring me into joy and fulness. I will never be happy letting my thoughts drip away and ignoring my God-given design.

Finally, I cannot do anything without Jesus. I have learned that I have to ask my Wonderful One to help me walk in His design for me *every day* and He is faithful to empower and enable me. I *cannot* overcome the inertia of sin and self unless I appeal to God - Father, Son, and Holy

RESOLVED.

Spirit - to supernaturally enable me... and He is a willing and ready Help to me! He never wearies of my asking or fails to empower for His service. *I mean that.*

Overcoming apathy and walking in purpose is, for me, often a matter of simply 'doing the next thing'. It does not have to be amazing. I just need to get going: do the dishes, walk the dog. Purpose might not start with a mission trip to the Congo, but it might end up there. It is more likely to start with getting off the sofa, taking the garbage out, and going to check on my neighbour. What as-yet-to-be-realized purposes and treasures are just waiting for you to discover and enjoy to the Glory of God and the good of others? Might you be overdue in asking Jesus for yet another helping of grace (He has plenty!) to get going?

Therefore, I urge you, brothers and sisters, in view of God's mercy, to offer your bodies as a living sacrifice, holy and pleasing to God – this is your true and proper worship. Do not conform to the pattern of this world, but be transformed by the renewing of your mind. Then you will be able to test and approve what God's will is – his good, pleasing and perfect will.
(Romans 12:1,2)

'Do the next thing.'[2]
(Elizabeth Elliot)

'Take yourself by the scruff of the neck and shake off your incarnate laziness.'[3]
(Oswald Chambers)

---

[2] From an anonymous poem referenced by Elizabeth Elliot in her series of radio talks, *Gateway to Joy,* (1991), found at https://elisabethelliot.org/resource-library/gateway-to-joy/do-the-next-thing-practical-holy-living/

[3] Chambers, O. *My Utmost for His Highest.* ' Can You Come Down?' April 16th.

Resolved 62

Resolved to be ever ruled by the Law of Love, cheerfully and willingly serving others, but not so much to please people, as to please the Lord Himself, knowing that the good that a Christian does to a person in need is simply enabled by the Lord and is in the end done unto the Lord.

[O]bey your earthly masters with respect and fear, and with sincerity of heart, just as you would obey Christ. Obey them not only to win their favour when their eye is on you, but as slaves of Christ, doing the will of God from your heart. Serve wholeheartedly, as if you were serving the Lord, not people, because you know that the Lord will reward each one for whatever good they do, whether they are slave or free.
(Ephesians 6:5-8)

Dear Friends,

Are you a 'people server' or a 'people pleaser'? There is a big difference!

Martin Luther came out with a zinger when he rightly reminded us that, '[a] Christian man is the most free lord of all and subject to none; a Christian man is the most dutiful servant of all and subject to everyone'.[1]

Free and subject to no-one.
   Slave and servant of all.
      A servant of Christ who will bow in homage to no person.
      A servant of Christ who will wash the feet of any person.

---

[1] Luther, M. (2008). *The Freedom of a Christian: Concerning Christian Liberty*, p.1. Pennsylvania: 1517 Media, Fortress Press.

RESOLVED.

Jonathan resolves to be ruled by one great law, the Law of Love. Jesus summed up the Law of Love - the *Royal* Law of Love – as:

> *Love the Lord your God with all your heart and with all your soul and with all your mind and with all your strength. The second is this: Love your neighbour as yourself. There is no commandment greater than these.*
> (Mark 12:30,31)

Augustine of Hippo summed it up, perhaps with a wry smile:

> Love, and do what you please.[2]

That is radical freedom. That is radical slavery.

The Christian life is meant to be *simple*. I did not say *easy*. It is meant to be uncomplicated. I am to be ruled not by a ledger of edicts, but by the Law of Love. The love of Christ is to motivate, constrain, control, and empower me. But hear this: It is *supernatural*. It is the result of the regenerating act of God's Spirit filling the heart of the believer. I *cannot* love without divine empowerment. But God is ready and willing to empower! He *wants* to enable. He *wants* to give what He commands. He *never* asks without enabling. We must be sure of His heart in this matter.

When we are ruled by love, it is inevitable that our lives will spill over into service for others. I can ask God to make my dry and crusty heart to be like a river in flood-stage, ready to burst its banks in love and service towards others.

---

[2] Augustine of Hippo, Seventh Homily on 1 John 4:4-12.

RESOLVED.

The Royal Law of Love is not just an idea or a theory. It is a life lived for the sake of others …

But … (and this is a *big* But!) …

…with the goal of pleasing the Lord, and not those whom we serve.

If we do not get this clear and right, we will become slaves, not to those whom we serve, but to the *opinions* of those whom we serve. Being slaves to their opinions, to what they *think* of our service will eventually and inevitably lead to bitterness and sourness in our service.

Oh, please hear this! The Royal Law of Love leads us to *serve* people, but not to be people *pleasers.* Being a people pleaser is an impossible bondage. People pleasers serve out of obligation. Soon, service becomes a drudgery and resentment sets in. We feel unappreciated. It all becomes a chore. Relationships suffer and the spirit sags.

It is nice to be appreciated, and by all means we should show appreciation toward those who serve us, but when we serve people with a *goal* of being appreciated, we are setting ourselves up for bitterness and disappointment. Think about this: when we serve others to gain their approval, we are actually … serving *ourselves.* People may see and appreciate, or they may not. *Their* opinion must not be our goal.

Here is the freedom formula in the Royal Law of Love:

We serve *people* with the goal to please the *Lord.*

Let me write that again with different emphasis:

We *serve* people with the *goal* to please the Lord.

RESOLVED.

And ... good news ... God is easy to please! He is far easier to please than people.

He is impossible to impress. (Don't even try. He made the Universe.)

But he is easy to please.[3] (For He loves us through His perfect Son.)

When we serve with an eye toward our Heavenly Father, we see His smile and bright countenance towards us. He is moment by moment empowering, we are moment by moment receiving. He has already ordained the work; we are now walking in the work. He has brought the need to our attention; we are obeying Him in serving to meet that need. The people we serve may or may not 'get it'. They may or may not appreciate what we do. You might please them, or you might not. They may be quite hard to please. You might feel as though you never can do enough.

But ... (another *big* But!)...

God is not like them (or us!) and the Law of Love sets you free from trying to please them. It invites you to serve with an eye to your wonderful Heavenly Father who, through your union with His Son, is happy to say to *you* the very words He said to Jesus:

> *This is my Son [daughter], whom I love; with him*
> *[her] I am well pleased.*
> (Matthew 3:17)

Breathe this in. Stop striving. This entire Christian life is an enterprise in grace. We live in the unmerited favour of our super-abundant God and we serve in the crystal current of that favour.

---

[3] See also **Resolved 27.**

RESOLVED.

He sees.

He smiles.

He appreciates.

He rewards.

How many dear mothers need to know this! How many children serving their elderly parents need this good news! How many pastors, physicians, teachers need to be set free from the devil-inspired tyranny of trying to make others happy with their man-pleasing service!

I am called to love God and to love others. And I can do this because God loved me first. And His divine love can and will spill over and out into service for others. And He will see that service. And He will be pleased with it for He ordained it from the start.

Let's go live, love, serve, all under the watchful and smiling face of our Heavenly Father.

Let me leave you with a mini feast of truths to confirm this within you. Please, please feed on them:

His divine power has given us everything we need for a godly life
through our knowledge of him who called us by his own
glory and goodness.
(2 Peter 1:3)

For we are God's handiwork, created in Christ Jesus to do good
works, which God prepared in advance for us to do.
(Ephesians 2:10)

RESOLVED.

But when you give to the needy, do not let your left hand know what your right hand is doing, so that your giving may be in secret. Then your Father, who sees what is done in secret, will reward you.
(Matthew 6:3,4)

Slaves, obey your earthly masters in everything; and do it, not only when their eye is on you and to curry their favour, but with sincerity of heart and reverence for the Lord. Whatever you do, work at it with all your heart, as working for the Lord, not for human masters, since you know that you will receive an inheritance from the Lord as a reward. It is the Lord Christ you are serving.
(Colossians 3:22-24)

'One of the principal rules of religion is to lose no occasion of serving God. And, since he is invisible to our eyes, we are to serve him in our neighbour, which he receives as if done to himself in person, standing visibly before us.' [4]
(John Wesley)

---

[4] Wesley, J. (1844) *A Plain Account of Christian Perfection,* p.53. New York: G. Lane & P.P. Sandford.

RESOLVED.

Resolved 63

Resolved, understanding that there is not, nor never has been, one person who in every respect is a shining and true example of a faithful follower of Jesus, but imagining that at a given time there is *one* such person in all of the earth, I resolve - with all my strength –
to live as though I might be that one.

Teach me Your way, O Lord; I will walk in Your truth; unite my heart to fear Your name. I will praise You, O Lord my God, with all my heart, and I will glorify Your name forevermore. For great is Your mercy toward me, and You have delivered my soul from the depths of Sheol.
(Psalm 86:11-13)

Not that I have already obtained all this, or have already arrived at my goal, but I press on to take hold of that for which Christ Jesus took hold of me.
(Philippians 3:12)

Dear Jesus-Following Friend,

In the 1870's the American evangelist D.L. Moody was visiting and preaching in England when he was arrested by an observation from the British preacher Henry Varley: 'Moody, the world has yet to see what God will do with a man fully consecrated to him.'

Moody later recalled how those words pierced his heart:

Ah … those were the words sent to my soul … from the Living God. As I crossed the wide Atlantic, the boards of the deck of the vessel were engraved with them, and when I reached Chicago, the very paving stones seemed marked with 'Moody, the world has yet to see what God will do with a man fully consecrated to him.' [1]

Now I love that story and have for many years been affected by it for my good. But I have to temper it with some wisdom born of years following Jesus, wisdom that is found in Jonathan's magnificent *Resolution* given at the top of the page.

So, in wanting Jonathan's *Resolution* - and Varley's words to Moody - to have their full affect upon us, please consider first the following truths:

- No-one has ever been, or will ever be, fully consecrated to Jesus in this life. In the best hearts there are always dark corners where sin lurks and battlefronts yet to be conquered and claimed for Jesus.

- The most consecrated followers of Jesus are actually desperately aware of their remaining sin, of the divisions in their hearts, and of the inconsistencies of their lives.

- We are not saved by being fully consecrated to Jesus, but by His mercy to ruined sinners like us who have approached Him with weak, faulty faith.

- As our Saviour and Shepherd, *Jesus* is fully consecrated to *us* and that is why we can be assured that we are safe in His care in the midst of our broken, flawed discipleship.

Those things being said: It is *a good thing* to want to be, and to strive to

---

[1] https://www.christianitytoday.com/history/issues/issue-25/world-has-yet-to-see.html

RESOLVED.

be, as consecrated, as all out for Jesus, as we can be this side of Heaven. The grace of God is not given that we might be lazy and, as the hymnist said, '*be carried to the skies on flowery beds of ease ...*'[2] The grace of God, His undeserved favour poured out to us through Jesus, not only brings salvation from the *penalty* of sin, but from its *power*. We are supernaturally given a new life and, therefore, we cannot help but begin to want to please God and to walk in a new way. Salvation is not just 'going to Heaven' (or 'not going to Hell'). It is the ongoing restoration of the Image of God within us which was so tragically marred by sin. It, therefore, follows that a true Child of Grace will *want* to be as like Jesus as she can be this side of Heaven and will want to be all that she can be for Jesus during her brief sojourn here on Earth.

All of the Christian's life is sustained and fuelled by the grace and power of God. None of this is of us. But that grace and power is given that we may live new lives, under the Lordship of Jesus, for new purpose. Hear the Apostle Paul:

And he died for all, that those who live should no longer live for themselves but for him who died for them and was raised again.
(2 Corinthians 5:15)

I have been crucified with Christ and I no longer live, but Christ lives in me. The life I now live in the body, I live by faith in the Son of God, who loved me and gave himself for me.
(Galatians 2:20)

To this end I strenuously contend with all the energy Christ so powerfully works in me.
(Colossians 1:29)

---

[2] From the hymn, *Am I a Soldier of the Cross,* by Isaac Watts.

RESOLVED.

My response to God's unceasing flow of undeserved favour is often so paltry and pathetic. It is not compatible with the goodness He continually shows me. It is incongruous. It does not fit. It does not make sense.

> Jonathan's does.
> Dwight Moody's does.
> The Apostle Paul's does.

I can hear these guys in their misunderstood zeal (misunderstood by everyone except Jesus!) spurring one another on:

'I'm all in!'
> 'I want to be that 100% Jesus-follower the world needs!'
> > 'Let's go for it with all we have!'

A blood-bought, grace-empowered follower of Jesus should forever have the attitude of a kid at game-time:

> 'Put me in coach!'
> > 'Watch me go!'
> > > 'Give me the ball!'

Jesus does not mind you or me striking out. What he does mind is if we do not even want to step up to the plate and swing the bat. At least Jonathan is swinging for the fence!

I want, by the grace of God, to be all that *I* can be for Jesus this side of Heaven. I do not have to be *you* (phew!). Even though sin did its best to ruin me, I now just want to be the *me* that Jesus created: that the Gospel redeemed, and grace is reclaiming. It just makes no sense to want to be anything less than 100% for Jesus … even if I know I won't be 100% until I die and see Him face to face.

RESOLVED.

I must not let fear of failure or love of ease hold me back. I live under the banner of God's love (Song of Solomon 2:4), and under that banner I can:

> risk, stretch, fail, get back up, try again,
> make a mess of things, start over, keep going,
> stumble, strike out, and dream big.

What I cannot do is not bother.

Thank you, Jonathan, Dwight, Paul for spurring me on and for stirring me up. Without friends like you (and I could add Joni Erickson-Tada, Amy Carmichael, Hudson Taylor, Gladys Aylward, George Verwer and many others to this list), I would lapse into offering Jesus my second-hand love and my left-over strength ... after I had given my best to this world. Keep speaking into my life, guys and gals. I need it.

Brothers and sisters, I do not consider myself yet to have taken hold of it. But one thing I do: forgetting what is behind and straining towards what is ahead, I press on towards the goal to win the prize for which God has called me heavenwards in Christ Jesus.
(Philippians 3:13,14)

'I wasn't God's first choice for what I've done in China ... I don't know who it was ... it must have been a man ... a well-educated man. I don't know what happened. Perhaps he died. Perhaps he wasn't willing ... and God looked down ... and saw Gladys Aylward ... and God said, "Well, she's willing."'[3]
(Gladys Aylward)

---

[3]For her story see Burgess, A., & Bergman, I. (1957). *The Small Woman*. Evans.

341

Resolved 64

Resolved to never ignore, but to act upon the 'groanings' and 'longings' of my deep soul, embracing them fully and not tiring of the soul work of pouring out my deepest heart to God, knowing that I am sure to reap a great benefit.

Likewise, the Spirit also helps in our weaknesses. For we do not know what we should pray for as we ought, but the Spirit Himself makes intercession for us with groanings which cannot be uttered.
(Romans 8:26 NKJV)

My soul is consumed with longing for your laws at all times.
(Psalm 119:20)

My soul yearns for you in the night; in the morning, my spirit longs for you.
(Isaiah 26:9)

Dear Friend,

God wants your heart. He is not just interested in your service. He is not interested in your money. He is not interested in your outward obedience.

Those things are not unimportant, but they are no replacement for your heart.

God the Holy Spirit indwells every believer that He might move our spirits toward God the Father. God orders our lives to create in us a soul-thirst, that we might embark upon a pursuit of God at heart-level. Every Christian should live in dread of the words uttered by Jesus, lest they be found to be true of them:

RESOLVED.

*These people honour me with their lips, but
their hearts are far from me.*
(Matthew 15:8)

Do not be satisfied with the shallows. God is inviting you to the depths. God is inviting you to step out where your feet cannot touch bottom. I am not just talking about 'doing' things for God. I am referring to our hearts being drawn out by Him and toward Him. I am speaking of realizing that every lesser love, every rival for our heart's affection, is a pretender to the throne and must be banished.

When we sense these deeper longings, when we recognize an emptiness and a dissatisfaction with all that is about us, *God* is summoning us onward, outward, deeper. The challenge from Jonathan is to *respond* to those inconsolable longings, and not just numb them or ignore them. That groan from your heart may well be God trying for your deeper attention. That sigh in your spirit is probably God's Spirit summoning yours to Himself.

Deep calls to deep ...
(Psalm 42:7)

The very depth of God is trying to get the attention of the very depth of us. But we seek to be satisfied with the lesser when God is inviting our hearts to an adventure with Himself. We need to learn to heed the longings and not just shrug them off. We need to learn to pay attention to the deep groans of the soul, knowing that God is graciously wooing us to himself.

The little book, Song of Solomon, thought by the rabbis to be the 'Holy of Holies' of the sacred Scriptures, is given to us by God to be, among other things, a picture of the love Jesus has for the simple believer. In that wonderous book, the bridegroom's heart is actually *affected* by the response of the bride. He yearns, she sometimes disregards. He invites,

343

she sometimes refuses. He pursues, she retreats. But the love song gives us a portrait of the very heart of God for us. It is a heart that seeks response. It is a heart that provokes a response. Listen to the bridegroom (Jesus) and imagine yourself to be the beloved bride:

> *You have stolen my heart, my sister, my bride; you have stolen*
> *my heart with one glance of your eyes…*
> (Song of Solomon 4:9)

Can it be? Can it be that God, the Eternal Uncreated, the All-Sufficient *God* of the Universe has so ordered things that He actually wants a deep relationship with you and me? That it is actually a part of His essential being to love deeply and to be *affected* by those whom He has created in His image and redeemed through the blood of His son?

Lord, can I really touch your heart when the eyes of my soul look in love toward You?

Augustine rightly said that God has made us for Himself and that our hearts are restless until they find rest in Him.[1] Dare I venture to say that this God, who made us for Himself, likewise is restless until we rest in Him?

> *I belong to my beloved, and his desire is for me.*
> (Song of Solomon 7:10)

> *As a bridegroom rejoices over his bride,*
> *so will your God rejoice over you.*
> (Isaiah 62:5)

---

[1] Augustine, S. (1876). *The Confessions*. Paraphrase of i1, p. iii. Ed, Clarke, G. University of Liverpool.

RESOLVED.

We believe that the transient things that we can see, feel, taste, buy, build, and touch will satisfy our deepest desire, so, we acquire, we date, we build, we marry, we invest, we procreate, we do all these things. But, if we will be still for a moment, can we not still hear that inward groan and feel that inconsolable longing? *God* put that there. It is Jesus calling. Deep calls unto deep. Stop and listen! Respond to the invitation. As I have said before, Christianity is not just a legal arrangement between us and God whereby, through the wonders of justification, our sin is removed, and we can now get on with our own God-ignoring lives. We are justified *so that we can draw near*.

'You, God, are my God, earnestly I seek you; I thirst for you, my whole being longs for you, in a dry and parched land where there is no water.'
(Psalm 63:1)

God repeatedly arranges things so that the visible and transient disappoint and decay. He does this for our good. He does this because He loves us. Otherwise, we will be satisfied at mere 'animal level' and forget we even have a soul and that there is a wooing God for whom we have been created and redeemed. My dog is totally satisfied with his bowl of food, a scratch around the ears, and a snooze on the lawn.

But I dare not be satisfied at that level.

Alas! Our entire culture believes it can be satisfied at mere animal level!

No!

I need to hear the words of Blaise Paschal (1623-1662), the French mathematician and theologian. Though he managed only 39 years on this planet, he left his mark, not the least of which is this great observation:

> What else does this craving, and this helplessness, proclaim but that there was once in man a true happiness, of which all that now remains is the empty print and trace? This he tries in vain to fill with everything around him, seeking in things that are not there the help he cannot find in those that are, though none can help, since this infinite abyss can be filled only with an infinite and immutable object; in other words, with God himself.[2]

Don't ignore the inner longing. Don't pacify it. Turn it into a relentless pursuit of God. It is soul work, and it will reap the reward of a deep and real knowledge of the Holy One.

Lord Jesus! Keep loving me too much to let me be satisfied with the trivial! Do not take away that deep groan in my soul! Do not allow my inconsolable longing to be falsely filled with foolishness! Keep me thankful for what you have given me in this life but dissatisfied with it. Give me grace to open my Bible and get on my knees and seek You like a thirsty man seeks water or a hungry man bread or a miser gold. Be *jealous* over me, Lord, as a bridegroom is over his bride. Keep me from wandering the streets looking for what cannot satisfy. *Make me* want You!

> *My beloved spoke and said to me,*
> *'Arise, my darling,*
> *my beautiful one, come with me.*
> *See! The winter is past; the rains are over and gone.*
> *Flowers appear on the earth;*

---

[2] Pascal, B. (1966). *Pensées*, p. 75. New York: Penguin Books.

RESOLVED.

the season of singing has come,
the cooing of doves is heard in our land.

The fig-tree forms its early fruit;
the blossoming vines spread their fragrance.

Arise, come, my darling; my beautiful one, come with me.'
(Song of Solomon 2:10-13)

'All of humanity's problems stem from man's inability to
sit quietly in a room alone.'[3]
(Blaise Pascal)

---

[3] Pascal, B. (1999). *Pensées and Other Writings*, p 44. Oxford University Press.

Resolved 65

Resolved, in all of my life, and for all of my life, to lay my heart and soul open to God - meaning, all of my temptations, my sins, my sadness, my fears, my hopes, and my desires - holding nothing back from my Lord in any and every circumstance.

But the Lord God called to the man, 'Where are you?'
He answered, 'I heard you in the garden, and I was afraid
because I was naked; so I hid.'
(Genesis 3:9,10)

Dear Friend in Jesus,

Since the dawn of time, we have been hiding. God has been looking. Since Adam and Eve, we have shied away from God, from being real, from coming clean. Their attempt to cover their nakedness with scratchy fig leaves (Genesis 3:7) was the first 'religious' event in human history. It did not work. God saw right through it.

We are ever holding back; God is forever coming forth.

All through the Bible we find a seeking God and a hiding sinner. Finally, we encounter Jesus who plainly and wonderfully tells us that he came 'to seek and to save the lost' (Luke 19:10).

Jonathan wants to be done with hiding, with lurking, with the excuses, with the shadows. He knows the character of God toward him. He knows that the God of the Bible (the only God that there is!) is a *willing, consistent* God, not a capricious, grudging God. He knows that God only has Jonathan's best in mind, and that it is foolish to hide *anything* from such a God (as though it was possible to do so).

348

RESOLVED.

David, who knew as well as any of us the folly of covering-up and the wonder of opening-up, counsels us:

> *Blessed is the one ... in whose spirit is no deceit.*
> (Psalm 32:2)

There is a freedom to being open with God. There is a freshness of spirit for the one who daily, even moment by moment, brings all that they are before their loving and all-knowing Heavenly Father. Listen to God's word though David:

> *I will instruct you and teach you in the way you should go; I will counsel you with my loving eye on you. Do not be like the horse or the mule, which have no understanding but must be controlled by bit and bridle or they will not come to you.*
> (Psalm 32:8,9)

Your view of God, your understanding of His character and of His heart toward you is vital in all of this. I cannot be 'open' with God if I am not sure of His heart toward me. Is He really good? Does He truly always have my best in mind? Will He always and only deal with me through the covenant His Son Jesus has made by His blood on my behalf? Does He care about the details of my life? Is He concerned with my heart, or does He just want my obedience? Can I pour everything out to Him? Can I tell Him of my hopes and dreams? Can I tell Him of my sins and failures? Does He see me? Does He understand me?

There are many who believe in Jesus, who call themselves Christians, but who have a sad view of God. Many of us think that God, at best, puts up with us. Sure, He has forgiven us through the Gospel, but He does not *like* us. Certainly, He is not *interested* in us. I could never open my heart to Him.

349

RESOLVED.

Some of us think that the Gospel is God saying, 'OK. I forgive you. Now go away...', when in fact it is God saying, 'I have removed your transgressions from you and clothed you in the very Righteousness of my Son. Now *come to me.*'

Do you know that God has an open heart for you and that therefore you will not be rebuffed if you open your heart to Him?

It is revolutionary to open up one's entire self to God. Sin leads to hiding. And, even for a Jesus-follower who knows the forgiveness of his sins and crimes, there can still be a residue of guilt and grime causing an unwillingness to come, a shyness to open oneself, a reticence to let all be seen. There can be a fear born of a wrong view of God and the Gospel. There can be a constant looking over one's shoulder, a nervousness, a looming sense of unworthiness and guilt.

All this leads to a spiritual poverty, to distance, to coldness with God.

And – guaranteed – if your heart is not open to Jesus, it is not open to others either. Every human relationship springs from our relationship with God, and to the degree that you are available to intimacy with God, you are available to intimacy with people. (That is why one of the first questions I often ask when counselling friends concerning their human relationships is, 'Tell me about your life with Jesus'.)

Oh, please hear this! Through Christ, because of His blood shed once for our sins, there *need be no hindrance* in our approach to God. We could marshal Scripture passages all day to prove God's heart toward us. Just meditate on a few:

The Lord will fulfil his purpose for me; your steadfast love, O Lord,
endures forever. Do not forsake the work of your hands.
(Psalm 138:8 ESV)

RESOLVED.

*Let us then approach God's throne of grace with confidence, so
that we may receive mercy and find grace to help us
in our time of need.*
(Hebrews 4:16)

*Lord, all my desire is before You; and my sighing
is not hidden from You.*
(Psalm 38:9)

*Trust in him at all times, you people; pour out your
hearts to him, for God is our refuge.*
(Psalm 62:8)

We will spend eternity marvelling at this wonderful God who, though
uncaused and without any need, has chosen to want us and desires to
walk in intimacy with us. So many of the word pictures in the Bible
describing Jesus' relationship with us depict intimacy, union,
friendship, openness:

Shepherd and sheep,
    Vine and Branches,
        Bridegroom and bride,
            Friend and befriended,
                Head and body.

Indeed, He is our Boaz, we are His impoverished Ruth. He is our
David, we His lowly Mephibosheth. Every picture seems to point to
willingness on God's part and need on ours. It is our union with Him
by faith, His openness to us, and our openness to Him in response, that
brings us life and wholeness. God did not create us and redeem us so
that we could simply be workers – drones - who do our duty. He seeks a
bride, friends, members of His Body.

RESOLVED.

He understands when no one else tries to.
He forgives when no one else wants to.
He feels when no one else cares to.
He is willing when no one else dares to.
He sees what no one else can see.
He hears when no one else will listen.

Wonderful, wonderful Jesus.

Jonathan's *Resolution* is timeless and as needed today in my life and yours as it once was in his. Will you resolve, by the grace of God, to open up your entire self to Jesus? Daily? Yes, even moment by moment? Because of Jesus you will always find a warm welcome, a willing ear, a watchful eye, and a tender voice. Wait not in resolving to lay your heart and soul open to the Lord.

Mother-in-law Naomi's advice to the poor widowed Ruth (us) regarding strong Boaz (Jesus) and his heart to redeem her, is a word for us today. Believe it and stop holding back from the One who loves you so!

Wash, put on perfume, and get dressed in your best clothes [open
your whole self to Jesus]...For the man will not rest
until the matter is settled today.'
(Ruth 3:3;18)

'God is more concerned with winning all of me for Christ than in me
winning all the world for Christ.'[1]
(David Wilkerson)

---

[1] See also this citation in Resolved 21: Wilkerson, D. (1987). *Taking Hold of Christ*, World Challenge Pulpit Series, accessible at
http://www.tscpulpitseries.org/english/1980s/ts870601.html.

RESOLVED.

Resolved 66

Resolved to seek, at all times, to act and speak in a gracious and benevolent manner, in all places and toward all people, unless faithfulness requires otherwise.

Love suffers long and is kind; love does not envy; love does not parade itself, is not puffed up; does not behave rudely, does not seek its own, is not provoked, thinks no evil; does not rejoice in iniquity, but rejoices in the truth; bears all things, believes all things, hopes all things, endures all things.
(1 Corinthians 13:4-7 NKJV)

Dear Friend in Christ,

Oh, to have a sweet, Christ-like spirit!

What would it be like to possess a heart which *always* believes the best about others, which *always* responds in grace, and which *always* acts in a manner appropriate to the need of the moment? Imagine having not one ounce of jealousy, not a grain of ill-will toward another, no grumbling bitterness, no lurking bad attitude. Consider a life with no little twists in your words, no sharp corners in your communications, no raised eyebrows, harrumphs, or rolls of the eye. Imagine never again tossing in your sleepless bed, rehearsing that 'giving him a piece of my mind' speech over and over. Think of life with no more sour feelings, not one other 'Why did I say that?' regret.

What would life be like if you only ever corrected another person when love required it, and then only ever with a humble heart behind your words and with a love-motivated desire to see the other blessed? Imagine never removing your friend's speck from his smarting eye until you had removed the log from your own. Think of relationships with no

353

arguments, no points to prove, no more walking away with that 'I wiped the floor with that guy' pride while leaving a relationship in shambles.

Such a heart, such a life, is what old-timers called ... *Holiness.*

It is not terribly *common* these days. But it is *normal,* sanctified Jesus-following.

My relationship with Jesus has to completely re-wire how I interact with others – both inwardly and outwardly – or it is suspect. Let the Apostle John speak:

> *Dear friends, let us love one another, for love comes from God. Everyone who loves has been born of God and knows God. Whoever does not love does not know God, because God is love. This is how God showed his love among us: he sent his one and only Son into the world that we might live through him. This is love: not that we loved God, but that he loved us and sent his Son as an atoning sacrifice for our sins. Dear friends, since God so loved us, we also ought to love one another. No one has ever seen God; but if we love one another, God lives in us and his love is made complete in us.*
> (1 John 4:7-12)

Living the 'crucified life', the life that says 'no' to self and 'yes' to God, inevitably spills over into our actions and attitudes towards others. Holiness as not a feeling one gets when the music is 'just right' and the (short) sermon makes one feel good. It is not a tingling in the spine so much as a trembling in the heart. It is personal but not private. It causes a believer in Jesus to see every person through the lens of the Gospel and act toward them remembering that they are divine image bearers for whom Christ has shed blood.

RESOLVED.

It *must* affect how I relate to people. John Wesley put it simply:

> Solitary religion is not to be found there [in the Bible]. 'Holy Solitaries' is a phrase no more consistent with the gospel than Holy Adulterers. The gospel of Christ knows of no religion, but social; no holiness but social holiness. Faith working by love, is the length and breadth and depth and height of Christian perfection.[1]

Holiness of heart and life is not so much a *negative* posture – a posture of *not* being sour and bitter - but a *positive* one – of being sweet and tender in spirit. It is about having a heart like Jesus'. It is about being 'gentle and humble in heart' (Matthew 11:29). This is what Jesus wants to form in us. What Jonathan is resolving is actually to open Himself up to a deep and wonderful work in his inner being that will produce a precious outer countenance toward those he walks with. Old-timers did not see this as optional. It was to them the tell-tale proof of God making them like Jesus. Allowing Jesus to do a work of gentleness and sweetness in them, training themselves to believe the best about others and treat others with all purity and holiness, was for them simple obedience to the Bible. Their writings brim with this. They sought a *deep* holiness that affected how they treated people.

They not only *believed* their Bibles, they *behaved* them. They wanted to be made like Jesus:

> *But the fruit of the Spirit is love, joy, peace, forbearance,*
> *kindness, goodness, faithfulness, gentleness and self-control.*
> *Against such things there is no law. Those who belong to Christ*
> *Jesus have crucified the flesh with its passions and desires.*
> (Galatians 5:22-24)

---

[1] Wesley, J. (1739). *Hymns and Sacred Poems,* p. viii. Bristol: Felix Farley.

RESOLVED.

Be completely humble and gentle; be patient,
bearing with one another in love.
(Ephesians 4:2)

Therefore, as God's chosen people, holy and dearly loved, clothe
yourselves with compassion, kindness, humility,
gentleness and patience.
(Colossians 3:12)

Sometimes faithfulness will require that we share a hard word with another. At such times it can actually be *un*loving to not speak. How thankful I am for those who have ventured to confront me when I have needed it! You can tell when someone has your best in mind, when their heart is gentle towards your heart, when their words are well chosen and seasoned with salt. Perhaps they have wept first for your situation. Certainly, they have prayed before they have spoken.

There is a remarkable order given in Luke's Gospel regarding Jesus' cleansing of the Jerusalem Temple from those merchandising in God's house. It is instructive for us:

As he approached Jerusalem and saw the city, he wept over it
...When Jesus entered the temple courts, he began to drive out
those who were selling. 'It is written,' he said to them, '"My
house will be a house of prayer"; but you have made it
"a den of robbers"'.
(Luke 19:41;45,46)

Do you see the order? He *wept* before He *whipped.* His heart, defined by gentleness, broke before He bruised. As Dane Ortland, in his remarkable book, *Gentle and Lowly,* tells us, kindness and gentleness are Christ's 'natural work', judgement and rebuke, while necessary, are His 'strange work'.[2] So should it be with us. What is to be natural to

356

us (in fact, *super*naturally natural!) is to be kind, sweet, and gentle. What is to be strange to us – though sometimes necessary – is to express judgement and rebuke.

Alas! How often with us it is our 'natural work' is to be negative, cross, corrective, and censuring, and our 'strange work' to be gracious, edifying, sweet, and gentle!

Lord Jesus! Change me! Work in me a transformation that makes me like You. May there be in me a true and genuine sweetness of spirit that controls my thoughts, words, and actions toward others. May it become my nature to see others through the Gospel, and to regard even the bothersome as being of eternal value in Your eyes and, therefore, in mine. By your grace, do a *supernatural* work in me that causes love, sweetness, and kindness toward others to be *natural* to me!

> *For he does not willingly bring affliction or grief to anyone.*
> (Lamentations 3:33)

> *The tongue of the righteous is choice silver ...*
> *The lips of the righteous nourish many ...*
> (Proverbs 10:20,21)

> 'Growing up involves the work of the Holy Spirit forming
> our born-again spirits into the likeness of Christ.' [3]
> (Eugene H. Peterson)

---

[2] 'When God deigns to lavish goodness on his people, he does it with a certain naturalness reflective of the depth of who he is. For God to be merciful is for God to be God.' (Dane Ortland, (2020), *Gentle and Lowly*, The Good Book Company, p.144)

[3] Peterson, E., (2010), *Practice Resurrection: A Conversation on Growing Up in Christ, p.2.* Cambridge, England: W.B. Eerdman's Publishing Company.

RESOLVED.

Resolved 67

Resolved, after suffering afflictions and trials, to discover in what ways I am now better for having experienced them. I will ask, 'What good have I received from them? What new insights do I now have because of them?'

And we all, who with unveiled faces contemplate the Lord's glory, are being transformed into his image with ever-increasing glory, which comes from the Lord, who is the Spirit.
(2 Corinthians 3:18)

It was good for me to be afflicted so that I might learn your decrees.
(Psalm 119:71)

Dear Friend in Jesus,

God wants to make us like Jesus. His love is real and purposeful. It has a goal in mind, and when He takes on 'projects' - you and me - He does not intend to do a partial job.

... being confident of this, that he who began a good work in you will carry it on to completion until the day of Christ Jesus.
(Philippians 1:6)

His transformation of us, from creatures accustomed to lurking in dark corners to sons and daughters of the Light, usually requires a major demolition work. This does not happen without pain, trial, and affliction. But His purposes are sure, and His hand is steady (even if ours is trembling). He is a master artist, a most skilful surgeon, an expert craftsman, a precision builder.

RESOLVED.

There is *purpose* in all that God does in our lives, including sufferings and afflictions. When we kick against Him, we only delay His purposes. I think there is a sad sense in which almost every western Christian has been poisoned by the 'prosperity gospel'. By that I mean, we all have been infected by the notion that if we are following Jesus, everything should go well with us most, if not all, of the time. We think, 'Certainly, God wants us healthy and wealthy, doesn't He? He would not put us through tough trials, would He? He would not take a surgeon's knife to our plans and purposes and passions, would He?'

Ah, but we forget that He has *eternal* purposes for us. We forget that our addiction to sin and self has ravaged us and warped every faculty of ours, and that salvation is not just avoiding Hell, but being restored to glory and prepared to inhabit eternity with Him.

We need to learn to learn from afflictions and trials.

We need to learn to submit to His skilful, precise, purposeful work in our lives.

How well I remember being with a dear friend on the day he was diagnosed with the cancer that would kill him. I can never forget his words, 'I am not going to waste this!' His determination was that if God had ordered this hard providence, he was going to let it do its good work of refining his soul. How well I remember watching his refinement during that last year of his earthly life! How can I ever forget his final days when he freely confessed that God had been *good* to him in weaning him from sin and making him more like Jesus? He told me without hesitation that he would not want to turn back the clock and be the strong young man he had been just a year ago, because now he was in fact a 'new man' ready to be with Jesus. He recited 1 Peter 4:1 to me the last time I was with him:

RESOLVED.

*Therefore, since Christ suffered in his body, arm yourselves also
with the same attitude, because whoever suffers in
the body has finished with sin.*

He rejoiced that *finally* he was free from sin (to my friend, being free
from sin was a greater victory than being hale and hearty).

Trusting God's goodness in the midst of afflictions is a faith issue. It
boils down to our view of God, and our understanding of the purpose
behind His saving work in us. Can it really be true that '…in all things
God works for the good of those who love him, who have been called
according to his purpose' (Romans 8:28)? Can we truly 'lean in' to
God's providential workings in our lives, trusting that He only desires
our good? Jonathan's resolve to not waste his trials reveals his
confidence in God's goodness toward him, and his trust in God's long-
range purposes concerning him:

'What good have I received from them?'

'What new insights do I now have because of them?'

'In what ways am I being made more like Jesus because of them?'

He is not kicking and squirming. He is trusting and submitting. He is
allowing the Artist to work His master strokes. He is submitting to the
Surgeon's necessary knife. He is letting the Potter work the lump of
clay. He is trusting the Builder to demolish and build.

Remember that Jonathan recited this *Resolution* weekly until his death
at the age of 55. Let's go there now. In the dim eyes of men, what an
untimely death it was! Having just become president of what was to be
Princeton University, he received a small-pox vaccination, but the dose

RESOLVED.

was too powerful, and he contracted the deadly malady. For weeks he suffered an excruciating sickness and then a painful death.
But grace had well-instructed His soul! Forgive me for being long in unpacking this *Resolution*, but I cannot explore it without quoting from his attending physician, Dr. Shippen. Oh, to see the value of learning to learn from our trials and afflictions. That will make us strong, willing, resolute, and conformed to the very image of Christ!

Please read these words slowly and let the truth of them sink in.

In a letter to Jonathan's daughter, Sarah, he writes:

> This afternoon, between two and three o'clock, it pleased God to let him sleep in that dear Lord Jesus, whose kingdom and interest he has been faithfully and painfully serving all his life. And never did any mortal man more fully and clearly evidence the sincerity of all his professions, by one continued, universal, calm, cheerful resignation, and patient submission to the divine will, through every stage of his disease, than he; not so much as one discontented expression, nor the least appearance of murmuring, through the whole.... I conclude with my hearty prayer... that you may be enabled to look to God, whose love and goodness you have experienced a thousand times, for direction and help, under this most afflictive dispensation of His providence, and under every other difficulty, you may meet with here, in order to your being more perfectly fitted for the joys of heaven hereafter.[1]

Dr. Shippen tells of Jonathan's dying words to his dear daughter, Lucy. You can hear this very *Resolution,* to not waste this trial but learn from it, in his words:

---

[1] *The Works of Jonathan Edwards*, Vol. 1. p. clxxix. (1974). Edinburgh: Banner of Truth.

RESOLVED.

...and I hope she [Lucy's mother and Jonathan's wife, Sarah] will be supported under so great a trial & submit cheerfully to the Will of God; and as to my Children, you are now like to be left Fatherless which I hope will be an Inducement to you all to seek a Father who will never fail you ...[2]

Jonathan's dear wife, Sarah, with whom he had shared what he called 'an uncommon union' was not with him at his death. But upon receiving word from Dr. Shippen of her husband's death, she, in consort with this *Resolution,* was able to write to a daughter:

My very dear child,
What shall I say? A holy and good God has covered us with a dark cloud. The Lord has done it. He has made me adore his [God's] goodness, that we had him so long. But my God lives; and he has my heart. O what a legacy my husband, and your father, has left us! We are all given to God; and there I am, and love to be.
Your ever affectionate mother,
Sarah Edwards.[3]

Beloved, learning to learn from afflictions is not optional if you want to grow in Christlikeness, and live fearlessly and joyfully until you enter Heaven! You will not live or die well if you have not learned to trust the careful providences of God all through your life. God is good. His ways are good. His mysteries are good. His designs are good. Let us learn to learn.

---

[2] *The Works of Jonathan Edwards,* Vol. 1, p. clxxviii. (1974). Edinburgh: Banner of Truth.
[3] Ibid. p. clxxix.

RESOLVED.

*For our light and momentary troubles are achieving for us an
eternal glory that far outweighs them all.*
(2 Corinthians 4:17)

'Trust in God, and ye need not fear.'
(Jonathan Edward's last words in this life)[4]

Deep in unfathomable mines
Of never failing skill
He treasures up His bright designs
And works His sov'reign will.
(William Cowper)

---

[4] Ibid. p. clxxviii.

RESOLVED.

Resolved 68

Resolved to be honest with myself regarding my own weaknesses and sins, being diligent regarding my spiritual health, to confess my whole heart to God, asking for, and trusting Him for, His needed help.

For we do not have a high priest who is unable to feel sympathy for our weaknesses, but we have one who has been tempted in every way, just as we are – yet he did not sin. Let us then approach God's throne of grace with confidence, so that we may receive mercy and find grace to help us in our time of need.
(Hebrews 4:15,16)

My dear children, I write this to you so that you will not sin. But if anybody does sin, we have an advocate with the Father – Jesus Christ, the Righteous One.
(1 John 2:1)

Dear Friends,

Do you know that we have a *willing* God? He is actually motivated to help His children through their weaknesses and failures. His desire for us is that we live lives that honour Him, know fulness and blessedness, and bring blessing to our world. It is this desire that motivated Jesus to leave Heaven and come on His saving errand to this fallen, rebel planet.

Because of the heart of God to alleviate our guilt and lift us from our shame, there is no reason for us to hesitate for an instant to be honest in regard to our sins and to bring our whole hearts often before Him for cleansing and help. Why wait? Why hide? Why make excuses?

Confession and repentance are the meat and potatoes of the Christian life. Martin Luther ignited his world by nailing *Ninety-Five Theses* to

RESOLVED.

the door of All Saints' Church in Wittenberg, Germany in 1517. His
opening salvo summed up the Christian's life:

> When our Lord and Master, Jesus Christ, said, 'Repent' (Mt
> 4:17), he willed the entire life of believers to be one of
> repentance.

But…the sad fact is that sin has so deceived us, so perverted our view
of God and His goodness, that we hide in the shadows rather than come
out into the light. We hold on to our sins as though they were of benefit
to us when, in fact, they are killing us. We shy away from God. We
deceive ourselves. We make up excuses. We cast blame. All the while
God is ready, willing and waiting:

> *All day long I have held out my hands to an obstinate people,*
> *who walk in ways not good, pursuing their own imaginations.*
> (Isaiah 65:2)

Indeed,

> *Whoever conceals their sins does not prosper, but the one*
> *who confesses and renounces them finds mercy.*
> (Proverbs 28:13)

There is *freedom* in confession. There is *joy* in repenting. There is
liberty in bringing one's messed up heart before a willing God. Jesus'
blood, shed once and for all on Calvary, forever speaks a word of
pardon on our behalf. His grace is an inexhaustible river, not a muddy
little pool.

> *On that day a fountain will be opened to the house of David and*
> *the inhabitants of Jerusalem, to cleanse them from*
> *sin and impurity.*

RESOLVED.

(Zechariah 13:1)

*But if we walk in the light, as he is in the light, we have fellowship
with one another, and the blood of Jesus, his Son,
purifies us from all sin.*
(1 John 1:7)

When we are willing to 'walk in the light', we are willing to see our sins and confess them. Then and there, we are cleansed by the blood of Jesus which was once shed for all sins for all time. *And* – BONUS - there in the light, where we are confessing and being cleansed, 'we have fellowship with one another'. For there, while we are confessing, we find others doing the same. What sweet fellowship exists between repenting believers as Christ cleanses and restores!

This is nothing short of revival and the more repenters join in, the farther the revival spreads. Families, churches, whole nations have experienced such wonders.

But - let me say this again - the only heart I have any jurisdiction over is my own. So, as far as *I* am concerned, revival needs to begin with me – with me being ready and willing to be real with myself and with God regarding my sin and coming without delay to Him. When *I* deal with *my sin* before Jesus, *my* world changes. Marriages, families, churches, friendships, workplaces can be transformed when *one* person deals with their hearts before their welcoming God.

I cannot say this better than Roy Hession does in his remarkable little book *The Calvary Road.* I recommend (again!) that you get his wonderful book and read it over and over.

Roy! Forgive me for quoting you at length! You say it better than I can!

RESOLVED.

The only basis for real fellowship with God and man is to live out in the open with both. *'But if we walk in the light, as He is in the light, we have fellowship one with another.'* To walk in the light is the opposite of walking in darkness. Spurgeon defines it in one of his sermons as 'the willingness to know and be known.' As far as God is concerned, this means that we are willing to know the whole truth about ourselves, we are open to conviction. We will bend the neck to the first twinges of conscience. Everything He shows us to be sin, we will deal with as sin - we will hide or excuse nothing. Such a walk in the light cannot but disclose sin increasingly in our lives, and we shall see things to be sin which we never thought to be such before. For that reason, we might shrink from this walk, and be tempted to make for cover. But the verse goes on with the precious words, *'and the Blood of Jesus Christ, His Son, cleanseth us from all sin.'* Everything that the light of God shows up as sin, we can confess and carry to the Fountain of Blood and it is gone, gone from God's sight and gone from our hearts. By the power of the precious Blood, we can be made more stainless than the driven snow; and thus, continually abiding in the light and cleansed by the Blood, we have fellowship with God.

But the fellowship promised us here is not only with God, but 'one with another', and that involves us in walking in the light with our brother too. In any case, we cannot be 'in the open' with God and 'in the dark' with him. This means that we must be as willing to know the truth about ourselves from our brother as to know it from God. We must be prepared for him to hold the light to us (and we must be willing to do the same service for him) and challenge us in love about anything he sees in our lives which is not the highest. We must be willing not only to know, but to be known by him for what we really are. That means we are not going to hide our inner selves from those with whom we ought to be in fellowship; we are not going to window dress and put on appearances; nor are we going to whitewash and excuse ourselves. We are going to be honest about ourselves with them. We are willing to give up our spiritual privacy, pocket our pride and risk our reputations for the sake of being open and transparent with our brethren in Christ. It means, too, that we are not going to cherish any wrong feeling in our hearts about another, but we are first going to claim deliverance from it from God and put it right with the one concerned. As we walk this way, we shall find that we shall have fellowship with one another at an altogether new level, and we shall not love one another less, but infinitely more.[1]

Oh, let us learn the holy habit of dealing with our own sins quickly. Let us each have a path worn to the cross. May Jesus find us often there, for there He will always be ready to receive us.

In repentance and rest is your salvation,
in quietness and trust is your strength.
(Isaiah 30:15)

'Life changing repentance begins when blame shifting ends.'[2]
(Tim Keller)

---

[1] Hession, R. (1990). *The Calvary Road,* p.38. CLC Publications.
[2] Keller, T., tweet @timkellernyc, Dec 11, 2018.

RESOLVED.

Resolved 69

Resolved, when I see others do something admirable which I wish
I had done, to make it my habit to do it.

One who walks with wise people will be wise ...
(Proverbs 13:20 NASB)

Whatever you have learned or received or heard from me,
or seen in me – put it into practice. And the God of peace
will be with you.
(Philippians 4:9)

Dear Friends,

We saw in an earlier *Resolution* that envy is destructive, but admiration
can be constructive. To see something good in another's character or
actions, and to desire it in your life, can be the beginning of
transformation.

There is humility and a teachable spirit in this *Resolution*. It is quite
remarkable that it comes from the pen of such a young man. Young
men tend to be hard to teach, feeling that they have cornered the market
on wisdom. But grace is clearly at work in young Jonathan. It is not
unusual, when we see something admirable in another to envy them.
Nor is it unusual to find some way to criticize them or to begin to seethe
against them. But not Jonathan. His humble sprit wants to learn all he
can as he applies himself to being all that he can be for Jesus. This is as
rare as it is beautiful.

But, beware! If youngsters can be brash and unteachable, older men
(and women!) can be crusty, stuck and unwilling to learn and grow and
change.

RESOLVED.

The story of Saul in the Old Testament is instructive here. Instead of admiring the gifts and deeds of young David, he allowed jealousy and a mean spirit to grow within him which would eventually destroy him.

When the men were returning home after David had killed the Philistine, the women came out from all the towns of Israel to meet King Saul with singing and dancing, with joyful songs and with tambourines and lyres.

> *As they danced, they sang:*
> *'Saul has slain his thousands,*
> *and David his tens of thousands.'*

Saul was very angry; this refrain displeased him greatly. 'They have credited David with tens of thousands,' he thought, 'but me with only thousands. What more can he get but the kingdom?'
(1 Samuel 18:6-8)

No humble, teachable, ready spirit there! Go read the sad story of Saul and see where his envious heart got him…

A teachable spirit is a peaceful spirit with which God can do great things. To look on another's good accomplishments and 1) praise God for them, 2) desire them in your own life, and 3) emulate them with a humble spirit, is a remarkable accomplishment of grace in the soul.

In almost any and every situation, there is going to be someone better at something than I am. There is always going to be someone doing something I realize I should be doing. If I am humble and teachable, I will actually seek out such people. I will want to be around them. I will pursue relationship with them.

RESOLVED.

Think about this with me: a good athlete wants to be in the presence of a great one. A journeyman craftsman wants to be in the workshop with a master. A second-chair violinist wants to learn all she can from the first chair. Translate that into the Kingdom:

Who can I run with?
Who is excellent in prayer and godliness?
Where is a better preacher than I from whom I can learn?
Where is that godly grandmother who can teach me to be a godly mother?
Where is the young man who is running hard after God, overcoming lust, and bad habits that I can grab onto?

> Mary had her Elizabeth.
> Timothy had his Paul.
> Elisha had his Elijah.
> Joshua had his Moses.
> Ruth had her Naomi.

Look at Paul's instruction to young Timothy. In addition to exhorting young Tim to emulate Paul (Philippians 4:9), Paul urges Timothy to '[f]lee the evil desires of youth and pursue righteousness, faith, love and peace, *along with those who call on the Lord out of a pure heart'* (2 Timothy 2:22, italics mine).

'Timothy! Find those sold-out Jesus followers, grab on, and then hang on for dear life!'

Let me ask you and let's be honest with one another. Do you have a teachable spirit? When you see someone excel you in some desirous area, or when someone does something excellent or praiseworthy, is your reaction one of joy and praise to God, soon followed by a desire for God to work something of that into you, or does that horrible feeling of envy steal into your heart?

Jonathan's *Resolution* has a sweet freedom to it. We have all been around those … bores … who just cannot handle someone else doing something they wish they had done or something better than they can do it. They always have to come up with a better story. Behind them is insecurity and a sense of inferiority. But, as Jesus' followers, we can be secure in who we are in Him, and thus be delivered from such destructive complexes. This sets us free to rejoice in the good things others do and desire to do them, but without the attending bitterness of spirit. Such a free spirit enables a lifetime of growth! I remember hearing the story of Billy Graham, that great and wonderful evangelist, when he was well over eighty years of age, having preached all over the world, having written endless books … sitting the front row of a meeting, with Bible open and notebook and pen in hand!

> Teach me!
> What can I learn?
> I am ready!

I want such a child-like spirit of teachable humility to follow me through to the very end of my days on earth.

It is good to ask God the Holy Spirit the following questions:

Lord God, as I engage with this person, will You please grant me a humble and teachable spirit?

Lord, what is it in this person that You would like to work in me?

What is this person doing which, were I walking in step with You, I would be doing?

RESOLVED.

And, if needed,

Lord, why is my spirit disturbed over their good work? Why am I envious? Please grant me a spirit of repentance here and now!

It is good to remember that *everyone* is the best in the world - World Number One - at *something* and, therefore, can inspire and motivate me to some good end. Each and every person I walk through life with can move me forward... if I have a humble and teachable spirit.

This is really just about being sanctified, growing in grace, and walking in the purposes for which God has created and redeemed us. It cannot happen without a humble spirit which always seeks to be learning and growing and is willing to be challenged and inspired by the graces evidenced in those around us.

For we are God's handiwork, created in Christ Jesus to do good works, which God prepared in advance for us to do.
(Ephesians 2:10)

May the Lord Jesus grant us humble, teachable, godly spirits that are easily inspired by His wonderful work in others.

When pride comes, then comes disgrace, but with humility comes wisdom.
(Proverbs 11:2)

'No one has a corner on wisdom. ... Our acute need is to cultivate a willingness to learn and to remain teachable.'[1]
(Charles Swindoll)

---

[1] Swindoll, C. (2005). *Servant-Hearted Leaders* in *Day by Day*, Nashville, Tennessee: *Thomas Nelson, Inc.*

RESOLVED.

Resolved 70

Resolved that there be something good and helpful for others in everything that I speak.

A good man brings good things out of the good stored up in his heart, and an evil man brings evil things out of the evil stored up in his heart. For the mouth speaks what the heart is full of.
(Luke 6:45)

The mouth of the righteous is a fountain of life ...
The lips of the righteous nourish many...
(Proverbs 10:11,21)

Dear Friends,

This is the last of Jonathan's *Resolutions*. Here is his final 18th century promise to himself. What final encouragement and challenge does it hold for his 21st century readers – you and me?

We are people of words. Our inner life, thoughts and feelings are mediated outwards through words. And once out, like the feathers from the burst pillow, or the toothpaste from the tube, it is very hard to get them back in again.

Oh, to be a source, a channel of goodness and grace to all whom I encounter! Every day, in countless scenes, we have opportunity to bring life or death, healing or pain, hope or despair into the countless lives we rub up against through the words we speak.

You and I - through our words - might be the last source of hope for some broken soul, or the difference maker in some wayward son or daughter. Our words might be the answer to some pleading mother's

374

prayers, or the providential arrows of encouragement from God shot into the heart of a future soul-winner.

There is so much poison, so much vitriol, so much harm being done with words. Indeed, the abuse of speech we see all about us is proving the fallenness of our race:

Their throats are open graves; their tongues practise deceit. The poison of vipers is on their lips. Their mouths are full of cursing and bitterness.
(Romans 3:13,14)

But as redeemed people, those who have been transferred from the kingdom of darkness to light, our words should - *must* - be reflecting the wonders of our redemption. We actually have an opportunity with our speech to bring life into a world of death, grace into a culture of anger, hope into an age of despair.

The words of the reckless pierce like swords, but the tongue of the wise brings healing.
(Proverbs 12:18)

Jesus makes it plain, and there is no getting around it, that our mouths are the display if our hearts: 'For out of the abundance of the heart his mouth speaks' (Luke 6:45 NKJV). A true work of grace in the heart will inevitably have an effect upon the words that spring forth.

So, if I want my words to be life-giving and full of nourishment for many (and I do!), then I need to get grace into my heart. And because the effects of sin are so pervasive, it is in no way a given that grace will be brimming over. If I leave my heart alone, it will, just as surely as an unattended garden, very soon be over-run with the bitter weeds of sin and self. It takes almost no time! And then, sure to follow, my words will not be grace-filled and life-giving, but edgy, sarcastic, fault-finding, harsh, a reflection of my culture instead of a counter to my culture.

If I want my words to bless and not blast, then Jesus and His Word needs to be present and pre-eminent in my heart.

This requires deliberate attention and earnest intention!

I have an opportunity to be a world-changer. Every day. In every encounter. It is actually *fun* to speak words of grace and goodness into lives: '[a] person finds joy in giving an apt reply – and how good is a timely word!' (Proverbs 15:23). I am not talking about *flattery*. Flattery is manipulative and ungodly. I am talking about truly trusting Jesus to use little old me as a channel of life into lives. This is supernatural because it is not who I am naturally! Left to myself I will snipe and cut. But with Jesus in my heart, *I* can become a gospelling grace-spreader in countless encounters day in and day out.

> *Let your conversation be always full of grace, seasoned with salt,*
> *so that you may know how to answer everyone.*
> (Colossians 4:6)

> *Do not let any unwholesome talk come out of your mouths, but*
> *only what is helpful for building others up according to their*
> *needs, that it may benefit those who listen.*
> (Ephesians 4:29)

Even when I have to speak a 'hard word' into someone's life, and we have seen that this too is a part of having a benevolent heart toward others, if my words are sourced in a Jesus-filled heart they are going to be appropriate and medicinal. I can then trust the Holy Spirit to bring

RESOLVED.

the right result, using my words to do His work in the heart of one whom He loves with an everlasting love.

Blessed are those whose strength is in you ...As they pass through the Valley of Baka, they make it a place of springs...
(Psalm 84:5,6)

The use of our words for good or for evil is too big to ignore. It is not an 'elective subject' for some Christians to specialize in. It actually is integral to who God is, and to who we are as those made in His image. *God* is a speaking God. From the dawn of creation to the incarnation of Jesus, The Word Made Flesh, God speaks life into being. Being Divine image-bearers, we as the crown of His creation are most like Him when we are speaking. Nothing else, in all creation, save the angelic host, uses words. Words are the privilege and domain of God and humanity. It is any wonder that Satan wants to work his mischief with our words, and cause us to use words to destroy and tear-down? Is it any wonder that God will hold us accountable for the things we say?

A good man brings good things out of the good stored up in him, and an evil man brings evil things out of the evil stored up in him. But I tell you that everyone will have to give account on the day of judgment for every empty word they have spoken. For by your words you will be acquitted, and by your words you will be condemned.
(Matthew 12:35-37)

With the tongue we praise our Lord and Father, and with it we curse human beings, who have been made in God's likeness. Out of the same mouth come praise and cursing. My brothers and sisters, this should not be. Can both fresh water and salt water flow from the same spring? My brothers and sisters, can a fig-tree bear olives, or a grapevine bear figs? Neither can a salt spring produce fresh water.

377

RESOLVED.

(James 3:9-12)

If we will, we can submit our words to Jesus and allow Him to speak through us into this broken world. We can refuse to have our tongues be instruments of destruction and stop doing the devil's work! We can view our fellows - *everyone* - through the lens of the Gospel and seek supernatural power to speak beneficial words into their world - words inspired by the Holy Spirit to bring truth and life into lives that are battered and beaten down by life.

As we come to the end of this challenging list of *Resolutions,* perhaps nothing will better demonstrate how fully we are engaging with the beautiful change God wants to effect within us (with our full consent and partnership) than how we use words.

'Lord Jesus! Fill my heart with Your love, Your Spirit, and Your Word until it spills its banks in life-giving words to each and every person I encounter. Make me good at grace-spreading. May my words be a source of joy and life in a weary world. For the sake of the Gospel, for the sake of people, for the sake of your Glory enhanced in this day of need.'

> *May these words of my mouth and this meditation of*
> *my heart be pleasing in your sight, Lord,*
> *my Rock and my Redeemer.*
> (Psalm 19:14)

'Let nothing be said about anyone unless it passes through the
three sieves: Is it true? Is it kind? Is it necessary?'[1]
(Amy Carmichael)

---

[1] Widely attributed to Amy Carmichael.

RESOLVED.

Epilogue

By Dee Molton, Editor.

Six months ago, I agreed to edit *Resolved.* for John. We have been friends for a long time, and it is a friendship, together with our spouses, which has offered fun and laughter in good times and shared strength in hard times. John and I approach some subjects under discussion in this book differently, but we share a love of Jesus and a commitment to the hard work of thinking and talking through our differences.

We represent the spectrum of Christians and seekers, hopers, doubters and enthusiasts who will read this book and for whom it will raise questions and offer challenge and encouragement. I do not think John anticipates that everything will resonate perfectly with every reader. I think he hopes you will talk things over with a friend: work hard. Jonathan and John offer you this opportunity to think! In today's polarised world where we all, to some extent, occupy a chamber of echoes, a dialogue over centuries, contexts and cultures is a great gift. This is a dialogue deeply rooted in friendship with God, in the Bible, and in lives – both Jonathon's and John's - which have experienced the reality of the Spirit at work in and around them.

Jonathan is long gone. Each of us soon will be. How are we growing our soul? What will we leave behind of value? How well are we loving others? How high is our excitement level at the prospect of seeing Jesus?

These are the questions John has explored through the 70 short but passionate promises Jonathan made to himself, kept, and now offers to us over a bridge of years. He was a man of a different era

RESOLVED.

but of exactly the same tests and calls upon his integrity as we face. John offers us the opportunity to listen and to learn with a view to action!

As you have taken the time to read this book and have come to the Epilogue, I think I can guarantee that you will have been 'stirred', that any slackness in your walk with Jesus will have been exposed to your own spiritual eyes, that even a few of these *Resolutions* - adopted as regular habits - will be making a difference to your joy and excitement in life and in God and to your relationships with others.

That is good!
That is investment well worth making!
That is action well worth taking!

Blessings!

Dee.

If you don't quit …
you win
Heidi Baker

RESOLVED.

The *Resolutions* of Jonathan Edwards[1]
1722-1723

"Being sensible that I am unable to do anything without God's help, I do humbly entreat him, by his grace, to enable me to keep these Resolutions, so far as they are agreeable to his will, for Christ's sake."

Remember to read over these Resolutions once a week.

1. *Resolved,* That *I will do whatsoever* I think to be most to the glory of God, and my own good, profit, and pleasure, in the whole of my duration; without any consideration of the time, whether now, or never so many myriads of ages hence. *Resolved,* to do whatever I think to be my *duty,* and most for the good and advantage of mankind in general. *Resolved,* so to do, whatever *difficulties* I meet with, how many soever, and how great soever.

2. *Resolved,* To be continually endeavouring to find out some *new contrivance* and invention to promote the forementioned things.

3. *Resolved,* If ever I shall fall and grow dull, so as to neglect to keep any part of these Resolutions, to repent of all I can remember, when I come to myself again.

4. *Resolved,* Never *to do* any manner of thing, whether in soul or body, less or more, but what tends to the glory of God, nor *be,* nor *suffer* it, if I can possibly avoid it.

5. *Resolved,* Never to lose one moment of time, but to improve it in the most profitable way I possibly can.

6. *Resolved,* To live with all my might, while I do live.

7. *Resolved,* Never to do anything, which I should be afraid to do if it were the last hour of my life.

---

[1] *The Works of Jonathan Edwards*, Edinburgh, The Banner of Trust. 1974. p xx

RESOLVED.

8. *Resolved*, To act, in all respects, both speaking and doing, as if nobody had been so vile as I, and as if I had committed the same sins, or had the same infirmities or failings, as others; and that I will let the knowledge of their failings promote nothing but shame in myself, and prove only an occasion of my confessing my own sins and misery to God. *Vid.*July 30.

9. *Resolved*, To think much, on all occasions of my dying, and of the common circumstances which attend death.

10. *Resolved*, when I feel pain, to think of the pains of martyrdom, and of hell.

11. *Resolved*, When I think of any theorem in divinity to be solved, immediately to do what I can towards solving it, if circumstances do not hinder.

12. *Resolved*, If I take delight in it as a gratification of pride, or vanity, or on any such account, immediately to throw it by.

13. *Resolved*, To be endeavouring to find out fit objects of liberality and charity.

14. *Resolved*, Never to do anything out of revenge.

15. *Resolved*, Never to suffer the least motions of anger towards irrational beings.

16. *Resolved,* Never to speak evil of anyone, so that it shall tend to his dishonour, more or less, upon no account except for some real good.

17. *Resolved*, That I will live so, as I shall wish I had done when I come to die.

18. *Resolved*, To live so, at all times, as I think is best in my most devout frames, and when I have the clearest notions of the things of the gospel, and another world.

19. *Resolved*, Never to do anything, which I should be afraid to do, if I expected it would not be above an hour before I should hear the last trump.

20. *Resolved*, To maintain the strictest temperance in eating and drinking.

RESOLVED.

21. *Resolved*, Never to do anything, which if I should see in another, I should count a just occasion to despise him for, or to think any way the more meanly of him.

22. *Resolved*, To endeavour to obtain for myself as much happiness in the other world as I possibly can, with all the power, might, vigour, and vehemence, yea violence, I am capable of, or can bring myself to exert, in any way that can be thought of.

23. *Resolved*, Frequently to take some deliberate action, which seems most unlikely to be done, for the glory of God, and trace it back to the original intention, designs, and ends of it; and if I find it not to be for God's glory, to repute it as a breach of the fourth Resolution.

24. *Resolved*, Whenever I do any conspicuously evil action, to trace it back, till I come to the original cause; and then, both carefully endeavour to do so no more, and to fight and pray with all my might against the original of it.

25. *Resolved*, To examine carefully and constantly, what that one thing in me is, which causes me in the least to doubt of the love of God; and so direct all my forces against it.

26. *Resolved*, To cast away such things as I find do abate my assurance.

27. *Resolved*, Never wilfully to omit anything, except the omission be for the glory of God; and frequently to examine my omissions.

28. *Resolved*, To study the Scriptures so steadily, constantly, and frequently, as that I may find, and plainly perceive, myself to grow in the knowledge of the same.

29. *Resolved*, Never to count that a prayer, nor to let that pass as a prayer, nor that as a petition of a prayer, which is so made, that I cannot hope that God will answer it; nor that as a confession which I cannot hope God will accept.

30. *Resolved*, To strive every week to be brought higher in religion, and to a higher exercise of grace, than I was the week before.

31. *Resolved*, Never to say anything at all against anybody, but when it is perfectly agreeable to the highest degree of Christian honour, and of

love to mankind, agreeable to the lowest humility, and sense of my own faults and failings, and agreeable to the golden rule; often, when I have said anything against any one, to bring it to, and try it strictly by, the test of this Resolution.

32. *Resolved*, To be strictly and firmly faithful to my trust, that that, in Prov. xx. 6. 'A faithful man, who can find?' may not be partly fulfilled in me.

33. *Resolved*, To do always what I can towards making, maintaining, and preserving peace, when it can be done without an overbalancing detriment in other respects. Dec. 26, 1722.

34. *Resolved*, In narrations, never to speak anything but the pure and simple verity.

35. *Resolved*, Whenever I so much question whether I have done my duty, as that my quiet and calm is thereby disturbed, to set it down, and also how the question was resolved. Dec. 18, 1722.

36. *Resolved*, Never to speak evil of any, except I have some particular good call to it. Dec. 19, 1722.

37. *Resolved*, To inquire every night, as I am going to bed, wherein I have been negligent, - what sin I have committed,— and wherein I have denied myself;—also, at the end of every week, month, and year. Dec. 22 and 26, 1722.

38. *Resolved*, Never to utter anything that is sportive, or matter of laughter, on a Lord's Day. Sabbath evening, Dec. 23, 1722.

39. *Resolved*, Never to do anything, of which I so much question the lawfulness, as that I intend, at the same time, to consider and examine afterwards, whether it be lawful or not; unless I as much question the lawfulness of the omission.

40. *Resolved*, To inquire every night before I go to bed, whether I have acted in the best way I possibly could, with respect to eating and drinking. Jan. 7, 1723.

41. *Resolved*, to ask myself, at the end of every day, week, month, and year, wherein I could possibly, in any respect, have done better. Jan. 11, 1723.

RESOLVED.

42. *Resolved*, Frequently to renew the dedication of myself to God, which was made at my baptism, which I solemnly renewed when I was received into the communion of the church, and which I have solemnly re-made this 12th day of January, 1723.

43. *Resolved*, Never, henceforward, till I die, to act as if I were any way my own, but entirely and altogether God's; agreeably to what is to be found in Saturday, Jan. 12th. *Jan.* 12, 1723.

44. *Resolved*, That no other end but religion shall have any influence at all on any of my actions; and that no action shall be, in the least circumstance, any otherwise than the religious end will carry it. Jan. 12, 1723.

45. *Resolved*, Never to allow any pleasure or grief, joy or sorrow, nor any affection at all, nor any degree of affection, nor any circumstance relating to it, but what helps religion. Jan. 12 and 13, 1723.

46. *Resolved*, Never to allow the least measure of any fretting or uneasiness at my father or mother. *Resolved,* to suffer no effects of it, so much as in the least alteration of speech, or motion of my eye; and to be especially careful of it with respect to any of our family.

47. *Resolved*, To endeavour, to my utmost, to deny whatever is not most agreeable to a good and universally sweet and benevolent, quiet, peaceable, contented and easy, compassionate and generous, humble and meek, submissive and obliging, diligent and industrious, charitable and even, patient, moderate, forgiving, and sincere, temper; and to do, at all times, what such a temper would lead me to; and to examine strictly, at the end of every week, whether I have so done. Sabbath morning, May 5, 1723.

48. *Resolved*, Constantly, with the utmost niceness and diligence, and the strictest scrutiny, to be looking into the state of my soul, that I may know whether I have truly an interest in Christ or not; that when I come to die, I may not have any negligence respecting this to repent of. May 26, 1723.

49. *Resolved*, That this never shall be, if I can help it.

50. *Resolved*, That I will act so, as I think I shall judge would have been best, and most prudent, when I come into the future world. July 5, 1723.

51. *Resolved*, That I will act so, in every respect, as I think I shall wish I had done, if I should at last be damned. July 8, 1723.

52. I frequently hear persons in old age say how they would live, if they were to live their lives over again: *Resolved*, That I will live just so as I can think I shall wish I had done, supposing I live to old age. July 8, 1723.

53. *Resolved*, To improve every opportunity, when I am in the best and happiest frame of mind, to cast and venture my soul on the Lord Jesus Christ, to trust and confide in him, and consecrate myself wholly to him; that from this I may have assurance of my safety, knowing that I confide in my Redeemer. July 8, 1723.

54. *Resolved*, Whenever I hear anything spoken in commendation of any person, if I think it would be praiseworthy in me, that I will endeavour to imitate it. July 8, 1723.

55. *Resolved*, To endeavour, to my utmost, so to act, as I can think I should do, if I had already seen the happiness of heaven and hell torments. July 8, 1723.

56. *Resolved*, Never to give over, nor in the least to slacken, my fight with my corruptions, however unsuccessful I may be.

57. *Resolved*, When I fear misfortunes and adversity, to examine whether I have done my duty, and resolve to do it and let the event be just as Providence orders it. I will, as far as I can, be concerned about nothing but my duty and my sin. June 9, and July 13, 1723.

58. *Resolved*, Not only to refrain from an air of dislike, fretfulness, and anger in conversation, but to exhibit an air of love, cheerfulness, and benignity. May 27, and July 13, 1723.

59. *Resolved*, When I am most conscious of provocations to ill nature and anger, that I will strive most to feel and act good-naturedly; yea, at such times, to manifest good nature, though I think that in other respects

it would be disadvantageous, and so as would be imprudent at other times. May 12, July 11, and July 13.

60. *Resolved*, Whenever my feelings begin to appear in the least out of order, when I am conscious of the least uneasiness within, or the least irregularity without, I will then subject myself to the strictest examination. July 4 and 13, 1723.

61. *Resolved*, That I will not give way to that listlessness which I find unbends and relaxes my mind from being fully and fixedly set on religion, whatever excuse I may have for it—that what my listlessness inclines me to do, is best to be done, &c. May 21, and July 13, 1723.

62. *Resolved*, Never to do anything but my duty, and then, according to Eph. vi. 6-8. to do it willingly and cheerfully, as unto the Lord, and not to man: knowing that whatever good thing any man doth, the same shall be receive of the Lord. June 25, and July 13, 1723.

63. On the supposition, that there never was to be but one individual in the world, at any one time, who was properly a complete Christian, in all respects of a right stamp, having Christianity always shining in its true lustre, and appearing excellent and lovely, from whatever part and under whatever character viewed: *Resolved*, To act just as I would do, if I strove with all my might to be that one, who should live in my time. Jan. 14, and July 13, 1723.

64. *Resolved*, When I find those *"groanings which cannot be uttered,"* of which the apostle speaks, and those *"breathings of soul* for the longing it hath,"* of which the psalmist speaks, Psalm cxix. 20. that I will promote them to the utmost of my power; and that I will not be weary of earnestly endeavouring to vent my desires, nor of the repetitions of such earnestness. July 23, and Aug. 10, 1723.

65. *Resolved*, Very much to exercise myself in this, all my life long, *viz.* with the greatest openness of which I am capable, to declare my ways to God, and lay open my soul to him, all my sins, temptations, difficulties, sorrows, fears, hopes, desires, and every thing, and every circumstance, according to Dr. Manton's Sermon on the 119th Psalm,. July 26, and Aug. 10, 1723.

66. *Resolved*, That I will endeavour always to keep a benign aspect, and air of acting and speaking, in all places, and in all companies, except it should so happen that duty requires otherwise.

67. *Resolved*, After afflictions, to inquire, what I am the better for them; what good I have got by them; and, what I might have got by them.

68. *Resolved*, To confess frankly to myself, all that which I find in myself, either infirmity or sin; and, if it be what concerns religion, also to confess the whole case to God, and implore needed help. July 23, and August 10, 1723.

69. *Resolved*, Always to do that, which I shall wish I had done when I see others do it. Aug. 11, 1723.

70. Let there be something of benevolence in all that I speak. Aug. 17, 1723.

RESOLVED.

Also by John Gillespie and available on Amazon

Beholding Jesus: Letters to My Children

Ideas Matter: Considering Jesus Christ

Be Encouraged! Letters That Will Build You Up in a Tear You Down World

Jesus is the Best – A Simple Discovery in Hebrews

The Gospel and Charles Finney: The Tragic Pastoral Results of Bad Theology

The New Life of God in the Soul of Man: An Interpretation of Henry Scougal's Classic

The Believers' Eternal Rest: An Interpretation of Richard Baxter's The Saints' Everlasting Rest.

Available from the Author at jgille8134@aol.com

Beware of Living too Long!